Effective Project Management

Effective Project Management

How to Plan, Manage, and Deliver Projects On Time and within Budget

Robert K. Wysocki

Robert Beck, Jr.

David B. Crane

John Wiley & Sons, Inc.

New York • Chichester • Brisbane • Toronto • Singapore

Associate Publisher: Katherine Schowalter

Editor: Theresa Hudson

Managing Editor: Mark Hayden

Text Design & Composition: SunCliff Graphic Productions

This text is printed on acid-free paper.

Library of Congress Cataloging-in-Publication Data

ISBN: 0-471-11521-5

Printed in the United States of America

1 0

Contents

Preface

Project management has become a habit with us. It was not an easily acquired habit. You must know that. To become an effective project manager will require behavioral changes—and those aren't easy. Our best advice is to find a few *getting started* pearls in the pages of this book. Use them. Get comfortable with them. Make them part of your life. Make them indispensable so that you feel shortchanged if you neglect to use them. Once you have reached that point, you are ready for more. Add another tool. Add another technique. In time you will find that your project management arsenal is complete, and you have the confidence to go forward into the unpredictable and exhilarating world of the project manager fully ready to do your best.

We have tried to be as helpful as possible by making our book a useful addition to your library. Much of what you find in the pages that follow is the compendium of many years experience by all three authors. In fact, we total over 70 years experience between us. We've been through a lot. We've made a lot of mistakes. Follow our advice and you will not repeat history.

In writing this book we found, as so many other writers have, that we could have gone on for several more months with additional tools and techniques honed through years of experiences. Our editor would not have been pleased had we done that. We have however put much good practical advice and many exercises in these pages. Our hope is that you will come to appreciate the value from the fruits of our labor. We truly want this to be your single guide to learning project management. We think we have a unique approach and would like to hear from you as you try to use our materials.

PART 1
PREVIEW

We think you will find our treatment of project management a refreshing change to the usual fare you have been subjected to. As the title of our work suggests, there will be plenty of opportunity to practice the tools and techniques that we have used successfully for many years and are now sharing with you. We offer a rich source of materials, many of which are not to be found in other books on the subject. We also offer a broad sampling of problems through a simulated company, which we call O'Neill & Preigh, a manufacturer of church furnishings and equipment. In their attempt to remain competitive O&P is introducing three projects that you will follow from day one to day last. Along the way we will create a number of computer-based problem situations that you will solve using Microsoft Project.

We introduce our competency model and the three projects that will be our guide throughout the book. Each chapter presents problems from these three projects. You will have to analyze the situation, discover the problem, and look for alternative solutions. Most of your work will take place within our simulated environment, using Microsoft Project. Within the simulation tool a mentor will watch your analysis and decisions, and offer further advice and suggestions as requested. We hope you will find it a stimulating and enjoyable experience.

Good luck!

OVERVIEW

PART 1

Introduction

Practice is everything.

Diogenes Laertius
Greek historian and writer

CHAPTER

WHAT THIS BOOK IS ALL ABOUT

CHAPTER LEARNING OBJECTIVES

As a result of participating in the learning experiences in this chapter you will be able to:

1. Explain how the changing business climate has impacted project management.
2. Understand the growing importance of project management to contemporary organizations.
3. Appreciate the need for project management training and the specific training needs of project managers.

Changes in the Business Environment

Change is constant! We hope that does not come as a surprise to you. Change is always with us and seems to be happening at an increasing rate. Every day we are presented with new challenges and the need to improve what we did yesterday. As John Naisbett says in *The Third Wave*, "Change or die." For project managers and wanna-be project managers the road to breakthrough performance is paved with uncertainty and the need to be creative and adaptive in how we manage our projects. If we simply rely on a routine application of someone else's methodology, we are sure to fall short of the mark.

Organizational Structures

The familiar command and control structures introduced at the turn of the century are rapidly disappearing. In their place we have task forces and self-directed work teams. Empowerment of the worker lies at the foundation of these new structures. With that empowerment comes the need for solid project management skills.

Software Applications

Many of our readers may remember the days when a computer application had to meet the needs of only a single department. If there was a corporate data base, we accessed it to retrieve the required data and passed the data through an applications program to produce the requested report. If there was no data or we simply did not know of its existence, we created our own database or file and proceeded accordingly. In retrospect our professional life as systems developers was relatively simple. Not so anymore. We are now developing applications that cross departmental lines, applications that span organizations, applications that are not clearly defined, and applications that will change because the business climate changed. All of this means that we will have to anticipate change in our projects and be skilled at the management of that change.

Cycle Time

The window of opportunity is narrowing and constantly moving. Organizations that can take advantage of these opportunities are organizations that have addressed the problem of reducing cycle time. Taking too long to roll out a new or revamped product may mean missing a business opportunity. Project managers must know how and when to introduce multiple release strategies and project schedule compression strategies to help meet requirements that happen at unexpected times even though we knew to expect them.

Rightsizing

With the thinning of depth and breadth in many organizations there is a need for the continuing professional staff to find ways to work smarter, not harder. Project management includes a number of tools and techniques that help the project manager respond to the increased work loads.

Middle Management

Peter Drucker, in a landmark paper ("The Coming of the New Organization," *Harvard Business Review*, Jan/Feb 1988), depicts middle managers as those who either receive information from above, reinterpret it, and pass it down; or people who receive information from below, reinterpret it, and pass it up the line. Given the politics and power struggles at play, not only is quality suspect, but also the need for such activities when the computer is perfectly capable of delivering that information to the desk of any manager who has a need to know. As a result, we have seen the thinning of the organization's layers of middle management. Do not expect them to come back. They are gone forever.

The Growth of Project Management as a Profession

We are beginning to see companies implementing career-pathing programs for project managers. Projects are classified according to such characteristics as risk, business value, length, complexity, and so on. Project management skill sets are mapped into this structure, and project managers chosen based on a skill-set match. Project management curricula are matched to this classification so that project managers can develop their skills by managing projects of a certain classification and participating in the training associated with that project class.

The Project Management Institute has developed a Project Management Body of Knowledge (PMBOK), a curriculum outline to accompany it, and an examination for the professional certification of project managers. The topics in this book relate closely to the PMBOK so that the reader has reasonable assurance that they are learning project management as defined by its premier professional society.

The Need for a New Training Paradigm for Project Managers

We would like to think that all organizations recognize how important project management is to the success of their business activity. Unfortunately they do not. Thankfully, however, many of their professional staff do. They have seen radical changes in their jobs in the last few years. As organizations *rightsized*, many of the responsibilities of those who were let go passed on to those who remained. We are not sure who the winners and losers were in these cases. Jobs changed radically. New responsibilities were added and often without the benefit of training in how to carry out those new responsibilities. In many cases professionals had to rely on their own resources to find a way. For many, however: Where do they turn when they want to learn how to be a good project manager?

Many have come to the conclusion (and rightly so) that they are in charge of their careers and professional development. Congratulations if you are one of them. We understand and we are here to help you.

Why We Wrote This Book

We believe there are a number of professionals like those just described who are looking for some help. Hopefully we have filled their needs with this book. When scheduled training is not available, or is but cannot be utilized because of scheduling conflicts, a book such as ours can help. It is written to be studied. It is written to be a guide as you attempt to learn project management. And finally it is written to be a self-paced resource—one that will immerse you in managing projects through a simulated company and a number of projects active in that company.

How the Book Is Structured

The book consists of four parts organized into seventeen chapters, an additional part, and three appendixes. In writing it we have deliberately chosen to follow the PMBOK, but not necessarily in the order in which PMBOK presents the material. Once you have completed this book you will have covered the PMBOK except for the contract negotiations topic.

Part I introduces the topic and builds a case for more emphasis on developing project managers to meet the changing needs of the contemporary organization.

In Part II we set the stage for the rest of the book. Here we define the project and introduce our five-phase model for project management. While the principles of management apply to project management, there are a number of collateral principles that are peculiar to project management which we want to get on the table early. You need to be thinking about the management dimensions just as you will be thinking about the block and tackle of project management.

Part III is the heart of the book. It contains seven chapters that lead the reader through the details of developing a project plan. The reader will follow the chronology of events that begin with developing a clear understanding of the request and the deliverable, followed by the detailed development of the work to be done, the resources required to do the work, and the timeline for completing the work. The treatment is applications-oriented and includes several example problems from the simulated exercises in O'Neill & Preigh.

Part IV covers the implementation of the project plan. Once the concepts and principles of status reporting, change management, and problem resolution are discussed, we immerse the reader in a number of exercises from O'Neill & Preigh. These exercises are designed to test your mettle. A variety of projects and project situations are presented.

In Part V we explore the environment in which project management is practiced and will be practiced in the near future. A variety of organizational structures are discussed, with focus on how they support or hinder good project management. We also consider the broader picture, wherein organizations are evolving into more open forms, and how project management plays an ever growing role in these migrations.

How to Use This Book

You will find the book adapts very well, whatever your current knowledge or experience of project management might be. Those totally unfamiliar with project management can learn the basics by simply reading and reflecting. If you wish to take it to the next step we offer a wealth of practice opportunities through the simulation exercises. You will, of course need access to MS Project for Windows to use the simulation package.

For those who have some experience and knowledge there are several ways to use our materials. Perhaps you need to strengthen one or more areas of project management. Either the book and/or the simulation package can help you.

The seasoned professional project manager will find value in the book as well. We have gathered a number of tools and techniques that we have originated. The Joint Project Planning session, the use of sticker notes and whiteboards for building the project network, work packages for professional staff development, and milestone trend charts are a few of our more noteworthy contributions.

How to Use PM/Simulator

We want you to test your mettle on a project that has some substance. We often observe seminars and workshops that use building birdhouses as a test of your mastery of the tools and techniques of project management. We will not insult you with yet another birdhouse-type project. Instead we are going to guide you through a potentially real project, and expose you to the warts and traps that you might expect to encounter in a real project. Those of you who survive will understand what we have been trying to teach you. Congratulations!

For details on how to get into PM Simulator, please consult Appendix D. There you will find some basic *getting started* information. The details of navigating the simulator can be found in the ReadME file on the enclosed diskette.

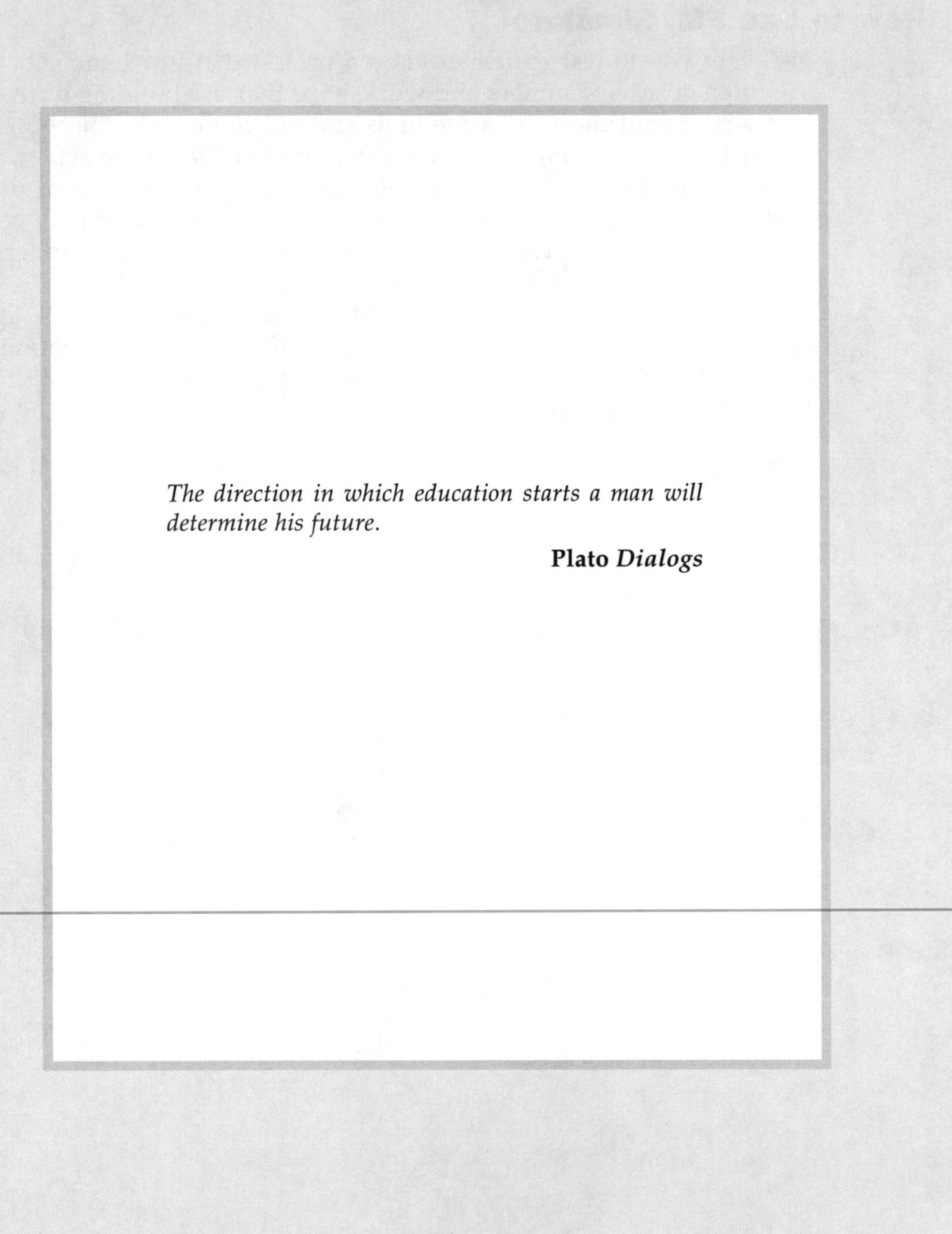

The direction in which education starts a man will determine his future.

Plato *Dialogs*

CHAPTER

SKILLS AND COMPETENCIES FOR EFFECTIVE PROJECT MANAGEMENT

CHAPTER LEARNING OBJECTIVES

As a result of participating in the learning experiences in this chapter you will be able to:

1. Identify the skills required to be a successful project manager.
2. Assess your current skill levels as a project manager.
3. Establish a vision of the perfect project manager.
4. Identify the specific skills that you personally wish to develop.

Project Manager: Competencies, Functions, Tasks

If anyone has a foolproof method of identifying a professional who will make a competent project manager, please contact one of the authors. We can show you how to make a lot of money. In fact, it is very difficult to identify someone with the requisite skills and competencies. Figure 2.1 conveys the reason why it is so difficult. There are two levels of characteristics that determine success or failure as a project manager. At the visible level are skills that can be observed and can be acquired through training. That is the easy part. More difficult are those traits that lie below the surface, out of the range of the visible. We can see them in practice but we cannot measure them in the sense of determining whether a particular person has them and, if so, to what degree. They are also the traits that are more difficult to develop through training. Some of them may in fact be hereditary.

Before we embark on this journey to learn about projects, project management, and project managers, it is instructive to lay out a plan of action. Part of that plan involves specifying our own individual learning program.

This section gives an overview of the competencies, functions, and tasks common to the discipline of project management. It is meant to give you a general sense of what is required to be an effective project

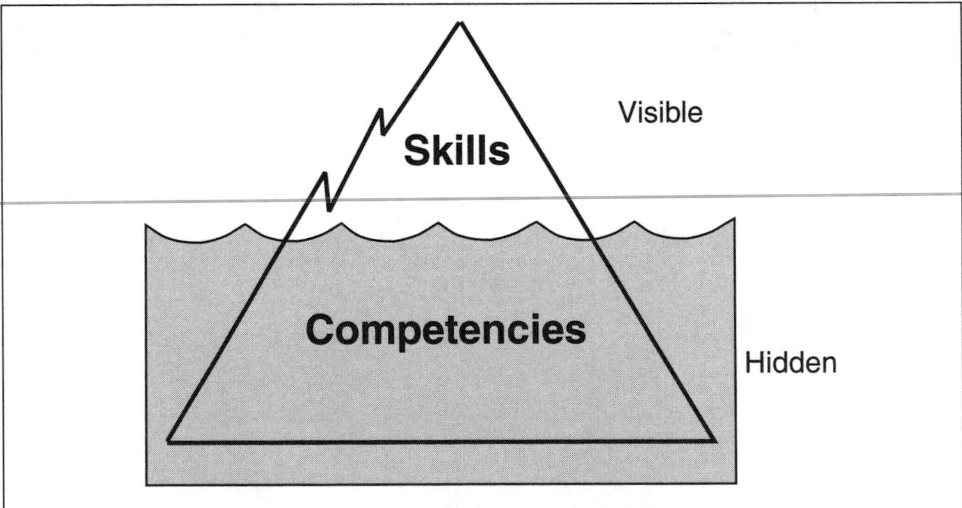

Figure 2.1 Project manager competencies and skills.

manager and to match your current competencies against those required of project managers. What results from this examination is a gap between the knowledge and skills you now have and those you will need as project manager. This forms the basis of your personal learning contract.

The following list provides a capsule description of the competencies required to be an effective project manager. As we begin, it would be a good exercise to review this list and consider how your competencies measure up against this list. The list was developed by the Corporate Education Center of Boston University in cooperation with their major corporate accounts, and is reproduced here with permission.

Business Achievement Competencies

1. *Business Awareness*
   - Ensures that the project is linked to the organization's business plan and satisfies a business objective by solving a business problem.
   - Stays current and evaluates the impact of industry and technology developments.
   - Balances ideal technical approaches and project scope against business deadlines and priorities to find the best compromise (doesn't seek perfection).
   - Works with business financial management to understand the financial implications of the project (for example: cost-benefit analysis, capitalization vs. expensing).
2. *Business Partner Orientation*
   - Meets frequently with business partners throughout the cycle of the project to ensure full understanding of the business partners' needs and concerns.
   - Builds business ownership by seeking extensive business area interactive participation during the design process.
   - Co-locates the business and systems project team members if possible.
   - Conducts business-oriented walk-throughs.
   - Structures the activities of the project team so that systems staff members work closely with a business partner.

- Follows up with business partners during and after the project to make sure their needs have been met.

3. *Commitment to Quality*

   - Pushes for more efficient ways to do things.
   - Sets and enforces high standards of quality for self and others.
   - Staffs the project with people with the skills and attitudes necessary for the project to be successful.
   - Develops a quality plan based on objectives, and coordinated with the project plan.
   - Monitors performance against quality plan and objectives.

Problem-Solving Competencies

4. *Initiative*

   - Develops innovative and creative approaches to problems when faced with obstacles or limitations.
   - Takes calculated risks.
   - Takes persistent, repeated action to overcome obstacles and achieve solutions.
   - Puts in whatever effort is needed to get the job done.

5. *Information Gathering*

   - Identifies all groups that may be affected by the project, and involves them—actively soliciting their input.
   - Seeks information or data from various sources to clarify a problem.
   - Identifies and consults individuals and groups that can expedite project activities or provide assistance.
   - Obtains sufficient factual information to develop and support the design and implementation decisions.

6. *Analytic Thinking*

   - Breaks down a large or complex project into meaningful subprojects.
   - Develops an overall project plan to determine resource needs, budget, and time.

- Translates the business goals into project goals, and the project goals into detailed work-breakdown structure.
- Uses project management software tools to develop detailed project plans and to track status.
- Sorts or organizes data to facilitate dealing with it systematically.
- Generates and presents logical, clearly reasoned alternatives to stimulate decision making and action.
- Assimilates diverse information and assesses the impact on each piece of the project as well as on the project as a whole.
- Assesses project design and implementation approach often to ensure that the project properly addresses the business problem to be solved.

7. *Conceptual Thinking*

- Considers the project within the context of a broader view of how the business and technology will be changing over the next several years.
- Uses understanding of business and technical objectives to prioritize effectively (for example: project tasks, test cases, issues to be resolved).
- Anticipates and plans for the impact of the project on other systems.
- Develops a clear vision or conceptual model of the system to be developed.

Influence Competencies

8. *Interpersonal Awareness*

- Tries to get to know team members and potential team members to understand what motivates them.
- Understands the issues and concerns of other individuals and groups.
- Notices and interprets nonverbal behavior.
- Is objective when mediating conflicting positions of members of the project team.

9. *Organizational Awareness*

    - Identifies and seeks the support of key stakeholders affected by the project.
    - Proactively engages groups and individuals with technical and/or financial overseeing responsibilities.
    - Takes the time to understand and consider the political dynamics among groups involved in the project.
    - Uses relationships with people from other units within the organization to resolve issues or provide assistance.
    - Takes the organization's budgetary cycle into account when developing project schedules.

10. *Anticipation of Impact*

    - Adapts style or approach to achieve a particular impact (for example: use of media, adaptation of presentation style to the audience, selection of a meeting site to make management's commitment visible to the project team).
    - Manages expectations by ensuring that what is promised can be delivered.
    - Arranges for a senior manager to attend the initial project meeting and explain the project's mission and objectives.
    - Considers the short-and-long term implications of project decisions (for example: design vs. maintenance activities).

11. *Resourceful Use of Influence*

    - Develops strategies that address other people's most important concerns or needs.
    - Approaches senior managers and seeks their support for the project.
    - Enlists the support of his or her own management to influence other senior managers.
    - Enlists support of others by appealing to their management.
    - Enlists cooperation by appealing to people's unique expertise.
    - Involves project team members in the detail planning of the project so that they will have ownership of the plan.

People Management Competencies

12. *Motivating Others*
    - Ensures that team members understand the project's goals and purpose.
    - Provides opportunities or rewards that are tailored to each individual's interests.
    - Provides rewards and recognition to people as intermediate milestones are reached on or ahead of schedule.
    - Initiates informal events to promote teamwork.
    - Takes appropriate action to assist and counsel marginal performers.
13. *Communication Skills*
    - Plans ahead for meetings (for example: prepares an agenda).
    - Ensures a common understanding and agreement on the project scope and objectives and on any subsequent changes.
    - Organizes and meets regularly with a management team composed of representatives from all areas affected by a project.
    - Holds regular, frequent meetings with the project team to discuss status, resolve issues, and share information.
    - Ensures that presentations are well organized.
    - Tailors his or her language to the level of the audience.
14. *Developing Others*
    - Gives team members assignments or training to provide opportunities for growth and development.
    - Provides direct, specific, constructive feedback and guidance to others regarding their performance.
    - Empowers team members to create challenge and stretch their abilities.
    - Provides more supervision for inexperienced people.
15. *Monitoring and Controlling*
    - Maintains a detailed master plan that shows at all times what people are working on and what must be done by when.

- Regularly obtains status information from each project team member on his or her assigned tasks.
- Monitors the project status to ensure effective use of resources.
- Keeps team members focused on project goals and deliverables.
- Identifies the economic and project schedule consequences of requested and/or mandated scope changes and communicates these to management.
- Maintains control of accepted changes to the project plan and ensures that any changes are communicated to all team members.
- Accepts responsibility for resolving project issues, focusing on solutions and action, and buffering criticism.
- Takes appropriate corrective action to keep the project on track or to get the project back on track.
- Conducts a postproject review to identify what went well, what should have been done differently, and what lessons were learned.

Self-Management Competencies

16. *Self-Confidence*
    - Presents a confident, positive attitude to set the tone for the project team.
    - Takes a firm stand in the face of opposition.
    - Confronts problems with others quickly and directly.
17. *Stress Management*
    - Controls own feelings and behavior in stressful situations.
    - Works effectively under pressure.
18. *Concern for Credibility*
    - Maintains credibility by consistently delivering what had been promised.
    - Stays on top of the details of his or her project effort to be able to answer questions authoritatively and maintain credibility.

- Answers questions honestly, to maintain credibility even if it is awkward to do so.
- Informs management and customer management promptly about any difficulties.

19. *Flexibility*

    - Adjusts readily to changes in the work environment.
    - Adjusts own managerial style, depending on the people and situation.
    - Uses or shares resources to best accomplish organizational goals.
    - Delegates tasks and activities to others.

Job Functions and Tasks for Project Management

Project managers are called upon to perform a variety of functions and tasks. Many might seem to be removed from the direct management of the project. In order to set the stage for what those expectations are, we provide the following list.

1. Project Planning (Strategic and Tactical)

    - Develops preliminary study with project team, identifying business problem, requirements, project scope, and benefits.
    - Identifies key project results and milestones.
    - Develops project plan and work-breakdown structure, and communicates to team and client.
    - Determines needed resources, including client involvement.
    - Estimates timelines and phases.
    - Influences selection of project team members.
    - Assigns project responsibilities based on assessment of individual skills and development needs.
    - Defines clear individual roles and performance expectations.
    - Establishes acceptance criteria.
    - Determines appropriate technological approach, including use of prototyping CASE or other tools.

2. Managing the Project
   - Continually reviews project status.
   - Reviews work against key results criteria.
   - Uses systematic method for logging project status—checking against schedule.
   - Uses change management/request procedure.
   - Uses project meetings to measure progress against plan; communicates changes and issues.
   - Assesses skill-needed documentation of meetings, work, conversations, and decisions.
   - Measures quality through testing against requirements.
   - Conducts project reviews and walk-throughs (with appropriate client involvement).
3. Lead Project Team
   - Involves team in planning.
   - Uses both formal and informal methods to track project status.
   - Recognizes individual and team accomplishments or results.
   - Manages performance issues in a timely manner.
   - Delegates tasks effectively based on understanding individual strengths and weaknesses.
   - Maintains open door for staff ideas and concerns.
   - Sets performance and development objectives for staff.
   - Schedules and holds regular team meetings.
4. Building Client Partnerships
   - Involves working jointly with client in defining project goals and key results.
   - Works with client to ensure alignment of project to overall business goals.
   - Listens and responds actively; documents client needs, changes, and demands.
   - Implements procedures for controlling and handling change.
   - Develops client understanding of the system, and trains in systems use.

- Presents and reports periodically to client.
- Establishes lines of responsibility and accountability to client.

5. Targeting to the Business
   - Manages in accordance with I/S visions and values.
   - Links overall I/S architecture principles.
   - Interfaces effectively with Corporate Database Management.
   - Plans for impacts on related systems/departments to achieve maximum efficiency.
   - Understands business needs, time, and cost pressures.
   - Keeps current with business and technology developments among competitors.
   - Aligns project with corporate and business priorities and direction.

Project Management Competency Levels

The project manager will eventually gain a high level of competency in each of the identified areas. Those new to project management may have acquired some of the competencies through other responsibilities. In any case you already have some level of competency in many of the areas common to effective project management. While this course is comprehensive of many of the needed competencies, it will not address each. In fact it will address some competencies at a rather superficial level, while others in considerable depth.

To help you understand the emphasis placed on each competency, we have prepared a graphic based on Bloom's Taxonomy of Educational Objectives—Cognitive Domain. Following is a definition of each of the six levels we will be using.

1. Knowledge (I Can Define It)—Knowledge, as defined here, involves *the remembering or recalling* of ideas, materials, or phenomena. For measurement purposes, the recall situations involve little more than bringing to mind the appropriate material. Although some alteration of the material may be required, this is a relatively minor part of the task. The process of relating and judging is also involved to the extent that the student is expected to answer questions or problems that are posed in a different form in the test situation from in the learning situation. To use an

analogy, if one thinks of the mind as a file, the problem in a knowledge test situation is that of finding in the problem or task the appropriate signals, cues, and clues that will most effectively bring out whatever knowledge is filed or stored. Knowledge does not mean that the student can actually perform or use the knowledge in a practical manner.

2. Comprehension (I Understand It)—Those objectives, behaviors, or responses that represent an understanding of the literal message contained in a communication. In reaching such understanding the student may change the communication in his mind or in his overt responses to some parallel form more meaningful to him. There may also be responses that represent simple extensions beyond what is given in the communication itself.
3. Application (I Have Used It)—The use of abstractions in particular and concrete situations. The abstractions may be in the form of general ideas, rules of procedures, or generalized methods. The abstractions may also be technical principles, ideas, and theories that must be remembered and applied. A demonstration of application is that the student will use an abstraction correctly, given an appropriate situation in which no mode of solution is specified: the ability to apply generalizations and conclusions to real-life problems, the ability to apply science principles, postulates, theorems, or other abstractions to new situations.
4. Analysis (I Know How Each Part Works)—The breakdown of a communication into its constituent elements or parts so that the relative hierarchy of ideas is made clear and/or the relations between the ideas expressed are made explicit. Such analyses are intended to clarify the communication; to indicate how the communication is organized and the way in which it manages to convey its effects, as well as its basis and arrangement. Analysis deals with both the content and form of material.
5. Synthesis (I Can Adapt It to Other Uses)—The putting together of elements and parts to form a whole. This involves the process of working with pieces, parts, elements, and so on; and arranging and combining them in such a way as to constitute a pattern or structure not clearly there before.
6. Evaluation (I Know When to Use It)—Judgments about the value of material and methods for given purposes. Quantitative and qualitative judgments about the extent to which material and

methods satisfy criteria. Use of a standard appraisal. The criteria may be those determined by the student or those given to him.

Using these definitions, the extent to which this book covers the project management competencies is given in Figure 2.2.

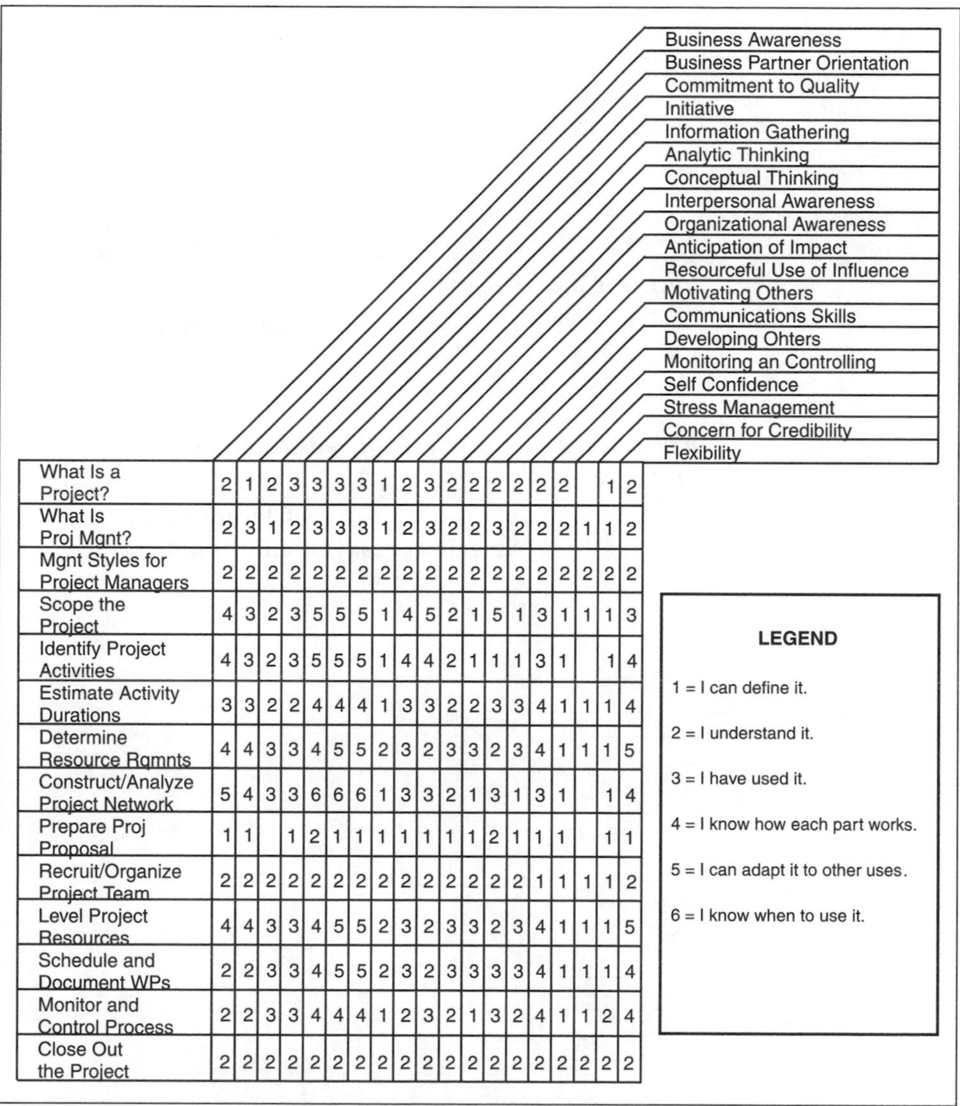

	Business Awareness	Business Partner Orientation	Commitment to Quality	Initiative	Information Gathering	Analytic Thinking	Conceptual Thinking	Interpersonal Awareness	Organizational Awareness	Anticipation of Impact	Resourceful Use of Influence	Motivating Others	Communications Skills	Developing Ohters	Monitoring an Controlling	Self Confidence	Stress Management	Concern for Credibility	Flexibility
What Is a Project?	2	1	2	3	3	3	3	1	2	3	2	2	2	2	2	2		1	2
What Is Proj Mgnt?	2	3	1	2	3	3	3	1	2	3	2	2	3	2	2	2	1	1	2
Mgnt Styles for Project Managers	2	2	2	2	2	2	2	2	2	2	2	2	2	2	2	2	2	2	2
Scope the Project	4	3	2	3	5	5	5	1	4	5	2	1	5	1	3	1	1	1	3
Identify Project Activities	4	3	2	3	5	5	5	1	4	4	2	1	1	1	3	1		1	4
Estimate Activity Durations	3	3	2	2	4	4	4	1	3	3	2	2	3	3	4	1	1	1	4
Determine Resource Rqmnts	4	4	3	3	4	5	5	2	3	2	3	3	2	3	4	1	1	1	5
Construct/Analyze Project Network	5	4	3	3	6	6	6	1	3	3	2	1	3	1	3	1		1	4
Prepare Proj Proposal	1	1		1	2	1	1	1	1	1	1	1	2	1	1	1		1	1
Recruit/Organize Project Team	2	2	2	2	2	2	2	2	2	2	2	2	2	2	1	1	1	1	2
Level Project Resources	4	4	3	3	4	5	5	2	3	2	3	3	2	3	4	1	1	1	5
Schedule and Document WPs	2	2	3	3	4	5	5	2	3	2	3	3	3	3	4	1	1	1	4
Monitor and Control Process	2	2	3	3	4	4	4	1	2	3	2	1	3	2	4	1	1	2	4
Close Out the Project	2	2	2	2	2	2	2	2	2	2	2	2	2	2	2	2	2	2	2

LEGEND

1 = I can define it.

2 = I understand it.

3 = I have used it.

4 = I know how each part works.

5 = I can adapt it to other uses.

6 = I know when to use it.

Figure 2.2 Project manager's competency matrix.

Practice is the best master.

Latin Proverb

Information's pretty thin stuff, unless mixed with experience.

Clarence Day
American essayist and humorist

CHAPTER 3

Case Study: O'Neill & Preigh

Overview of the Business Situation

O'Neill & Preigh is an 800-year-old manufacturer of church equipment. Originally established in a small village on the outskirts of Rome, they now operate out of their corporate offices in Lancaster, Pennsylvania. They are clearly recognized as the market leader in both stock and custom-built furnishings for churches of all denominations. Their quality and craftsmanship are undisputed as the best in the industry. They sell their products in international markets through their own sales staff as well as through distributor channels in major cities around the world.

All is not good, however. For the past six quarters business has dropped off dramatically. It is generally agreed that their problems are both internal as well as external.

Internally they have always operated rather loosely. Operating budgets are held at the officer level so that department managers have not been involved in operational-level details. Their long history as an organization has been to focus on the highly skilled craft of building custom furnishings, for which they are very proud and for which they are considered world-class. One could say that they are more an organization of artisans than an organization of business managers. An obvious consequence is poor cost control. Until recently they never had to worry about efficiency and effectiveness. In keeping with that environment, the computer has made little inroad into business operations. Their accounting office has computerized payables, receivables, payroll, and inventory, but little else.

Externally their market is changing and they are concerned. Their president, Del E. Lama, has just concluded the quarterly State of the Business meeting of the senior officers, at which he reported that part of their problem was the result of the aggressive pricing strategies of a Southeast Asian conglomerate that recently introduced their product into the American market. While the Asians do not compete on quality, it seems that the American market is more price sensitive than in the past. Del exhorted his management team to take a good, hard look at the business. "Leave no stone unturned" were his exact words. He went on to talk about a likely reengineering effort. (He attended the Chamber of Commerce breakfast that week, at which the speaker was a reengineering consultant from a large Philadelphia firm.)

The management team should also take a good, hard look at the information systems that supported the business. Here Del's concern was that the few computer applications they had were developed in the decentralized, laissez-faire style of the company. Maybe it was time to look at information as a competitive weapon to see what might be done to increase its impact on their future.

Del has also heard so much about information technology and automated manufacturing that he wonders whether the company, in its zeal for craftsmanship, hasn't overlooked opportunities to remain competitive without sacrificing quality. To spearhead this computerization effort he hired his grandson, Sal Vation, to join the firm as Director of Information Resources. Sal had just graduated from a prominent New England business school with an MBA in Information Systems.

Needless to say, the management team was taken aback. They certainly used computers, but only as a backroom tool. They ran their accounting functions and that was just fine. Del was talking about a whole new way of doing business. Many would find that discomforting.

Description of Project Initiatives

As a result of Del's bleak report, several managers stepped forward with ideas for projects that might help pull the company back to its former greatness and still maintain its image of world-class quality. They were after all quite committed to the company and were proud to be associated with O&P. Three projects will soon be proposed to the management team. They are briefly described in the following.

Project 1: E-Mail System

Sal is aware of the culture and traditions of O&P and that there will be some resistance to his efforts. He reasons that a quick, low-risk project with direct benefits to each manager should be his first initiative. Implementing an e-mail system seems to meet all the conditions Sal requires.

Project 2: Office Supplies Containment

The management team has a long history of not bothering department managers with operating issues. Times were good and there was little reason to be heavy-handed. The budget for office supplies was always administered by the Vice President of Finance, Nick Uldyme. Departments charged their office supplies expenses against a corporate budget. They did not have departmental office supply budgets. Nick was happy reporting the numbers but not too interested in procedures and controls for controlling expenses. The result was that the corporate budget for office supplies was generally overspent by 4 percent. Until now no one expressed much concern.

Project 3: Touch Screen Gold Medallion Organ

Hal E. Lewya is the Vice President of Manufacturing for O&P. He has been with the company only a few years, having been aggressively recruited away from a leading manufacturer of church musical instruments. Hal has always been the champion for new and innovative instrumentation. In fact, after only a few weeks on the job he presented an idea for a new line of church organs. He believed strongly in using current technology and had devised an idea for replacing the usual pulls and stops with a touch screen. The performer could easily configure the organ with a few quick finger moves, rather than the physical process heretofore required. His idea was not received very well by the old guard. They saw it as a compromise of the traditions that O&P had been known for. Somehow computers and craftsmanship didn't mix very well in their minds. Del's proclamation changed the game, however, and Hal was preparing to resurrect his idea once more. Surely they would buy it this time.

Professional Staff Resources

The following is a profile of a few of the key O&P professional staff who will be working on one or more of the three aforementioned projects. You will meet others as you work on specific projects using the PM Simulator.

Position Title	*Name*
President	Del E. Lama

Profile Del has been with O&P for longer than he or anyone else can remember. Del is steeped in the old ways, having designed and built many of the products that are still in the O&P product line and that have been among their most successful. He is not a strong leader but has done well in his job as president. The management team looks up to him because of his evenhandedness in dealing with personnel issues. He has nurtured a corporate culture that speaks of family values and concern for the individual. His openness is his greatest strength. He knows that business as usual is not going to work. It is time for change and he is opening the possibility for his senior managers to come forward with new ideas.

VP Finance Nick Uldyme

Profile Nick has been around for some time and has worked his way up from accounting clerk to his present position. He tends to spend his time on activities that are more operations-related and really hasn't established himself as a member of the senior management team. He is happy to report what happened with little interest in strategic issues, efficiency, or effectiveness.

VP Manufacturing Hal E. Lewya

Profile Hal has been with O&P for 30 years. He is a true craftsman who has been quite successful with O&P. Despite the fact that he has a high regard for the craft, he is open to new ideas to improve the business as long as quality is not sacrificed.

VP Marketing Clara Voyant

Profile Clara truly has the talent to design effective marketing programs. She has the uncanny ability to see pearls of wisdom in data, where others see only numbers. She welcomes the challenges that the business situation seems to be presenting.

VP Administration Olive Branch

Profile Olive doesn't make waves and avoids confrontation whenever possible. She would rather spend the time finding common grounds on which agreements can be reached than using the power of her position to dictate.

IS Manager Sal Vation

Profile Sal is the grandson of President Lama. He just received his MBA with a specialization in Information Systems from a prominent New England business school. His uncle hired him to bring O&P into the computer age, although he is not sure exactly what that will mean to the company. He is surely taking some risk, given the culture.

Programmer Sy Yonara

Profile Sy is unique among IS professionals. He is unequaled in his ability to solve very complex systems design problems. He is also unequaled in his ability to deliver complex solutions that no one can understand. He seems to delight in other people's confusion. Sy is very much a loner. He doesn't like to work with people and they share a like feeling for him. If it weren't for his exceptional analytic and programming skills he would be long gone.

Programmer Terri Tory

Profile Terri is definitely not a team player. She is a very skilled programmer but works effectively only if she is responsible for an activity from start to finish. She makes it very clear that she doesn't want to be assigned to complete work begun by others.

Programmer Manuel Labor

Profile Manuel is just a hard-working junior programmer. Give him a well-defined programming task and you can count on him to deliver. His skill set is limited but he is a good learner and has demonstrated a definite potential for growth.

Systems Analyst Anna Lyst

Profile Anna is the only systems analyst at O&P. Many have commented on her ability to see to the heart of the problem, offer a number of alternative solutions, and work with users through to implementation. She is an effective negotiator. Her only shortcoming is her intolerance of incompetent or poorly committed professionals. She makes no bones about letting them know not so much through words as through actions.

Senior Accountant Paul Bearer

Profile Paul has just been promoted to project manager for the Office Supplies Containment project. It is his first experience as project manager. He has just returned from a three-day seminar in project management and is looking forward to his first opportunity to *show his stuff*.

Receivables Clerk Bill U. Slowly

Profile Bill has been an accounts-receivable clerk ever since there were accounts receivable. He is trustworthy and accurate, but don't look to him for any breakthrough strategies.

PART 2

PREVIEW

In this part we set the foundation for our study of project management. The term *project* is defined in Chapter 4, and *project management* in Chapter 5. We next consider the many opportunities for the project manager to use projects for the career growth and professional development of staff.

We find this topic to be of great value to professionals but virtually ignored in the literature on project management. By introducing it at this early stage we can refer to it later in the context of our discussion of project management.

OVERVIEW

PART 2

Staging

Things are not always what they seem.

Phaedrus
Roman writer and fabulist

CHAPTER

WHAT IS A PROJECT?

CHAPTER LEARNING OBJECTIVES

As a result of participating in the learning experiences in this chapter you will be able to:

1. Define a project.
2. List a project's characteristics.
3. Distinguish a project from a program, activity, and task.
4. Understand the three parameters that constrain a project.
5. Define project management in terms of the principles of management.
6. Know how the *S curve* relates to project progress.

Definition of a Project

To put projects into perspective we need a definition—a common starting point. All too often people are wont to call any of their work a project. Projects actually have a very specific definition. If a set of tasks or work to be done does not meet the strict definition, then it cannot be called a project. To use the project management techniques presented in this book, we must first have a project. Our definition of a project is shown in Figure 4.1. This definition tells us quite a bit about a project. To appreciate just what constitutes a project let us look at each part of the definition.

Sequence of Activities

A project comprises a number of activities that must be completed in some specified order. At this point we simply say that an activity is a defined piece of work. That rather informal definition of an activity will be replaced later with a very precise definition. The sequencing is based on technical or best practice requirements, not on management prerogatives. It is often helpful to think in terms of input and output. The output of one activity or activities becomes the input to another activity or activities. In other words, what is needed in the way of input in order to begin working on this activity and what activities produce those as outputs. Avoid the trap of specifying sequence based on resource constraints or such statements as: Pete will work on activity B as soon as he finishes working on activity A. We are not going to ignore resource constraints when we actually schedule activities. That decision will come later in the project-planning activities.

WHAT IS A PROJECT?

A project is a *sequence of unique, complex,* and *connected activities* having *one goal* or purpose and that must be completed by *a specific time, within budget,* and *according to specification.*

Figure 4.1 Definition of a project.

Unique Activities

The project has never happened before and will never happen again under the same conditions. Something will always be different each time the activities that comprise this project are repeated. Usually the variations from time to time will be random in nature—a part is delayed, someone is sick, a power failure occurs, and so on. These are random events that we know will happen—but when, how, and with what impact on the schedule we are not exactly sure. It is these random variations that give rise to the challenge for the project manager.

Complex Activities

The activities that comprise the project are relatively complex. That is, they are not simple, repetitive acts, such as mowing the lawn, running the weekly payroll, washing the car, or loading the delivery truck. Rather they are new, and require special skill levels, creative input, and judgment to be done effectively.

Connected Activities

There is some order to the sequence in which the activities that make up the project must be completed. Connectedness follows from the fact that the output from one activity is input to another. The alternative is a list of tasks that are unconnected but must all be complete in order for the project to be complete. As a simple example, consider painting the interior rooms of a house. Except for rather unusual situations, the rooms can be painted in any order. The house is not completely painted until all its rooms have been painted but they may be painted in any order. Painting the house is a collection of tasks, but it is not a project in the sense that we have defined project.

One Goal

Projects must have a single goal as compared to a program, which can have many goals. Programs are therefore a collection of projects that may have to be completed in a specific order for the program to be completed. There will be situations where a project may be divided into several subprojects, which are each projects in their own right. For better management control this may happen in very large or complex projects. For example, subprojects may be defined at the department, division, or geographic level. The complicating factors may be that the projects are now interdependent. While this adds another layer of complexity and communication, it can be handled.

Specified Time

Projects have a specified completion date. This may be self-imposed by management or externally specified (as by a customer). Often the deadline is beyond the control of anyone, such as firing a rocket at a distant comet as it swings near the earth's orbit, or holding a trade conference. In both cases the project is over regardless of whether the project work has been completed.

Within Budget

Projects also have resource limits (people, money, machines). While these may be adjusted up or down by management, they are considered fixed resources by the project manager. We will have more to say on this later in the book.

According to Specification

The customer or recipient of the deliverables from the project expects a certain level of functionality and quality from the project. These may be self-imposed or customer-specified, and are fixed as far as the project manager is concerned. While the project manager treats them as fixed, that is not the reality of the situation. There are any number of factors that will cause the specification to change. For example, the customer may not have defined requirements completely, or the business situation may have changed (as happens in long projects). To expect the specification to remain fixed through the project is unrealistic. In fact, if it did, the job of project manager would be much less exciting and challenging. Systems specifications can and will change. This presents special challenges to the project manager. We will show you how to handle them effectively.

What Is a Program?

A program is different from a project. Programs are larger in scope and comprise multiple projects. For example, the United States government has a space program that includes several projects, such as the Challenger Project. Or construction company contracts a program to build an industrial technology park with several separate projects.

Project Parameters

Scope, cost, time, and resources define a system of four constraints that operate on every project. They are an interdependent set in the sense that as one changes it may cause us to change the others so that we can restore equilibrium to the system. Because they are so important to the success or failure of the project, we will spend a few minutes discussing them here.

Cost

Throughout the project management life cycle, cost is a major consideration. The first consideration occurs at an early and informal stage in the life of a project. The requesting client may simply offer a cost figure about equal to what they had in mind for the project.

Depending on how well thought out it was, their number could be fairly close to or far from the mark. Consultants will often encounter situations in which the client is willing to spend only a certain amount for the work: Do what you can with what you have. In more formal situations (the ones we will learn in this course) the project manager will prepare a proposal for the work to be done. That proposal will include a good estimate (perhaps even a quote) of the total cost of the project. Even if a preliminary figure had been given, the client's decision will be based on better estimates of cost and time. The decision is the second milestone.

Time

To a certain extent cost and time are trade-offs with one another. The time can be reduced but cost will increase as a result. Time is an interesting resource. It can't be inventoried. It is consumed whether we use it or not. For the project manager, the objective is to use the time allotted to the project in the most effective and productive ways possible. We will learn that time can be a resource to be traded within a project or across projects. Once a project has commenced, the prime resource available to the project manager to keep the project on schedule or get it back on schedule is time. Good project managers realize this and will protect their time resource jealously. We will have more to say about this later when we talk about scheduling project activities.

Resources

While all resources can be discussed in terms of cost, we choose to identify resources separately. We have in mind such resources as equipment, physical facilities, inventory, and others. These are capital assets that have limited availabilities, can be scheduled, or can be leased from an outside party. Some are fixed; others are variable only in the long term. In any case they are central to the scheduling of project activities and the orderly completion of the project. For systems development projects the people are the major resource. Another resource for systems projects is the availability of computer processing time (mostly for testing purposes), which can present significant problems to the project manager when it comes to project scheduling.

Classification of Project Types

We are seeing an increasing number of organizations adopt a project classification rule that is used to determine the parts of their project management methodology that will be used for the project. Our advice to you is that if a particular part of the methodology does not have clear value-added benefit for you on a particular project, don't use it! Such characteristics as project duration, business value, risk, complexity, and others are used in the rule. We caution you to be sensitive to the administrative cost of planning and controlling projects. You would not want to spend three weeks planning a two-month project. As part of defining your project management methodology you will certainly consider defining project classes. Here are a few suggestions:

Class	*Duration*	*Risk*	*Complexity*	*Technology*
Type A	18 months	High	High	Breakthrough; problems certain
Type B	9 to 18 months	Medium	Medium	Current; problems likely
Type C	3 to 9 months	Low	Low	Best of breed; some problems
Type D	< 3 months	Very Low	Very Low	Practical; no problems

Projects of Type A require the full methodology. Projects of Type B and C each require less of the methodology and leave optional certain other parts of the methodology. Project managers can use the optional parts if they see added value to their project management practice. Projects of Type D just meet the definition of a project and may require only a scope statement and a few scheduling pieces of information.

The Scope Triangle: Time, Cost, Resources

Projects are dynamic systems that must be kept in equilibrium. Not an easy task, as we shall see! Figure 4.2 is a simple graphic that will help you understand the dynamics of the situation. The scope and quality of the project are represented as the geographic area inside the triangle shown in the figure. Bounding scope and quality are time, cost, and resources. Time is the window of time within which the project must be completed. Cost is the dollar budget available to complete the project. Resources are any consumables used on the project. People, equipment availability, facilities, and so on, are examples.

While the accountants will tell us that everything can be reduced to dollars—and they are right—we will separate out resources as just defined. They are controllable by the project manager and need to be

Figure 4.2 The scope triangle.

separately identified for that reason. The project plan will have identified the time, cost, and resources needed to deliver the scope and quality. In other words, the project is in equilibrium at the completion of the project-planning session and approval of the commitment of resources and dollars to the project. That will not last too long however. Change is waiting around the corner.

The scope triangle offers a number of insights into changes that can occur in the life of the project. For example, before any project work has been done, the triangle represents a system in balance. The sides are long enough to encompass the area generated by the scope and quality statements. Not long after work commences something is sure to change. Perhaps the customer calls with a requirement to add a feature not envisioned during the planning sessions, or the market opportunities have changed and it is necessary to reschedule the deliverables to an earlier schedule, or a key team member leaves the company and will be very difficult to replace. Any one of these changes throws the system out of balance. Referring to the triangle, note that the project manager controls resource utilization and work schedules. Management controls cost and resource level. The customer controls scope, quality, and delivery dates. This suggests a hierarchy for the project manager as solutions to accommodate the changes are sought. We return to this topic in greater detail in Chapter 16.

Scope Creep

Change is constant. To expect otherwise is simply unrealistic. Changes occur for several reasons that have nothing to do with the ability or skill of the requestor or the provider. Market conditions are very dynamic. Competitors can introduce or announce that they are going to introduce a new version of their product. Your management might decide that it is necessary to get to the market before the competition. Your job as project manager is to figure out how that might be accomplished. Tough job but somebody has to do it! Regardless of how the scope change occurs, it is your job as project manager to figure out how, if at all, you can accommodate the change.

Hope Creep

This one is a major problem for the project manager. There will be several activity managers within your project. These are team members who manage a hunk of work. They do not want to give you bad news, so they are prone to tell you that their work is proceeding according to schedule, when in fact it is not. It is their hope that they will catch up by the next report period, so they mislead you into thinking that they are on schedule. Shame on you if you did not check the accuracy of their status report! In any case they hope that they will catch up by completing some work ahead of schedule to make up the slippage.

Effort Creep

Every one of us has worked on a project that always seems to be only 95 percent complete no matter how much effort seems to be expended to complete them. Every week's status report records progress but the amount remaining doesn't seem to decrease proportionately.

Feature Creep

Closely related to scope creep is *feature creep*. This is the same as scope creep except it is initiated by the provider, not by the customer. It occurs most frequently in systems development projects. Here the programmer or analyst decides to include a little extra because it will add sizzle to the steak. The customer didn't ask for it but they got it, anyway. This is a rather interesting phenomenon that we have seen quite often, especially in systems development projects. An example will suffice to illustrate the point: The programmer is busy coding a particular module in the system. He or she gets an idea that the customer might appreciate having another option included. The systems requirements document does not mention this option. It seems so trivial that the programmer decides to include it, rather than go through the lengthy change process.

While this may seem rather innocent, let us look at some possible consequences. First, since the feature is not in the system requirements document it is also not in the acceptance test procedure, the systems documentation, the user documentation, and the user training program. What will happen if something goes wrong with the *new option*? How will some other programmer know what to do? What will happen when the user discovers the option and asks for some modification of it? We think you can see the consequences of such an innocent attempt to please. The message here is that a formal change request must be filed and if approved, the project plan and all related activities will be appropriately modified.

Project Management Terminology

Unfortunately there are very few terms that are accepted standards in project management lore. While this is somewhat discomforting it will not cause us too many problems. We will point out the discrepancies as we go along. In all cases we will try to use what appears to be the most common usage.

The Project Scenario: Project Risk vs. Business Value

It will be helpful to consider two dimensions that impact project planning and execution. The first is business value. By that we mean the value senior management will place on the project you are proposing. As business value changes so will the priority that management is willing to place on the project. The other dimension is risk. As risk increases, business value will have to increase if management is to approve your project for funding and support. Let us look at how these two dimensions interact with one another. Figure 4.3 depicts the four categories we will consider.

Business Value Low—Risk Low

Projects that fall into this category are the *nice to have and not difficult to do* projects. They involve technologies that are stable and understood. The project itself is not high on management's list of importance to the business. Such projects often deal with internal improvements to existing systems rather than new development. In times of budget constraints these will often be the first to go—and they should. For the project manager it is important not to go to the mat defending these projects, or to be caught asking for more resources. Management expects them to be done and won't give them much time on their agenda, that is, unless things begin to go wrong. These are not the kind of projects that can make you a hero but they sure can contribute to your downfall.

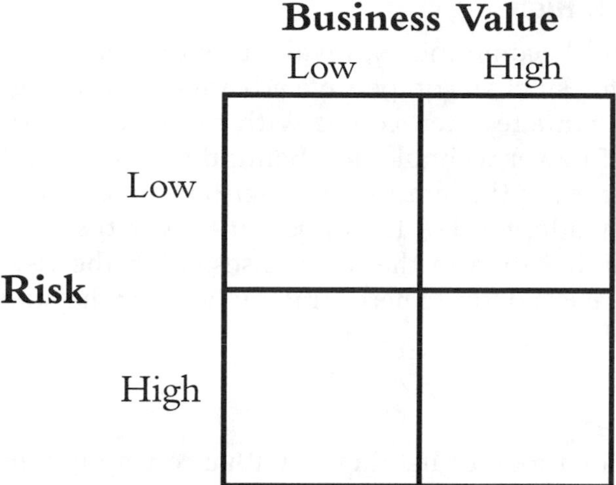

Figure 4.3 Risk/value project grid.

Business Value High—Risk Low

These projects have great business value, as perceived by senior managers. Management will be paying close attention to their progress. Since they are important you can expect to be reporting frequently on both a formal and informal basis. The risk of failure is low because you are working with established technology. Project managers would kill to get these assignments.

Business Value Low—Risk High

These are not the type of projects you want to have in your portfolio. They are high-risk and you will not have much management support if you run into difficulties. In such cases, however, it is important to be very careful in the planning stages. With any volatile technology it is to your advantage to pay closer attention to those activities that will use these types of technologies. This can be done by breaking activities down into subactivities so that better estimates of time and resource requirements can be made. We will have more to say about this later. High-risk projects require much closer management attention than do low-risk projects, and if business value is also high, then senior management attention is also more visible.

Business Value High—Risk High

These projects will become more prevalent as organizations look for any opportunity to establish competitive advantage over their competition. Strategic advantage often comes with the price of creative and innovative uses of newer technologies. Being the first to market with a product or service using the latest technologies has the advantages that accrue to the early adopter. For the project manager the risk of project failure is much higher than in the other cases. With the risk come the rewards, too! There is a definite hero strategy here for the stouthearted.

The S Curve

The *S curve* is another tool for helping us with a conceptual understanding of the project.

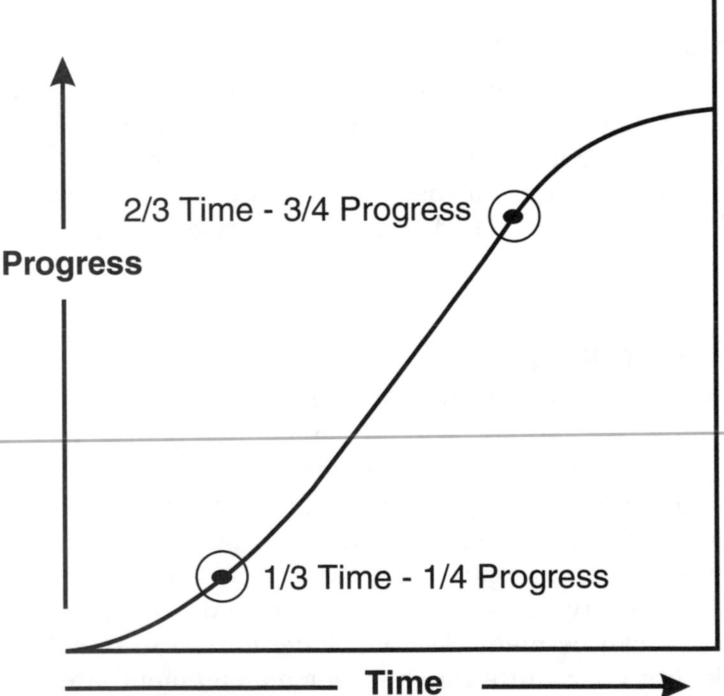

Figure 4.4 Standard S curve.

Normal Curve

As can be seen from Figure 4.4 the S curve models progress as well as other quantities of interest against time. Early in the life of a project the team is forming and learning to work together. Once the team has stabilized it can begin to work more effectively and the curve begins to accelerate rapidly. Toward the end of the project, work activity slows as the final touches are put on a successful project.

Aggressive Curve

Figure 4.5 depicts a somewhat different situation. Here the project plan is too aggressive and the team is eager to get started. Too much work is scheduled too early in the project before the team has even formed or begun to function as a team. The danger here is that mistakes will occur, rework will be required, and progress slows below the pace of

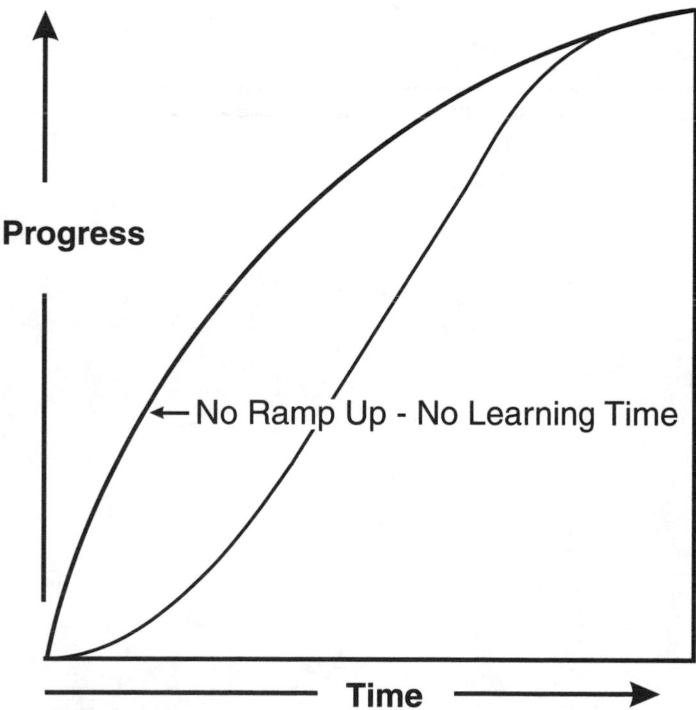

Figure 4.5 The aggresive curve.

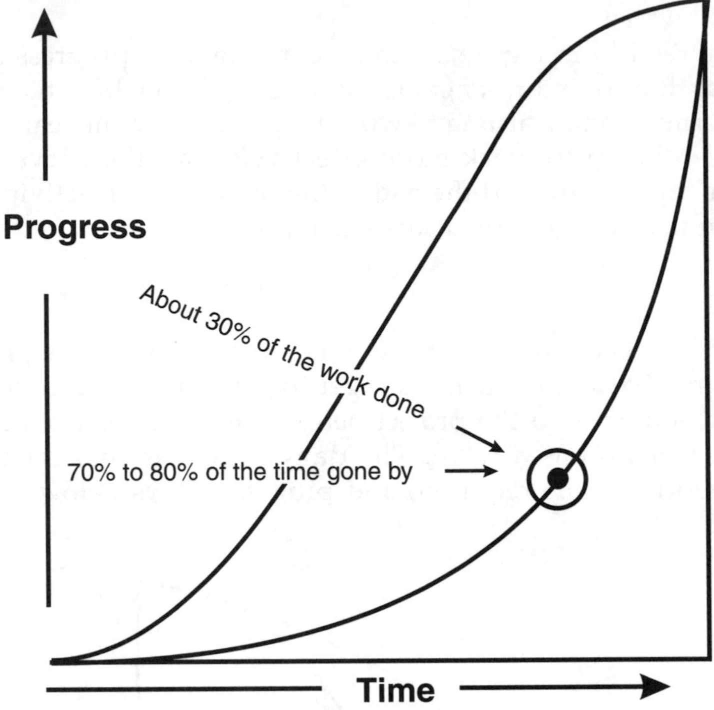

Figure 4.6 The curve to avoid.

the normal curve. The only exception that we have seen work is when the team has been together for some time, worked on projects together, and knows each other's strengths and weaknesses. Here one might see an aggressive curve that sustains a high rate of progress over the life of the project.

The Curve to Avoid

The next example is quite common. Figure 4.6 shows a project in which little work is accomplished early and the team puts on a full-court press as the deliverable dates approach. Too often the project team *can't get there from here*. Obviously this is the curve to avoid.

A manager . . . sets objectives . . . organizes . . . motivates . . . and communicates . . . measures . . . and develops people. Every manager does these things—knowingly or not. A manager may do them well, or may do them wretchedly but always does them.

Peter Drucker

CHAPTER 5

WHAT IS PROJECT MANAGEMENT?

CHAPTER LEARNING OBJECTIVES

As a result of participating in the learning experiences in this chapter you will be able to:

1. Understand the relationship between people management and project management.
2. Understand the five phases of the project management life cycle.
3. Know what constitutes a Joint Project Planning (JPP) session and how to plan and conduct one.
4. Understand the deliverables from the JPP and how they relate to project success.

Definition of Project Management

When we think of the principles of management we usually associate them with the management of people. Those same principles also apply to projects, as we now illustrate.

Defining

One of the first tasks of managers is to define the work to be done in their area of responsibility. There is a parallel in project management. For the project manager this will often be a very preliminary phase of the project management life cycle but, as we shall see, it is a very important one. For it is here that the requestor and the project manager come to an agreement over several important aspects of the project. There are five questions to be answered by any good definition of a project:

1. What is the problem or opportunity being addressed?
2. What is the goal of the project?
3. What objectives are necessary in order to accomplish the goal?
4. How will we determine if the project has been successful?
5. Are there any assumptions, risks, or obstacles that may affect success?

The defining phase sets the scope of the project. It will be the basis for decisions as to whether a particular function or feature is within the scope of the project. Even the best of intentions in defining project scope is not enough. For a variety of reasons to be discussed later, the scope of the project changes—sometimes far more frequently than the project manager prefers. We call these changes *scope creep,* which is a way of life in today's organizations. It is the bane of the project manager but it must be dealt with effectively if the project is to be successful. It arises from several sources ranging from something the client forgot to include in the business requirements document, to a change in business priorities that necessitates scope change. For now it is sufficient to know that the project manager must respond to scope creep by documenting the alternatives and consequences of each that will result from the change of scope. A good project manager will have a formal change management process in place. We will have much more to say on this later.

Planning

Some would argue that planning is a waste of time. No sooner is the plan completed than something comes along to change it. These same naysayers would also argue that the plan, once done, is merely put on the shelf so that the team can get down to doing some real work. We will show you that the project plan is indispensable. Not only is it a roadmap to how the work will be done, but it is also a tool for decision making. Understand first that a project plan is dynamic. We expect it to change. A complete plan will clearly state what is to be done, why it is being done, who will do it, when it will be done, what resources will be needed, and what criteria must be met in order for the project to be declared complete and successful.

Planning reduces uncertainty. While we would never expect the project work to occur exactly as planned, having planned the work allows us to consider the likely outcome and to put the necessary corrective actions in place.

Planning improves efficiency. Once we have defined the work to be done and the resources needed to do the work, we are able to schedule work to take advantage of resource availability and to schedule work in parallel rather than in series. We are thus able to maximize our use of resources and complete the project work in less time than alternative approaches.

The mere act of planning gives us a better understanding of the goals and objectives of the project. Even if we were to discard the plan, we would have still benefitted from having done the exercise.

Just as Alice needed to know where in Wonderland she was going, so does the project manager. Not knowing where you are going prevents measurement of progress, and generates never knowing when the project is done. The plan also provides a basis for measuring work planned against work performed.

Executing

Executing the project plan involves a number of steps. In addition to organizing people, it includes the identification of the specific resources (manpower, materials, and money) for carrying out the work defined in the plan. It also involves scheduling workers to activities, and scheduling activities to start and end dates. As you will see, the final specification of the project schedule brings together all of the variables associated with the project. To facilitate this exercise we will introduce a number of tools and techniques that we have developed and use in our consulting practice.

Controlling

As part of the planning process an initial schedule is built. It specifies what is to be done, when, by whom, and what deliverables are expected. No matter how attentive the team is to creating the plan, the project work will not go according to plan. Schedules will slip. That is the reality of project management. In any case, the project manager must have a system in place to constantly monitor project progress or lack thereof. Not only will that monitoring system summarize completed work measured against the plan, but will also look ahead to forewarn of potential problems. Problem-escalation procedures and a formal change management process, which we discuss in Chapter 16, are essential to effective project control.

Closing

The closing phase is very important but it tends to be the part that is most often neglected by management. There is always the pressure to get on with the next project. There are several questions that should be answered as part of any closing:

1. Did the project do what the requestor said it would do?
2. Did the project do what the project manager said it would do?
3. Did the project team complete the project according to plan?
4. What information was collected that will help with later projects?
5. How well did the project management methodology work and how well did the project team follow it?

Closing therefore evaluates what was done and provides historical information for later projects. It is easy for management to skip this phase because it is perceived as an overhead expense, is easily overlooked, and delays getting the next project underway.

Project management is therefore seen as a method and a set of techniques based on the accepted principles of management used for planning, estimating, and controlling work activities to reach a desired end result on time—within budget and according to specification.

Causes of Project Failure

These causes are offered as an introduction to your workbook. Knowing who the *enemy* is gives us a competitive advantage. Projects that have failed generally display several of the following characteristics:

1. The customer's conditions of satisfaction have not been negotiated.
2. The project no longer has a high priority.
3. No one seems to be in charge.
4. The schedule is too optimistic.
5. The project plan is not used to manage the project.
6. Sufficient resources have not been committed.
7. Project status is not monitored against the plan.
8. No formal communications plan is in place.
9. The project has lost sight of its original goals.
10. There is no change management process in place.

Those of our readers with project management experience will recognize many of these causes. Now that you are forewarned , we hope that you will become forearmed.

An Overview of Project Management

Over years of consulting and training in project management we have observed a number of project management methodologies that would seem to differ from one another. On closer examination we have actually found that there are a number of underlying principles that are present in the more successful methodologies. From them we have fashioned a project management life cycle that was first published by Weiss and Wysocki.[1] Since then we have continued to compare this life

1. Weiss, Joseph W., and Robert K. Wysocki. 1991. *5-Phase Project Management: A Planning and Implementation Guide*. Reading, MA: Addison-Wesley.

cycle with client methodologies. The results confirm our assumption of recurring features in successful methodologies. More recently the Project Management Institute has circulated their Project Management Body of Knowledge, PMBOK, which has an underlying life cycle remarkably similar to the one we have adopted in our consulting practice. The one we share with you parallels PMBOK. If your organization has a methodology in place, compare it to the model given here. You should be able to map your methodology into this life cycle.

The Planning Process

Planning, or rather, effective planning, is painful. Planning doesn't seem like real work. Projects are always behind schedule, so we are tempted to skip planning so that we can get down to the real work of the project. Experience has shown that good planning can actually decrease the time required to complete a project, even taking the planning time into account. Planning reduces risk and increases productivity by 50 percent. We find it interesting that project teams do not have time to plan but they do have time to do the work over again. What insanity!

Goal Orientation

Every project has one goal. It is the agreement between requestor and provider as to what is to be accomplished from this project, the deliverable if you will. The goal tells us where we are going so that when we get there we will know it. In our project management life cycle the goal is bounded by a number of objective statements. These objective statements clarify the fuzzy boundary of the goal statement. Taken as a pair the goal and objective statements scope the project. They become the framework within which the entire project planning process is conducted.

Teamwork

Finally, projects are done by teams. We have to escape the notion that an individual is singly responsible for the success (or failure) of the project. True, you can point to examples in which the efforts of an individual brought the project to successful completion, but these are rare events. In contemporary organizations the project team is often cross-functional and spans organizational boundaries. We discuss the special problems that arise in these situations later in the workbook.

Levels of Project Management

The project management life cycle actually contains three cycles. Which cycle you use in a given project depends on what management needs you are trying to meet. Many organizations have defined a classification of projects based on such project characteristics as risk, business value, length, complexity, and cost. The project profile determines the classification and the classification defines the extent to which the project management methodology is to be used.

Defining, Planning, Organizing

This is the simplest of the three cycles and is concerned with getting the project going. There is no follow-up on performance against plan. I have encountered a number of situations in which one person will be singly responsible for completing all project activities. In such cases there is good value in planning the project but limited value in implementing the control and close phases. Here the project manager and client are the same person and are interested only in laying out a strategy for doing the work. Often this project will have to be planned in conjunction with one or more other projects. The intent is to set a timeline for completing this project in conjunction with others underway. This cycle is closely related to good time-management practices.

Defining, Planning, Organizing, Controlling

This is the version that is most often thought of as project management. Getting the project started is only half (or actually much less) of the effort. The more people, the more activities; and the more resources involved, the more likely the project manager will need to follow with the control function. Things will go wrong—you can bet on it! A mechanism needs to be in place to identify problems early on and do something to keep the project moving ahead as planned.

Defining, Planning, Organizing, Controlling, Closing

The astute project manager will want to learn from this project. Several questions can be answered from an audit of the records from completed projects.

In addition to these three levels, information systems organizations are beginning to introduce a classification scheme for their projects. Projects are typically classified based on length, cost, complexity, business value, risk, and other criteria. Four or five classifications are typical. Each classification has required and optional initiation, definition, planning, control, reporting, and closing requirements. The alternative of *one size fits all* doesn't make much sense in today's organization, where rightsizing, efficiency, and time to market are critical to success.

The Project Plan as a Model

The project plan is a description of events to come. In that sense it is a model. Furthermore, as events occur the model will be impacted by those events and will change and describe again how future events in the project are likely to occur.

Since it is a model, we will be able to test alternative strategies for redirecting future events. As project work commences the nature of the project will change—sometimes radically. Activities will get behind or ahead of schedule; team members will be reassigned, leave the company, get sick, and so on. Market situations will change, rendering all or some of the project objectives obsolete. These events can come one at a time or in clumps, and the project manager must be ready to analyze, decide, and act. You should already have an appreciation for the complexity of the project plan and work. There are in fact several dimensions to consider when trying to formulate a going-forward strategy. Here are just a few:

- If a project activity finishes earlier or later than the scheduled date, can the resource schedule for later activities be adjusted accordingly?
- If one or more project activities finish late, can other resources assigned to the project be reallocated to restore the project to its original schedule?
- How can the project manager simultaneously compress the project schedule while not creating unresolvable resource scheduling conflicts?
- What resources can be reallocated from one project to another without adversely affecting each project's schedule?

Any one of these decision situations involves a number of interdependent variables. It is unlikely that any project manager could process these variables and all of the possible variations without the aid of a computer-based project model and supporting software.

Management Principles Applied to Project Management

The Reactive/Proactive Roles of Information Services

Systems project initiation basically comes from two sources: from the I/S Department or not from the I/S Department. In the reactive role I/S responds to a request for a systems development project from the customer (internal/external). In such cases the business justification is the responsibility of the requestor, and it is the I/S Department that provides input to that justification. Roughly stated the customer is saying, "If you could provide a system with the following features, we would be able to impact business in the following ways...." These situations generally have a much lower risk of implementation failure and buy-in by the customer. The customer has a vested interest in the success of the project. Participation by the customer on the project team from planning inception through conversion is not a problem.

On the other hand, the proactive role for I/S is more difficult for the project manager. First, the business value of the project will often have been the responsibility of the I/S Department through the project manager. The customer's opinions may vary from very skeptical to very supportive and anywhere in between. The intended customer may not be as willing to fully participate on the project team as in the former case. Obviously there is a selling job to be done by the project manager. It is imperative that the customer have a responsible role on the project team. At the extreme the customer might be recruited to be the project manager, thus giving the customer a vested interest in the success of the project.

In either case there must be a meeting of the minds on what is being requested and what is being provided. This *clarity of purpose* or *Conditions of Satisfaction* should be taken seriously by both parties to the contract. We work in such complex and technically sophisticated environments that a clear and precise understanding of each party's needs is not easy. It is in the best interest of both parties to take as much care as possible in understanding what is requested and what is to be delivered.

We discuss in this section a number of methods that are available to help I/S professionals and their customers define the project.

An Overview of the Project Management Life Cycle

As we discuss project management at the 30,000-foot level in this section, many of our readers will discover that they have been doing bits and pieces of project management without realizing it. They will be saying: I've been doing that. I didn't call it by that name, but that is essentially what I have been doing all these years. Take comfort, for project management can be defined as nothing more than organized common sense. In fact, if it were not common sense, we would have a difficult time gaining any converts!

Please follow along with this discussion by referring to Figure 5.1. Note that the project management life cycle consists of five phases, with five steps in each phase. The five phases are done in sequence, with one feedback loop from the control phase to the planning phase. This model is adapted from the PMI PMBOK and from an earlier work of one of the authors (Weiss and Wysocki[2]).

Scope the Project

This phase of the project management life cycle is the one most often given the least attention. In this phase an initial statement of the project is put forward. A document called the Project Overview Statement (POS) is prepared. The POS is a brief document (usually one page) that describes, in the language of the business, what problem or opportunity is being addressed by the project; the project goal and objectives; how success will be measure; and what risks, obstacles, and assumptions may affect the project outcome. The purpose of the POS is to gain the approval of management to proceed to the next phase, which is the generation of the detailed project plan.

The Project Overview Statement, or some form of it, is in wide use. It is often called a Document of Understanding, Scope Statement, Initial Project Definition, or Statement of Work. In some cases attachments may be required. We are aware of organizations that require cost benefit analysis, return on investment analysis, internal rate of return esti-

2. Weiss, Joseph W., and Robert K. Wysocki. *5-Phase Project Management: A Planning and Implementation Guide.*

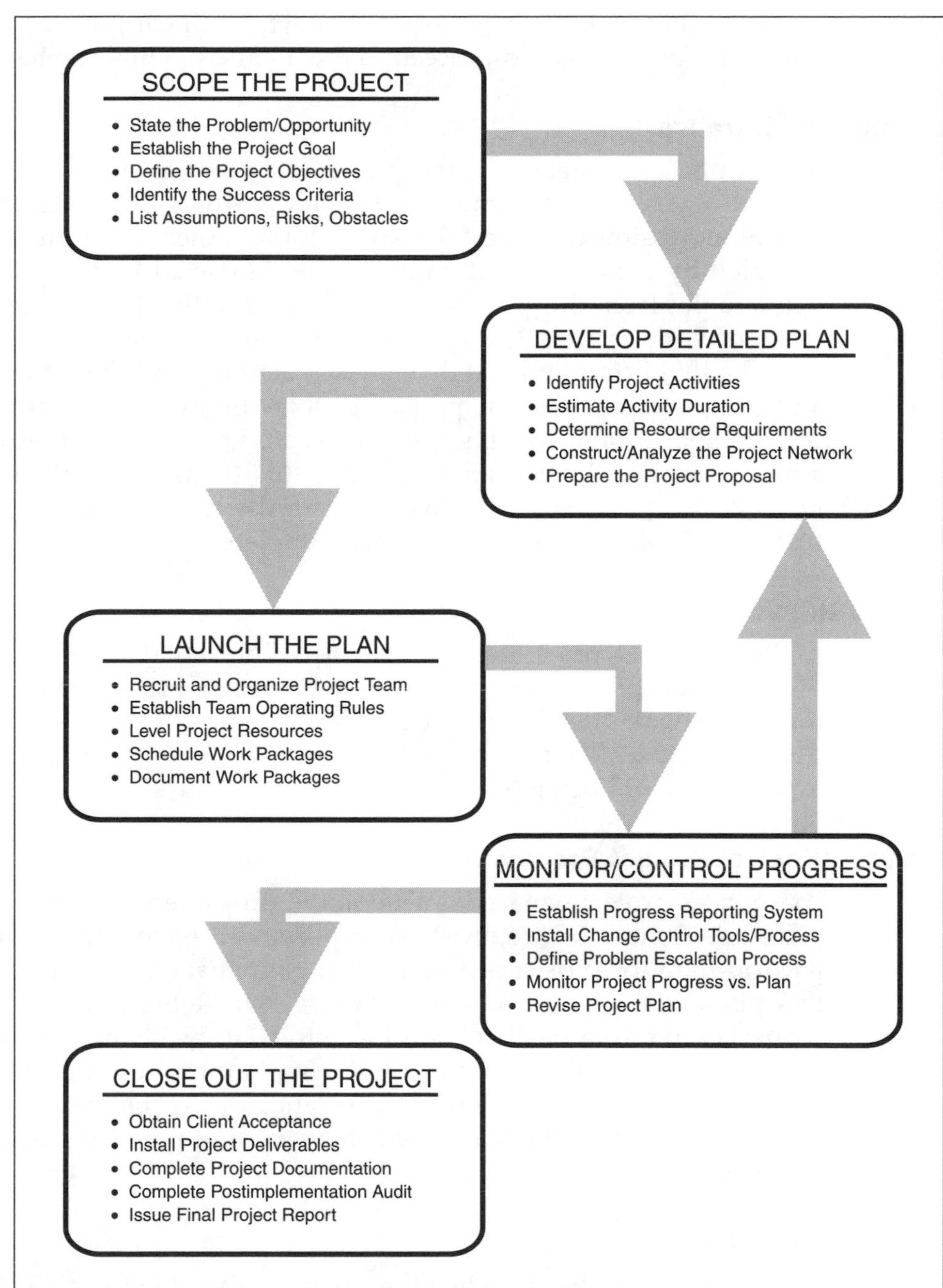
SCOPE THE PROJECT
• State the Problem/Opportunity
• Establish the Project Goal
• Define the Project Objectives
• Identify the Success Criteria
• List Assumptions, Risks, Obstacles
DEVELOP DETAILED PLAN
• Identify Project Activities
• Estimate Activity Duration
• Determine Resource Requirements
• Construct/Analyze the Project Network
• Prepare the Project Proposal
LAUNCH THE PLAN
• Recruit and Organize Project Team
• Establish Team Operating Rules
• Level Project Resources
• Schedule Work Packages
• Document Work Packages
MONITOR/CONTROL PROGRESS
• Establish Progress Reporting System
• Install Change Control Tools/Process
• Define Problem Escalation Process
• Monitor Project Progress vs. Plan
• Revise Project Plan
CLOSE OUT THE PROJECT
• Obtain Client Acceptance
• Install Project Deliverables
• Complete Project Documentation
• Complete Postimplementation Audit
• Issue Final Project Report

Figure 5.1 Project management life cycle.

mates, and break-even analysis as part of the input for deciding whether a project should proceed to the detailed planning phase.

Develop the Detailed Plan

In this phase the details of the project plan are developed. While this may be an exercise for one or a few individuals, it is often a formal planning session (see the following "Joint Project Planning" section) attended by those who will impact or be impacted by the project. The deliverables from this planning session include the detailed description of each work activity, the resources required to complete the activity, the scheduled start and end date of each activity, and the estimated cost and completion date of the project. In some organizations there may be any number of attachments, such as feasibility studies, environmental scans, or best-of-breed analyses. Once this document, called a *project proposal,* is approved, the project enters the next phase in which the final details of the work schedule are completed.

Launch the Plan

In this phase the project team is specified. The actual people assigned to work on the project will be identified, exact work schedules will be determined, and detailed descriptions of tasks to be done will be developed. The completion of this final planning activity signals the beginning of the monitoring phase.

Monitor/Control Project Progress

As soon as project work commences, the project enters the monitoring phase. A number of project status reports will have been defined and used to monitor project progress. Change management is a big part of this phase, and procedures will have been installed to process change requests. Here the feedback loop is activated, as change requests will always cause some amount of project replanning to take place. Problems will also occur as work finishes ahead of or behind schedule. A problem-escalation procedure will have been defined to handle these situations.

Close Out the Project

The final phase is begun when the customer says the project is finished. In this phase a number of closing activities are undertaken. Deliverables are installed, final reports and documentation filed, a postimplementation audit done, and a postproject celebration held.

Joint Project Planning (JPP) Sessions

The Project Management Life Cycle Pain Curve

Pay me now or pay me later applies equally well to project planning. When the team and your management are anxious for work to begin, it is difficult to focus on developing a solid plan of action before you are pressed into service. At times it would seem that the level of detail in the plan is overkill, but it is not. You will have to accept that on faith at this point in your learning. The project manager must resist the pressure to start project work and spend the time up front generating a detailed project plan. It has been demonstrated that a poor planning effort takes its toll later in the project as schedules slip, quality suffers, and expectations are not met.

The *pain curve* (Figure 5.2) is telling us that proper planning is painful but it pays off in lesser pain downstream in the project. To not plan is to expose yourself to significant pain as the project commences. In fact that pain usually continues to increase. It would continue to increase indefinitely except for the fact that someone usually pulls the plug on the project once the pain reaches unbearable levels. As one project manager puts it, "Pain me now or pain me later." Figure 5.2 is a graphical depiction of the project management pain curve.

We advocate and use a group process for generating the project overview statement and the detailed project plan. In this section we explain at a somewhat higher level how that process works, and leave to later chapters the specific how-to details of the process.

Our planning process shares many of the same features as Joint Requirements Planning (JRP) and Joint Applications Design (JAD) sessions. Ideally all of those affected by the project are invited to attend a planning session wherein the detailed plan for a project is to be developed and agreed to by all the stakeholders. Such planning sessions typically last from one to three days. They are intense. There is often conflict. But in the end there is agreement as to how this project can be accomplished within a specified time frame, budget, and customer specification.

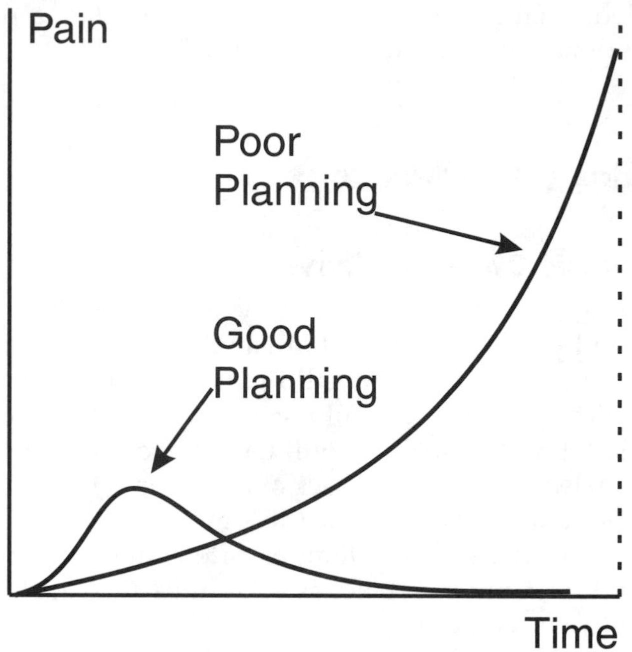

Figure 5.2 The project management pain curve.

Objectives

The objective of a JPP session is very simple: Develop a project plan that meets the conditions of satisfaction, as negotiated between the requestor and the provider. Sounds simple doesn't it? Unfortunately it doesn't happen with any regularity. There are many reasons for this. People are generally impatient to get on with the work of the project. After all, there are deadlines to meet and other projects demanding our attention. We don't have time for planning; we have too much work to do and customers to satisfy. Regrettably, at the project's eleventh hour when it is too late to recover from a poor plan, we bow in defeat. Next time, we promise ourselves, we will pay more attention to the planning details. Somehow that next time never seems to come. *It's time for change!*

Planning the JPP Session

Planning by the team and the stakeholders has always been viewed as having advantages over other forms of project planning. We have encountered many cases in which the synergy of the group provides far more accuracy of activity estimates, and we expect more complete information input to the planning process itself and more reasonable tracking requirements. Perhaps the best advantage of all is that it creates a much stronger commitment to the project for all those who lived through the pain of generating and agreeing upon the complete project plan. If all else fails, it is more fun than doing planning in isolation!

For many, we often feel that planning is at best a necessary evil. It is something we do because we have to and because we can then say that we have thought about where we want to go and how we are going to get there. Once written, plans are bound in a nice notebook and become bookends gathering dust on someone's shelf.

Make up your mind right now to change that! Planning is essential to good project management. The plan that you will generate is a dynamic document. It will change as the project commences. It will be a referent for you and the team members when questions of scope and change arise. We make no bones about it—to do good planning is painful, but to do poor planning is even more painful.

The first document to be developed in the JPP session is the Project Overview Statement (POS). We will return to the details of developing the POS in Chapter 7. The POS can be developed in a number of ways. If it is an idea for consideration, it will probably be developed by one individual—typically the person who will be the project manager. It can be departmentally based or cross-departmentally based. The broader the impact on the enterprise, the more likely it will be developed as the first phase of a Joint Project Planning (JPP) session.

The JPP session must be planned down to the last detail if it is to be successful. Understand ahead of time that it is a very intense session. Participants often get emotional and will even dig their heels into the process.

Attendees

The JPP participants will be anyone who might be affected by or have input into the project. If the project involves deliverables or is a new process or procedure, anyone who has input to the process, receives output from the process, or handles the deliverables should participate in the JPP. Obviously the customer falls into one or more of these categories and hence must be present at the JPP. The manager of the resources that may be required by the project team will attend the JPP.

In many organizations the project has a project champion (not necessarily the project manager or customer manager) who may wish to participate, too. A formal invitation, announcing the project, its general direction and purpose, and the planning schedule should be issued to all of these individuals. RSVPs are a must! Following is the list of participants for the JPP Session.

Facilitator

It requires an experienced facilitator to pull off a JPP session. We recommend a neutral party as the facilitator. It is important that the facilitator not have a vested interest or bring biases to the session. For this reason we strongly suggest that the project manager not facilitate the session. Another project manager might do. An outside consultant with experience conducting such sessions is usually the best choice.

Project Manager

Having the proposed project's project manager (if known) facilitate the JPP may seem to be an excellent choice but it may be the wrong choice. If the project is politically charged or has customers from more than one function, process, or resource pool, the JPP facilitator may need to be a neutral party. That may not be the project manager. The project manager must be comfortable with the project plan. After all, the project manager is the final responsibility when it comes to getting the project done on time, within budget, and according to specification.

Another Project Manager

Skilled JPP facilitators are hard to find. If the project manager is not a good choice for JPP facilitator, then maybe another project manager—presumably unbiased—would be a good choice, especially if he or she has JPP experience.

JPP Consultant

Project management consultants will often serve as another source of qualified JPP facilitators. Their broad experience in project management and project management consulting will be invaluable. This will be especially true in those organizations that have recently completed project management training and are in the process of implementing their own project management methodology. Having an outside consultant facilitate the JPP will be as much a learning experience as it is an opportunity to get off to a good start with a successful JPP.

Technographer

The JPP facilitator is supported by a technographer, a professional who not only knows project management, but also is an expert in the software tools to be used to support the project. While the JPP facilitator is conducting the planning activities, the JPP technographer is recording the plan in the computer. At any point in time—and there will be several—the technographer can print out or display the plan for all to see and critique.

Core Project Team

Commitment is so important that to exclude the core team from the JPP session would be foolish. Estimating activity duration and resource requirements will be much easier with professional expertise in the session. The core project team is made up of those individuals who will stay with the project from first day to last. This does not mean that they are with the project full time. In today's organization that is not to be expected unless the organization uses self-directed teams.

Client Representative

This is always a bit tricky. Let's face it: Some customers really don't want to be bothered. It is up to the project manager or champion to convince customers of the importance of their participation in the JPP session. We won't claim that this will be easy but it is nevertheless important. There must be customer buy-in to the project plan. That will not happen unless customers are involved in the planning session. To not have their buy-in is to court failure.

Resource Manager

These managers control the resources that the project will require. To put a schedule together without input from these managers would be a waste of time. They may have some suggestions that will make the plan all that more realistic, too. In some cases they may send a representative who might also be part of the project team. The important factor here is that someone from the resource area is empowered to make commitments of resources to the project schedule.

Project Champion

This person drives the project and sells it to senior management. In many cases the champion may be the customer—an ideal situation since commitment is already there. In other cases they may be the senior manager of the division, department, or process that will be the beneficiary of the project.

Functional Manager

Since they may provide input to or receive output from the project, they or a representative should participate in the planning session.

Process Owner

For the same reasons that functional managers should be present, so should process managers.

Facilities

Since the planning team may spend as many as three consecutive days in planning it is important that the physical facility be comfortable and away from the daily interruptions (off-site is best). While off-site seems preferable, we prefer on-site planning sessions. This has both advantages and disadvantages but, with proper planning, can be controlled. Easy access to information has been a major advantage in our experience.

Enough space should be allocated so that groups of four or five planning members each have separate work areas with tables, chairs, and flip charts at each. All work should be done in one room. We have found that breakout rooms tend to be dysfunctional. The room should have plenty of whiteboard space or blank walls. In many cases we have taped flip-chart paper or butcher paper to the walls. You can never have enough writing space in the planning room.

Equipment

An ample supply of sticker notes, tape, scissors, and colored marking pens are the supplies you will need. As for high-tech equipment: An overhead projector, graphics pad, and PC with the project management software is all you will need.

Agenda

The agenda for the JPP session (Figure 5.3) is straightforward. It may be completed in one, two, or three sessions. For example, an early meeting with the requestor may be scheduled, at which time the Conditions of Satisfaction are drafted. These will be input to the second session in which the POS is drafted. In those cases where the POS must be approved before detailed planning can commence, there will be an interruption until approval can be granted. Once approval is obtained, the third session can be scheduled. At this session (usually two or three days in length) the detailed project plan can be drafted for approval.

1. **Write the Conditions of Satisfaction.**
2. **Write the Project Overview Statement.**
3. **Create a first-level WBS (entire planning team).**
4. **Create a complete WBS (subteam exercise).**
5. **Present and critique the WBS.**
6. **Estimate activity durations and resource requirements.**
7. **Construct project network.**
8. **Determine critical path.**
9. **Revise and approve project completion date.**
10. **Schedule resources.**
11. **Gain consensus on the project plan.**

Figure 5.3 JPP session agenda.

Deliverables

The deliverables from the JPP session are given in the project management life cycle but are repeated in Figure 5.4 for completeness.

We will spend considerable time on each of the deliverables in the following chapters. For now we offer a brief definition of each.

Project Overview Statement

The Project Overview Statement is often the first deliverable from the planning session. This will occur in cases in which the Conditions of Satisfaction are yet to be negotiated. A statement of the request appears in the problem/opportunity section of the Project Overview Statement, while a statement of what will be provided is given in the goal and objective statements.

Work Breakdown Structure

The Work Breakdown Structure (WBS) is a graphical or indented outline list of the work (expressed as activities) to be done to complete the project. It is used as a planning tool as well as a reporting structure.

Activity Duration Estimates

The schedule is a major deliverable and it is developed from estimates of the duration of each work activity in the project.

- **Project Overview Statement**
- **Work Breakdown Structure**
- **Activity Duration Estimates**
- **Resource Requirements**
- **Project Network Schedule**

Figure 5.4 JPP session deliverables.

Resource Requirements

For each item of work in the project an estimate of the resources is required to perform the work. In most cases this will be the technical and people skills, although it may also include physical facilities, equipment, computer cycles, and so on.

Project Network Schedule

Using the WBS, the planning team will define the sequence in which the project activities must be performed. Initially this sequence is determined only by the technical relationships between activities, not by management prerogatives. That is, the deliverables from one or more activities are needed in order to begin work on the next activity. This sequence is most easily understood by displaying it graphically. The definition of the network activities and the details of the graphical representation are covered in Chapters 8 through 11.

Activity Schedule

With the sequence determined, the planning team will schedule the start and end dates for each activity. The availability of resources will largely determine that schedule.

Resource Assignments

The output of the activity schedule will be the assignment of specific resources (such as skill sets) to the project activities.

Project Notebook

Documentation of any type is always a chore to produce. Not so in the five-phase methodology we are using. Project documentation happens as a natural byproduct of the project work. All that is needed is to appoint a project team member to be responsible. His or her responsibilities include gathering information that is already available, putting it in a standard format, and electronically archiving it. This responsibility begins with the project planning session.

The productivity of a workgroup seems to depend on how the group members see their own goals in relation to the goals of the organization.

Paul Hersey and Kenneth H. Blanchard

When the best leader's work is done the people say, "We did it ourselves."

Lao-Tzu
Chinese philosopher

Leadership is the manager's ability to get subordinates to develop their capabilities by inspiring them to achieve.

John A. Reinecke and William F. Schoell

CHAPTER 6

MANAGEMENT STYLES FOR PROJECT MANAGERS

CHAPTER LEARNING OBJECTIVES

As a result of participating in the learning experiences in this chapter you will be able to:

1. Understand situational management and how to use it.
2. Know the factors that motivate and demotivate professional staff, and how to use them to improve professional staff productivity.
3. Use job design for staff development.
4. Discuss characteristics that an effective project manager must possess.
5. Understand the need for technical expertise by the project manager.
6. List the interpersonal skills needed by the project manager.
7. Discuss the factors that are important to selecting the project team members.
8. Organize the project team.
9. Know the difference between core and contract team members.

Directing, Coaching, Supporting, and Delegating

There is a cycle that manager/subordinate relationships follow. It begins at the time an employee begins a new job or new job responsibilities. While the pace of movement from stage to stage will vary with each employee, each stage will be represented in the building of the manager/subordinate relationship. Kenneth Blanchard in *Leadership and the One Minute-Manager* (Morrow, 1985) explains this concept. His model is depicted in Figure 6.1.

In most cases, when people first join a company their relationship with their manager is one of mentor and mentored. They are in a learning mode and close supervision is to be expected. After some time and at a point where the manager has some sense of how a person works, how much instruction is needed, and how self-managed they can be, they

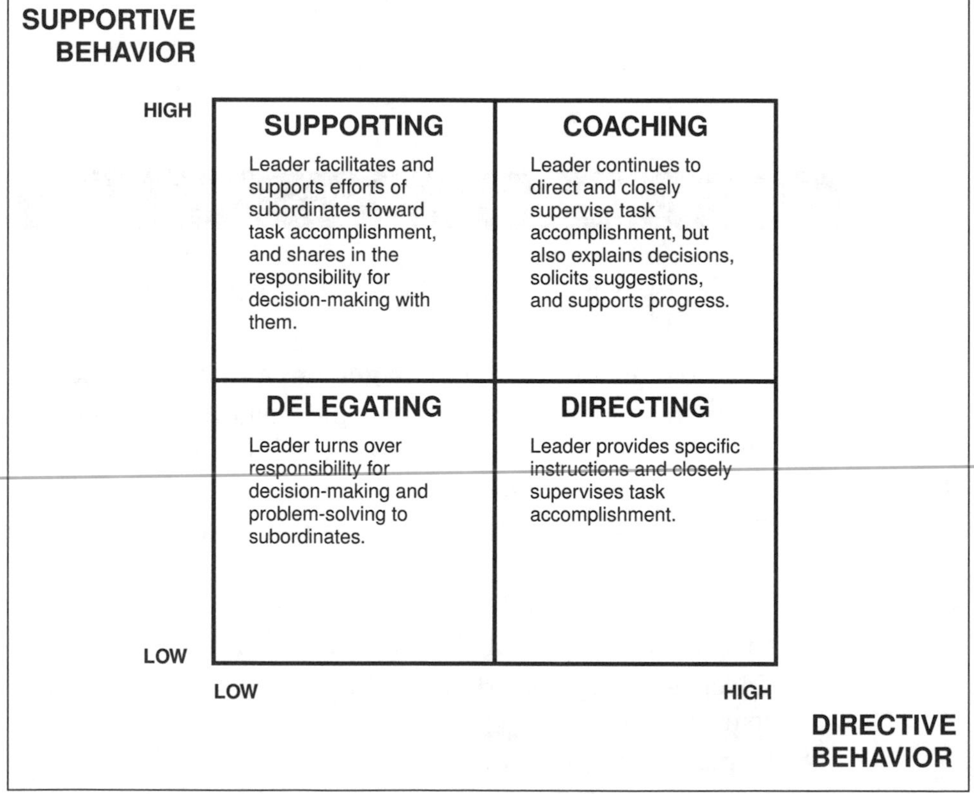

Figure 6.1 Management styles.

begin to loosen their control and direct supervision and move more toward a coaching role. The coaching role is one of offering advice, and suggestions, and evaluating the outcome. Finally the transition to a supporting role happens. Here the individual is operating quite independently of the manager. Some decision-making authority is vested in the person. At the last stage the person is vested with responsibility for carrying out the objectives of the unit in their area of interest.

Situational Management Styles

There are two scenarios to discuss: The first is the result of an initiative taken by the subordinate. The second is the result of an assignment given by the manager. Figure 6.2 illustrates the point of this discussion.

When the subordinate approaches the manager with an idea for a project, the question of commitment on the part of the subordinate is mute. Of course they are committed. The relationship between the manager and the subordinate in this case is clearly different from the case in which the manager suggests the project to the subordinate. While the subordinate may appear committed, there will always be that question. Is the subordinate committed or is the subordinate merely telling the manager what the manager wants to hear? Here the relationship between the manager and the subordinate is much closer than in the former case. The manager will want to closely monitor the subordinate, making sure that the project is moving along as requested. In the for-

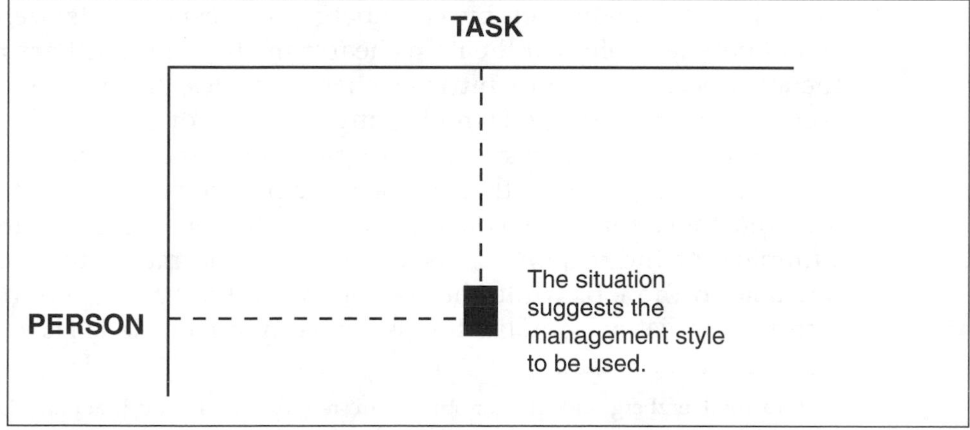

Figure 6.2 Situational management.

mer case, however, the manager will simply want a routine status report on how the project is going. There will be little need to direct the work of the subordinate except to make sure that the objective is clearly stated.

This relationship can change as the task changes, and will certainly change from one subordinate to another. For the project manager the challenge is to display an evenhandedness in working with members of the project team. Getting the project done on time, within budget, and according to specification is paramount for the project manager. Having to deal with project team-member relationships is important only in that it contributes or hinders project progress.

The Use of Projects for Motivation and Staff Development

Motivators and Demotivators

Not everyone can be motivated. In fact, in most cases all the manager can do is create an environment in which subordinates might be motivated and then hope that they are. It's really like farming. All the farmer can do is pick the crop to plant, the acreage to plant it on, the fertilizer to use, and then hope that mother nature supplies the right amounts of rain, wind, and sunshine. The same scenario applies to the subordinate.

Fortunately we do have some information on what professional staff perceive as motivators and demotivators on the job.[1] Figure 6.3 is data from a 1959 survey by Hertzberg. The respondents were professional people. Note that the items nearer the top of the list are related to the job, specifically to its intrinsic characteristics. A similar survey was conducted in 1988 by Daniel Cougar of Colorado State. Here the respondents were analysts and programmers, and the responses were grouped by those areas that the respondents considered to be motivators and those that they considered to be demotivators. Figure 6.4 is a summary of the responses. As you can see the motivators tend to be intrinsic to the job, while the demotivators tend to be environmental factors. The list of demotivators is probably mislabeled. These environ-

1. Both the Herzberg and Cougar studies are reported in Toledo Mata and Elizabeth A. Unger, "Another Look at Motivating Data Processing Professionals," Department of Computer Science, Kansas State University, Manhattan, KS, p. 4.

BACKGROUND
DEVELOPING AND MOTIVATING

MOTIVATORS

- Recognition
- Advancement and growth
- Responsibility
- The work itself

DEMOTIVATORS

- Company policy
- Administrative practices
- Working conditions
- Technical supervision
- Interpersonal relations
- Job security
- Salary

Figure 6.3 Motivators and demotivators.

ANALYST AND PROGRAMMER
RANKING OF
MOTIVATING FACTORS

- The work itself
- Opportunity for achievement
- Opportunity for advancement
- Pay and benefits
- Recognition
- Increased responsibility
- Technical supervision
- Interpersonal relations
- Job security
- Working conditions
- Company policy

Figure 6.4 Ranked motivators.

mental factors are what employees expect to have. Therefore having them is not a motivator, but not having them is definitely a demotivator. Managers should find it comforting that the list of motivators contains many areas that they control or influence directly. These are discussed in the following.

Challenge

Professionals have always responded to challenge. To tell professionals that something cannot be done is usually all that need be said to get their creative juices flowing. A solution will follow. Nothing is more dreaded by a professional to continue practicing skills long since mastered. This is the ground on which errors are grown. Being bored usually leads to daydreaming and lack of attention to detail. In any case errors result. Being challenged does not mean that every moment of every day is spent solving previously unsolved problems. For example, spending only an hour or two on a new and challenging task is sufficient to keep a professional motivated throughout the day.

Achievement

Professionals want to know that they are progressing toward some professional goal. Such is the case if their achievement is not only recognized but followed with another challenge. Success begets success, and challenge begets challenge.

Recognition

Achievement must be followed by recognition—especially among a person's peers. Recognition does not necessarily mean dollars or promotions—or titles.

Job Design

Since job is so important, let us look at job design for just a moment. Cougar has identified five dimensions needed to define a job (see Figure 6.5).

Skill Variety

Jobs that do not offer much task variety, and hence opportunity to learn and practice new skills, become boring for most people. In designing

CORE JOB DIMENSIONS

- Skill variety
- Task identity
- Task significance
- Autonomy
- Feedback

Figure 6.5 Core job dimensions.

jobs it is therefore advantageous to consider building in some task variety. This may provide only a diversion from what otherwise would be a tedious and boring work day. On the other hand, it might also provide a break in which the person can learn a new skill. With a little bit of forethought the manager can find opportunities for cross-training by introducing some task variety for new skills development. Of course, the manager will want to consider the risk involved in such actions. The person may not rise to the challenge of the new task or might not have the native ability to master the skills need to perform the new task.

Task Identity

People need to know what they are working on. This is especially true for contracted team members. Help them understand their work in relation to the entire project. Knowing that their task is on the critical path will mean a lot to their attitude and the quality of their work.

Task Significance

Does it make any difference if I am successful? Will anybody notice? Just how important is my work to the overall success of the project? Am I just doing busywork to pass the time of day? They need to know if it makes any difference to the success of the project whether they are successful and on schedule.

Autonomy

Professionals want to know what is expected of them—what are the deliverables? They don't want to hear the project manager tell them every detail of how they will accomplish their work. Systems people are rugged individualists. They want to exercise their creativity. They want freedom, independence, and discretion in scheduling their work and determining the procedures they will follow to carry it out.

Feedback

Good, bad, or indifferent, professionals want to know how effective they are in their work. Paying attention to a professional is motivating in itself. Having something good to say is even better. When performance is below expectations, tell them. If you can convince them that they own the problem, then ask them for an action plan to correct their marginal performance.

The Project Manager vis-à-vis the Functional Manager

Project Manager Objectives

The objectives of the project manager are clear. Complete the project on time, within budget, and according to the customer's conditions of satisfaction, that is, according to specification. Staff development is not on the list! The only cases when staff development is an objective of the project manager occur when the project manager also has line responsibility for the project team, in self-managed teams, or in project forms of organizational structures. In these cases staff development is definitely part of the project manager's objectives. They must develop the skills on their project team to handle whatever assignments come along.

Functional Manager Objectives

On the other hand, the resource manager's objectives include deployment of staff to projects, and development of staff skills to meet project requirements. These objectives pertain regardless of the organizational structure.

Conflicting Objectives

The project manager's objectives and the resource manager's objectives will often conflict. Part of the program for developing staff skills will occur through on-the-job training. Resource managers will look for opportunities to deploy staff to project assignments that provide opportunities to learn new skills. In other words, less than qualified staff will be assigned to project activities. The project manager, on the other hand, would rather have experienced staff assigned to project activities, especially activities that are critical to the completion of the project according to plan. They will not be interested in being the training ground for professional staff.

A further complication arises in those situations in which the resource manager is also a project manager. In matrix organizations this occurs frequently. Here the resource manager is torn between assigning the best professionals to the activity and assigning professionals for the purpose of learning new or enhanced skills.

The last conflict arises in the choice between assigning skilled professionals to projects not in their area of responsibility, and projects in their area of responsibility. In matrix organizations this can occur with regularity. The primary issues arise when the manager must assign staff to projects. He or she not only has to staff projects internal to their functional responsibilities, but also assign staff to projects outside their functional area. Questions arise, such as: What projects have priority? Should I assign my best staff to my projects (after all I do have to take care of my needs, which may be hard to explain to the other project managers)? Do I assign the best staff to outside projects (am I shooting myself in the foot; after all I do have responsibilities to meet and do want to succeed in doing them)? Always assigning the best professionals to projects within their area of responsibility will cause senior managers to wonder whether the resource manager has the proper corporate focus.

We don't want you to think that the project manager is totally insensitive to staff development and motivation. They need the commitment of each project team member, and in that sense will have to provide opportunities for development but only with the goal of the project in mind. To the extent that the two are compatible, development will be an objective of the project manager.

PREVIEW

PART 3

Planning a project involves answering several questions:

- What work is to be done?
- What conditions will determine that the work has been done as agreed?
- How long will it take to complete each item of work?
- What is the order of the work to be done?
- What resources are needed to complete each item of work?
- How can the work be scheduled to meet the requested deadlines?

The answers are certainly not independent of one another. Our minds, however, cannot absorb these six dimensions simultaneously, so we will consider them one at a time.

We begin in Chapter 7 by determining the boundaries of the project, and defining through goal and objective statements what is to be done to meet the deliverables negotiated between the requestor and the provider. Once the scope has been approved we will define the items of work (labeled *activities* in this book) needed to meet the requestor's requirements. This topic is considered in Chapter 8. In Chapter 9 we will estimate the clock time needed to complete each activity (labeled *activity duration* in this book), and then in Chapter 10 identify the resources required to complete each activity. With this data as our building blocks we construct, in Chapter 11, a graphical representation of the project work (labeled the *project network* in this book). An analysis of the project network will provide an estimate of when the project will be completed.

Finally, a detailed report (labeled the *project proposal* in this book) will be drafted in Chapter 12. The project proposal is submitted to senior management for final approval and hence the authorization to proceed with the project work.

PART 3 OVERVIEW

Planning

PART 3

OVERVIEW

Prediction is very difficult, especially about the future.

Neils Bohr

Define the problem before you pursue a solution.

John Williams
CEO, Spence Corp.

CHAPTER

SCOPE THE PROJECT

CHAPTER LEARNING OBJECTIVES

As a result of participating in the learning experiences in this chapter you will be able to:

1. Explain the process of developing the Conditions of Satisfaction.
2. Develop the Conditions of Satisfaction.
3. Define the basic parts and function of the Project Overview Statement.
4. Write a saleable Project Overview Statement for your project idea using the language of your business.
5. Know the role of the Project Overview Statement in the project management life cycle.
6. Write clear goal and objective statements.
7. Establish measurable criteria for project success.
8. Identify relevant assumptions, risks, and obstacles.
9. Understand the approval process for the Project Overview Statement.

The Project Overview Statement

Purpose

The most important and difficult part of the project is its beginning. It is here that the requestor and provider meet to define what is needed, and agree on what will be provided. If done carefully, the project has a chance for success. If done carelessly or not at all, the project is doomed to failure even before it starts.

In this section we focus on producing the Project Overview Statement (POS). You can think of it as a short (ideally one page long), crisply phrased information piece for review by those managers who are charged with setting priorities and deciding what projects will be supported. It is also a general statement that can be read by any interested party in the enterprise. That means it cannot have any technical jargon that is not generally used across the enterprise. It states what is to be done, why it is to be done, and what business value it will provide to the enterprise if it is done. The main purpose of the POS is to secure senior management approval and the resources to develop a detailed plan for the project.

Once approved the POS becomes the foundation for future planning and execution of the project. It becomes the reference for questions or conflicts regarding project scope and purpose.

Initiation

We have designed the POS so that it can be initiated by anyone in the organization. It is then a vehicle for quickly conveying an idea—however ill conceived or well thought out it might be. By allowing anyone to initiate an idea using the POS, the organization provides a way to encourage the submission of new ideas into the enterprise without the baggage of having to provide lengthy justifications for ideas that may not be approved. If the idea has merit, then it justifies spending the time developing a detailed plan of what it will take to make it happen. The desired result from having submitted a POS is to get management's approval to do a detailed project plan. Along with that approval is the commitment of resources needed to do a project plan.

What If You Inherit the Project?

There will be situations in which you have inherited the project. It has already been defined and scoped; a budget, staff resources, and completion date may also be given. You may well ask: Should I write a POS? Answer—an unqualified Yes! There are several reasons. The first is to level set your understanding of the project with management's expectations. We can't stress enough how important it is for requestor and provider to make sure that what will be delivered is what the customer expects to be delivered. For more on this check the "Developing Conditions of Satisfaction" section later in this chapter. The second reason is that the POS will become the referent for the planning team. In this case the project scope has been determined, and it will be up to the planning team to make sure that the resulting project plan is within the scope, as defined in the POS.

Approval Process

The approval process is far from a formality. Rather it is a deliberate decision on the part of senior management that the project as presented does indeed have business value and it is worth proceeding to the detailed planning phase. As part of the approval process you should expect senior management to ask several questions regarding the information presented. Remember, they are trying to make good business decisions and need to test your thinking along the way. Our best advice is for you to remember that the document must stand on its own. You will not be present to explain what you meant. Write in the language of the business, and anticipate questions as you consider the content of the project overview statement.

Expect several iterations. Despite your best efforts to make the POS stand on its own, you will not be successful. Rather senior management will have questions. For example, they may question the scope of the project—asking for some consideration of expanding or contracting it. They may ask for some backup on how you arrived at the results you claim in your success criteria. If financial analyses are attached, you may have some justification or explanation to give.

Definition

The POS has five component parts, as follows:

- Problem/Opportunity
- Project Goal
- Project Objectives
- Success Criteria
- Assumptions, Risks, Obstacles

The POS is designed to lead senior managers from a statement of fact (problem/opportunity) to a statement of what this project will address (project goal). Given that senior management is interested in the project goal and that it addresses a high enough priority concern, they will read more detail on exactly what it includes (project objectives). The business value is expressed as quantitative business outcomes (success criteria). Finally a summary of conditions that may hinder project success are identified (assumptions, risks, obstacles).

State the Problem/Opportunity

A statement of the problem or opportunity to be addressed by the project is the first part of the POS. It is a statement of fact, a statement that everyone in the organization will accept as true. This is critically important, for it puts a stake in the ground and gives a basis for the rest of the document. The POS may have to stand on its own and not have the benefit of the project manager being there to explain what is written or to defend the reason for proposing the project. Having a problem or opportunity statement that is an accepted truth gives the proposer a foundation on which to build a rationale for the project. It also sets the priority with which management will view what follows.

Your statement of the problem or opportunity must be well accepted by the enterprise. It does not need to be defined or defended, because it is a statement of well-known fact. If you are addressing a high-priority area or high business value area, your idea will get further attention and senior management will read on.

Unsolicited Individual Initiative

Many organizations are using the POS as a method for anyone in the organization to suggest an idea for increasing efficiency, improving productivity, or seizing upon a business opportunity. Because the POS can be drafted rather quickly by one person it is a way to capture a brief statement of the nature of the idea. It provides a document that senior management can react to without spending or wasting much time. If the idea has merit, the proposer will be asked to provide a detailed plan. On the other hand, the idea may be conditionally accepted, pending a little more justification by the proposer. Again, the idea is pursued further if it has merit. Otherwise it is rejected at this early stage and before too much time and too many resources are spent on needless planning.

Known Problem Area

Every organization has a collection of known problems. There may have been several attempts to alleviate part or all of the problem. The POS gives proposers a way to relate their idea to a known problem and to offer a full or partial solution. If the problem is serious enough and the proposed solution feasible, there will be further action taken. In this case senior managers will request a more detailed solution plan from the proposer.

Customer Request

Internal or external customers routinely make requests for product or service. The POS is an excellent vehicle for capturing the request and forwarding it to senior management for resolution. More recently with the empowerment of the worker, workers will not only receive the request, but also have the authority to act on the request. The POS coupled with the Conditions of Satisfaction (described following) establishes an excellent and well-defined starting point for any project. In this case the POS will be jointly developed by the requestor and the performer in the first phase of the Joint Project Planning session.

Corporate Initiative

Proposals to address new corporate initiatives should be started using the POS. There will be several ideas coming from the employees and the POS provides a standardized approach and document, from which senior management can prioritize proposals and select those that merit further planning. Having all responses to corporate initiatives follow the same documentation requirements simplifies senior managements' decision-making process for authorizing new projects.

Mandated Requirements

There will be several instances in which a project must be undertaken because of a mandated requirement. These could arise from market changes, customer requirements, or federal legislation, as well as other sources. The POS is a vehicle for establishing an agreement between performer and decision maker as to what will be done. Use of the POS clarifies for all interested parties exactly how the organization has decided to respond to the mandate.

Developing Conditions of Satisfaction

If we had to pick one area where the project runs into trouble it would be the very beginning. For some reason we have a difficult time understanding what we are saying to one another. How often we find ourselves thinking about what we are going to say while the other party is speaking. If you are going to be a successful project manager, you must stop that kind of behavior. A critical skill for you is good listening.

There are several dimensions to the conversations and negotiations that eventually lead to agreed-upon Conditions of Satisfaction. Basically the process of arriving at the Conditions of Satisfaction has four parts, as shown in Figure 7.1. A request is made, the provider explains what he or she heard as the request. A clear understanding of the request is established by both parties. The provider then states what he or she is willing to do to satisfy the request. The requestor then restates what he or she understands that the provider will provide. Again a clear understanding of the response is established by both parties.

Expecting that there will not be agreement on the first pass, this process repeats itself until there is an agreed-to request that is satisfied by an agreed-to response. Accompanying the agreement is a quantitative statement of when the request will have been satisfied. It is impor-

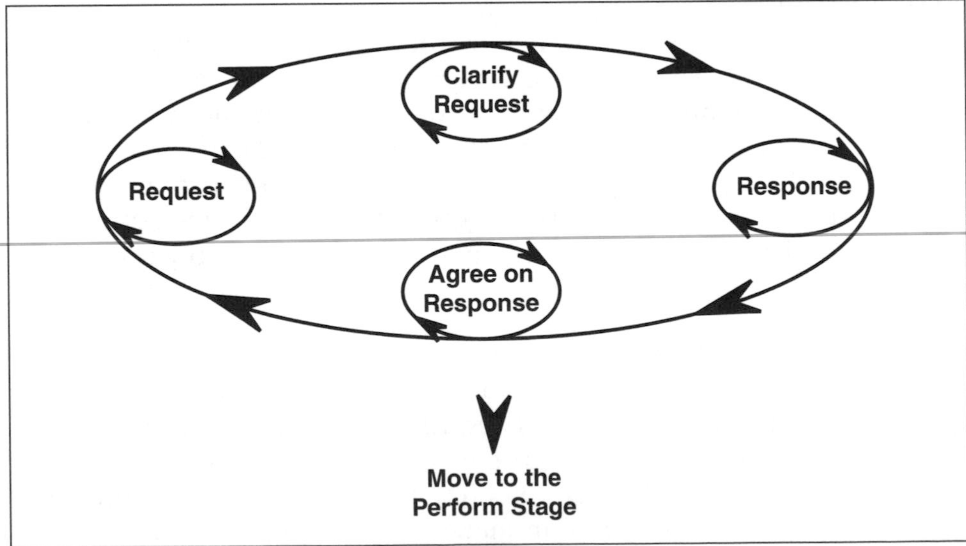

Figure 7.1 Establishing Conditions of Satisfaction.

tant that the statement be very specific. Do not leave to someone's interpretation whether the conditions have been met. An ideal statement will have only two results—the criteria was met or the criteria was not met. There can be no in-between answer here. This so called doneness criteria will become part of the POS. The result is documented as the Conditions of Satisfaction and becomes input to the POS.

We stress again the importance of this early step. It is especially difficult to do a thorough job, especially when everyone is anxious to get on with the work of the project. It is also painful. People will get impatient; tempers may flair. Remember, pain me now or pain me later. You choose what you are willing to live with.

The Conditions of Satisfaction is not a static document to be written and then filed. *It is a dynamic document that must become part of the continual project monitoring process.* Situations change and so will the needs of the customer. That means that Conditions of Satisfaction will change. At every major project status review, review the Conditions of Satisfaction. Do they still make sense? If not, change them and change the project plan accordingly.

Establish the Project Goal

This section of the POS states clearly and concisely what you intend to do to address the problem or opportunity previously identified. There may be several submissions from others, proposing to focus on the same issue. Yours will not be the only one submitted, and so you will want to have yours stand out among the crowd.

A project has one goal. The goal gives purpose and direction to the project by serving the following functions. It defines the final deliverable or outcome from the project so that all may know what is to be accomplished. By stating in clear terms what is to be accomplished, the goal statement will be used as a continual point of reference for any questions arising regarding scope or purpose.

The goal statement must be written in the language of the business so that anyone who reads it will understand it without further explanation from the proposer. Just as with the problem or opportunity statement, keep the goal statement short and specific. Do not volunteer any information that might commit the project to dates or deliverables that are not practical. Remember, you do not have much detail at this point. Under all circumstances avoid jargon. If jargon is used it is because everyone who might have reason to read the document understands the jargon.

Avoid giving a specific completion date (easier said than done, and we recognize that). If you expect that management will ask for a date, give it to the nearest quarter but with the caveat that improvements in the delivery date will be given as more is learned about project specifics. We have this peculiar habit of accepting as cast in stone any number that we see in writing regardless of the origin of the number. It is important that management understand just how some of the early numbers are estimated and that there is a great deal of variability in those early estimates. Assure them, however, that better estimates will be provided as the project plan is built and as the project work is undertaken. We will always know more about something tomorrow than we know today. And that applies to projects as well. Leave that for the detailed planning session when a more informed decision can be made. The exception will be for those cases where senior management expects a completion date and you know that without it your proposal may not get their approval. You might consider giving a date such as the third quarter of a specified year.

Next, writing the goal of the project follows from stating the problem and/or the opportunity. This may be a very short but specific statement, such as: Design and implement by the third quarter of the next budget year a new online customer order entry system. The important thing to remember is that the statement must be made using terms that anyone who might have reason to read it would understand.

Your purpose in writing the goal statement is to get senior management to value your idea enough to read on. In other words, they should think enough of your idea to conclude that it warrants further attention and consideration.

The goal statement should be short and to the point. It must not contain any language or terminology that might not be understandable to anyone having occasion to read it. In other words, no techie talk allowed. Remember, the more you write, the more you increase the risk that someone will find fault with something you have said.

Specific points to remember when writing a goal statement are given in Figure 7.2 as SMART characteristics.[1]

---

1. Doran, George T. 1981. "There's a SMART Way to Write Management Goals and Objectives." *Management Review*, November, pp. 35–36.

SMART CHARACTERISTICS OF AN OBJECTIVE STATEMENT

S pecific	Be specific in targeting an objective.
M easurable	Establish a measurable indicator(s) of progress.
A ssignable	Make the objective assignable to one person for completion.
R ealistic	State what can realistically be done with available resources.
T ime-related	State when the objective can be achieved; that is, duration.

Figure 7.2 SMART characteristics.

Define the Project Objectives

Think of objective statements as more detailed goal statements. The purpose of the objective statements is to clarify the boundaries of the goal statement. Taken together the goal and objective statements define the boundaries (the scope) of your project. In fact, the objective statements you will write for a specific goal statement are nothing more than a decomposition of the goal statement into a set of necessary and sufficient objective statements. That is, every objective must be accomplished in order to reach the goal, and no objective is superfluous.

Doran's method can also be used for forming objective statements. Doran's criteria are given in Figure 7.2.

Purpose of Objective Statement

Together with the goal statement the objectives statements define the scope of the project. By writing objective statements we clarify exactly what the boundaries of the project will be. In fact a good exercise to test the validity of the objective statements is to ask if it is clear what is in the project. Statements of objectives should specify a future state, rather than be activity based. We like to think of them as statements that clarify the goal by providing details about the goal. Think of them as subgoals and you will not be far off the mark.

It is also important to keep in mind that these are the current objective statements. They may change during the course of planning the project. This will happen as the details of the project work are defined. We all have the tendency to put more on our plates than we need. The result is to include project activities and tasks that extend beyond the boundaries defined in the POS. When this occurs, stop the planning session and ask whether the activity is outside the scope of the project, and if so, should the scope be adjusted to include the new activity or should the new activity be deleted from the project plan. Perhaps it is a good idea but not for this project. You will find that all through the project planning activities as discussed in this book there will be occasions to stop and reaffirm project boundaries. Boundary clarification questions will continually come up. Adopting this questioning approach is sound project management.

Characteristics of an Objective Statement

An objective statement should contain four parts, as follows:

1 An Outcome—a statement of what is to be accomplished
2. A Time Frame—the expected completion date
3 A Measure—metrics that will measure success
4 An Action—how the objective will be met

In many cases the complete objective statement will be spread across the Project Overview Statement, rather than be collected under the heading of Objectives. This is especially true for the timeframe and measures of success

Identify Success Criteria

This section of the POS answers the question, Why do we want to do this project? It is the measurable business value that will result from doing this project. It sells the project to senior management.

Purpose of Success Criteria

Whatever criteria is used it must answer the question, What must happen for us and the customer to say the project was a success? Obviously the Conditions of Satisfaction will contain the beginnings of a statement of success criteria. Phrased another way, success criteria is a statement of *doneness*. It is also a statement of the business value to be achieved, and therefore gives a basis for senior management to authorize the resources to do detailed planning. It is essential that the criteria be quantifiable and measurable, and if possible, expressed in terms of business value. Remember that you are trying to sell your idea to the decision makers.

In some cases it may take some creativity to identify the success criteria. For example, customer satisfaction may have to be measured by some pre- and postsurveys. In other cases a surrogate may be acceptable if it is impossible to directly measure the business value of the project. Be careful, however, and make sure that the decision maker buys into your surrogate measure. Also be careful of such traps as: We haven't been getting any customer complaint calls, therefore the customer must be satisfied. Did you ever consider the possibility that the lack of complaint calls may be the direct result of your lack of action in responding to complaints. Customers may feel that it does no good to complain, because nothing happens to settle their complaint.

Types of Success Criteria

The best choice for success criteria is to state clearly the bottom-line impact of the project. This may be expressed in such terms as increased margins, higher net revenues, reduced turnaround time, improved productivity, reduced cost of manufacture or sales, and so on. Since you want senior management approval of your proposal, you should express the benefits in terms that they routinely work with.

While you recognize bottom-line impact as the best success criteria, that may not be possible. As an alternative consider quantifiable statements about the impact your project will have on efficiency and effectiveness, error rates, reduced turnaround time to service a customer request, reduced cost of providing service, quality impact, or improved customer satisfaction. Management deals in deliverables, so always try to express your success criteria in quantitative terms. By doing this you avoid any possibility of disagreement as to whether the project was successful.

Senior management will look at your success criteria and assign business value to your project. In the absence of other criteria this will be the basis for their decision to commit resources to complete the detailed plan. The success criteria is another place to sell the value of your project. For example, you might state as one success criteria: This reengineering project is expected to reduce order entry to order fulfillment cycle time by 6 percent. Management may consider that number and conclude: If that is all you expect to gain from this project, we cannot finance the venture. Alternatively they may respond: If you can get 6 percent out of our current process, that will be a remarkable feat—so remarkable in fact that we would like more detail on how you expect to get that result. Can you provide some figures to substantiate your claim?

Measurability

Subjective measures of success will not do the job. You must speak quantitatively about tangible business benefits. This may require some creativity on your part. For example, when proposing a project that will have an impact on customer satisfaction, you will need to be particularly creative. There may be some surrogates for customer satisfaction. Avoid the common trap of saying that the number of complaints is an indication of customer satisfaction. Reasoning that the fewer the complaints the more satisfied the customer is not a fail-safe measure. Some customers are so frustrated with poor service that they see complaints as a waste of time. In other words, your nonresponse has caused them to not even try to complain.

List Assumptions, Risks, Obstacles

This section of the POS identifies any factors that may affect the outcome of the project. These factors may affect deliverables, the realization of the success criteria, the ability of the project team to complete the project as planned, or any other environmental or organizational conditions that are relevant to the project.

Purpose of Assumptions, Risks, Obstacles

The project manager uses this section to alert management to any factors that may interfere with the project work, or compromise the contribution that the project can make to the organization. Management may be able to neutralize their impact. On the other hand, the project manager will include in the project plan whatever contingencies may help reduce the probable impact and its effect on project success.

There are several areas where the project can be exposed to factors that may inhibit project success, as described in the following.

Technological

New technology, for example, creates a situation in which the company may not have much or any experience with the technology; whether it is new to the company or new to the industry makes little difference. The same can be said for rapidly changing technology. Who can say whether the present design and technology will still be current in three or six months.

Environmental

The environment in which the project work is to be done can also be an important determinant. An unstable or changing management structure can change a high-priority project to a low-priority project overnight. If your project sponsor leaves, will there be a new sponsor; and if so, how will he or she view the project? Will the project's priority be affected? High staff turnover will also present problems. The project team cannot get up on the learning curve because of the high turnover. A related problem stems from the skill requirements of the project. The higher the skill level required, the higher the risk associated with the project.

Interpersonal

Relationships between project team members are critical to project success. We don't have to be friends but we do have to be coworkers and team players. To the extent that this is not present among the project team or stakeholders, there will be problems. These should be called to the attention of senior management.

Cultural

How does the project fit with the enterprise? Is it consistent with the way the enterprise functions, or will it require a significant change in order to be successful?

Causal Relationships

We all like to think that what we are proposing will indeed correct the situation being addressed. This deserves some thought. In cases in which the project goal addresses a problem there will always be assumptions about cause and effect relationships. The proposer is assuming that the solution will in fact impact the problem. If such is the case, these assumptions need to be clearly stated in the Project Overview Statement. Remember, the rest of the world does not stand still waiting for your solution. Things continue to change and it is a fair question to ask whether your solution depends on all other things remaining equal.

Attachments to the Project Overview Statement

While we strongly recommend a one-page POS, there will be cases in which a longer document will be in order. As part of their initial approval of the resources to do detailed project planning, senior management will want some measure of the economic value of the proposed project. While they recognize that many of the estimates are little more than a guess, they will nevertheless ask for this information. In our experience we have seen five different analyses asked for with some frequency. They are discussed briefly in the following. Readers who wish more detail can consult the literature.

Risk Analysis

In the high technology industries risk analysis is becoming the rule rather than the exception. Formal procedures are becoming part of the initial definition of a project and continue through the life of the project. These analyses typically contain the identification of risk factors, the likelihood of their occurrence, the damage they will cause, and containment actions to either reduce their likelihood or their potential damage. The cost of the containment program is compared with the expected loss as a basis for deciding which containment strategies to put in place.

Financial Analysis

Some organizations require a preliminary financial analysis of the project before approval will be granted to do the detailed planning. While such analyses are very rough (remember, not much is known at this time) they will offer a tripwire for project planning approval. In some instances they may also offer a criteria for prioritizing all of the POSs they will be reviewing. Some of the possible analyses are briefly described in the following. More detailed explanations can be found in the many books devoted to such topics.

Feasibility Studies

The methodology to conduct a feasibility study is remarkably similar to the problem solving method, or scientific method if you prefer. The project manager will be asked to provide the feasibility study when senior management wants to review the thinking that led to the proposed solution. A more thoroughly researched solution may help build credibility for the project manager. The steps are shown in Figure 7.3.

Cost Benefit Analysis

These analyses are always difficult to do. The difficulty comes from the need to include intangible benefits into the decision situation. Such things as improved customer satisfaction cannot be easily quantified. One could argue that improved customer satisfaction reduces customer turnover, which in turn increases revenues—but how do you put a number on that? In many cases senior management will take these inferences into account but they still want to see hard dollar comparisons. Opt for the direct and measurable benefits to compare against the cost of doing the project and the cost of operating the new process. If

1. Clearly define the problem.
2. Describe the boundary of the problem; that is, what is in the problem scope and what is outside the problem scope.
3. Define the features and functions of a good solution.
4. Identify alternative solutions.
5. Rank alternative solutions.
6. State the recommendations along with the rationale for the choice.
7. Provide a rough estimate of the timetable and expected costs.

Figure 7.3 Methodology for conducting a feasibility study.

the benefits outweigh the costs over the expected life of the project deliverables, senior management may be willing to support the project.

Break-even Analysis

This will be a timeline that shows the cumulative cost of the project against the cumulative savings from the project. Wherever the cumulative savings line crosses the cumulative cost line is that point at which the project recoups the cost of doing the project. Usually senior management is looking for an elapsed time less than some threshold number. If the project meets that deadline date, it may be worthy of support.

Return on Investment

Over the life of the project deliverables, what are the total costs as compared with the increased revenue that will accrue? Here senior management can find a common basis for comparing one project against another. Obviously they are looking for the high ROI projects or at least for projects that meet some minimum ROI.

Approval Process

Approval of the POS commits the resources needed to complete a detailed plan for the project. It is not approval to do the project. That will come later with the approval of the detailed plan. At this early stage not too much is known about the project. Rough estimates (or WAGs, Wild A_ _ Guesses, or, if you prefer, SWAGs are the scientific version) are made as to what will be done and of what value it is to the enterprise. There might also be very preliminary estimates of time and cost to complete the work, although this is not even necessary. Meaningful estimates of time and cost will be part of the detailed plan.

Gaining management approval of the POS must be viewed as a significant event in the life of a project. The approving manager must put the project manager to task. There are a number of questions that should be asked and whose answers must be scrutinized very carefully. While the POS does not have a lot of detailed analysis supporting it, it is still of value to test the thinking of the proposer and the validity of the proposed project. It would not be unusual to have the project manager return to the drawing board perhaps several times for more analysis and thought as a prerequisite to management approval.

- **How important is the problem or opportunity to the enterprise?**
- **How is the project related to our CSFs?**
- **Does the goal statement relate directly to the problem or opportunity?**
- **Are the objectives clear representations of the goal statement?**
- **Is there sufficient business value as measured by the success criteria to warrant further expenditures on this project?**
- **Is the relationship between the project objectives and the success criteria clearly established?**
- **Are the risks too high and the business value too low?**
- **Can senior management mitigate the identified risks?**

Figure 7.4 Senior management POS review questions.

Let us put on the hat of the senior manager who is reviewing your POS, and examine the questions that might be asked. A list is given in Figure 7.4. The approval of the POS is not a perfunctory or ceremonial approval. By approving the document, professionals and managers are saying: Based on what we understand this project to involve and the business value to be derived, we believe that it makes good business sense to go to the next level; that is, to commit the resources needed to develop a detailed project plan. Several managers and professionals will have participated in that approval as discussed in the following.

At the preliminary stages of the project, a core project team may have been identified. These will be the managers, professionals, and perhaps the customer, who will remain on the project team from the beginning to the very end of the project. They will participate in developing the POS and reach consensus on what it contains.

Project Team

Some potential members of the project team are usually known beforehand. Their subject matter expertise and ideas should be considered as the POS is developed. At the least, you should have them review the POS before submission.

Project Manager

Ideally the project manager will have been identified and can participate in drafting the POS. Since they will manage the project, they should have a major role to play in its definition and its approval.

Resource Manager

Those who will be asked to provide the skills needed at the times when they will be needed are certainly important in the initial definition of the project and later in its detailed planning. There is little point in proposing a project if the resources are not or cannot be made available to the project.

Function/Process Manager

Project deliverables don't exist in a vacuum. Several units will provide input to or receive output from the project products/services. Their advice should be sought. Give them an early chance to buy into your project.

Customer

Our project management methodology includes a significant role for the customer. We have discussed the Conditions of Satisfaction as a prerequisite to, or concurrent exercise in developing, the POS. Many professionals are not skilled in interpersonal communications. Developing the Conditions of Satisfaction is a difficult task that focuses on having the customer state a request, and the performer repeating what the customer has asked for. This is followed by the performer stating what will be delivered, and the customer restating what the performer has offered. Negotiations will occur and finally both parties will agree as to what is being requested, what is to be delivered, and how success will be measured.

There will be situations in which the customer might be the project manager. We actually encourage this whenever it makes sense to do so. Commitment and buy-in are always difficult to get. Having the customer as project manager solves that problem. For such an approach to work the technical members of the project team take on the roles of advisor and consultant. It is their job to keep the feasible alternatives, and only the feasible alternatives, in front of the project manager. Obviously decision-making will be a little more difficult and time-consuming. By engaging the customer as project manager, the custiomer will not only appreciate the problems that are encountered, but also gain some skill in resolving them. We have seen marvelous learning-curve effects that have their payoff in later projects with that same customer.

Senior Management

Senior management support is a critical success factor in successful projects and successful implementation of the deliverables. Their approval says: Go and do detailed planning; we are authorizing the needed resources.

Exercise: Developing the POS

Figure 7.5 is an example of a POS from another O'Neill & Preigh project. Review it and then try to write the POS for your project. Figure 7.6 is a blank POS. Identify a project idea from your work situation and try to develop the POS for it. Pay particular attention to the language that you use. Remember that anyone in the enterprise who may have a reason to read your POS should be able to understand it. This is especially true for technically oriented projects whose readers may not be technically oriented. You are trying to convince senior management that your idea is worthy of support to the next level. They can know that only if you communicate to them in the language of your company's business.

How to Use a JPP Session to Scope the Project

There will be cases in which you will want to convene a planning session to draft the POS. Here is a process that we have followed with good success. First understand that this is the first part of the JPP. It may have to be completed in two parts. The first part drafts the POS. In

PROJECT OVERVIEW	Project Name MKTG. MIS	Project No. MKTG.9.1.01	Project Manager PAUL BEARER

Problem/Opportunity

THE LOSS OF MARKET SHARE OVER THE LAST SIX QUARTERS IS PARTIALLY ATTRIBUTABLE TO THE LACK OF TIMELY, ACCURATE, AND ACCESSIBLE INFORMATION ACROSS ALL UNITS IN THE MARKETING DIVISION.

Goal

DESIGN AND IMPLEMENT BY 7-1-93 AN INTEGRATED STRATEGIC MARKETING INFORMATION SYSTEM.

Objectives

1. DESIGN AN INTEGRATED MARKETING INFORMATION SYSTEM.
2. DEVELOP A PRODUCT LINE EVALUATION AND FORECASTING SYSTEM.
3. DEVELOP A DISTRIBUTION ANALYSIS SYSTEM FOR SALES TERRITORIES.
4. DEVELOP A SALES/PROMOTION SYSTEM.
5. DEVELOP A PRICING SYSTEM.
6. IMPLEMENT THE INTEGRATED SYSTEM.

Success Criteria

1. MARKET SHARE BEGINS TO INCREASE NO LATER THAN 1-1-94 AND IS RESTORED TO ITS 10-1-89 POSITION NO LATER THAN 1-1-95.
2. AT LEAST 80 PERCENT OF THE SYSTEM USERS RATE THE NEW SYSTEM AS AN IMPROVEMENT OVER THEIR EXISTING SYSTEM BASED ON AN EVALUATION AFTER THE FIRST SIX MONTHS OF OPERATION.

Assumptions, Risks, Obstacles

1. MARKET SHARE CAN BE INCREASED WITH THE IMPLEMENTATION OF AN INTEGRATED MARKETING INFORMATION SYSTEM.
2. AN INTEGRATED SYSTEM CAN BE DEVELOPED THAT WILL BE PERCEIVED AS AN IMPROVEMENT OVER THE INDEPENDENT SYSTEMS NOW IN PLACE.
3. USERS OF CURRENT SYSTEMS WILL PROBABLY BE RESISTANT TO CHANGING TO NEW SYSTEM AND MAY BE SOMEWHAT UNCOOPERATIVE.

Prepared By	Date	Approved By	Date
Sal Vation	3-1-91	Ben E. Dictus	3-3-91

Figure 7.5 POS for O&P Mktg. MIS project.

PROJECT OVERVIEW	Project Name	Project No.	Project Manager
Problem/Opportunity			
Goal			
Objectives			
Success Criteria			
Assumptions, Risks, Obstacles			
Prepared By	Date	Approved By	Date

Figure 7.6 POS form.

the second part you will complete the detailed plan after having received approval of the POS.

The first order of business is to come to agreement on the request and the response to the request. These are the Conditions of Satisfaction discussed earlier and become the problem/opportunity, goal, objectives, and success criteria parts of the POS. You are almost done. Next you will want to conduct a sanity check with those who were not party to developing the Conditions of Satisfaction. Discussion should follow until all parties are satisfied with the request and the response. Expect to add to the Conditions of Satisfaction in reaching a consensus.

The last item is to complete the Assumptions, Risks, and Obstacles portion. Here the planning participants will be able to offer a number of points to consider.

Any plan is bad which is not susceptible to change.

Bartolommeo de San Concordio
Florentine painter

Let all things be done decently and in order.

I Corinthians 14:40

CHAPTER 8

Identify Project Activities

CHAPTER LEARNING OBJECTIVES

As a result of participating in the learning experiences in this chapter you will be able to:

1. Understand the significance of the Work Breakdown Structure as a planning and reporting tool.
2. Know the importance of the completeness criteria to your ability to manage the work of the project.
3. Determine which of the approaches to use for generating the Work Breakdown Structure for a given project.
4. Generate a complete Work Breakdown Structure.
5. Conduct a Joint Project Planning session to generate a Work Breakdown Structure.

Definition of Project Activities

In order to develop good project plans we will first have to represent the project as a list of the work to be done. This list of work to be done will be generated in a top-down fashion, following a specific set of rules. Having defined the project work in this fashion, the work activities will have specific characteristics that allow us to estimate time, cost, and resource requirements first at an elementary level and then aggregate these figures to the project level. Project time, cost, and resource requirements will be much more accurately estimated if the project work is defined in this fashion than in any other manner we have seen. Once described we will be able to sequence the project work so that tasks can be done in parallel rather than in sequence. In other words, having defined the project as a list of activities, the activities can be sequenced so that the project duration (clock time needed to complete all project work) will be much less than the sum of all the times needed to complete each work activity.

Definition of the Work Breakdown Structure (WBS)

In order to facilitate our planning the work to be done, estimating the duration of the project, determining the resources that will be required, and scheduling the project work, we will need to view the project on a level that is more detailed than goal and objectives statements. To create this view we will decompose the project into chunks of work, proceeding from major chunks of work to smaller chunks of work and finally to a level of detail that meets our planning and scheduling needs. This process is exactly the same process we all used in grammar school to prepare a detailed outline of a research paper we were going to write. Despite the teacher extolling the value of preparing the outline before we wrote the paper, we chose to do it the other way around. That won't work in project planning. We have to define the work before we set about to do the work! Those who have experience in systems development should see the similarity to functional decomposition. The veterans might even see some similarity to stepwise refinement or pseudocode. These systems tools do in fact have a great deal in common with the techniques we use to generate the WBS. A generic example showing the hierarchical structure of the WBS is given in Figure 8.1.

Functional Decomposition

In principle there is no difference between a WBS and a functional decomposition of a system. Our approach to generating a WBS departs from the generation of a functional decomposition in that we follow a specific process with a stopping rule for completing the WBS. We are not aware of a similar process being reported for generating the functional decomposition of a system.

Granularity

In the final analysis it is the project manager who will decide on the architecture of the WBS and the level of detail required. This is important because the project manager is accountable for the success of the project. The WBS must be defined such that the project manager can manage the project. That means that the approach, detail, and so on in the WBS may not be the way others would have approached it. Apart from any senior management requirements for reporting or organizational requirements for documentation or process, the project manager is free to develop the WBS according to their needs and those of management. Because of this requirement, the WBS is not unique. That should not bother you because all that is required is a WBS that defines the project work so that you can manage it. Beauty being in the eyes of the beholder applies equally well to the WBS!

Approaches to Building the WBS

No one way can be said to be the best. Rather the choice is subjective and based more on the preference of the project manager than on any other requirements. In fact, apart from any management-imposed reporting requirements, the project manager is free to develop the WBS in any way that describes the project so that it can be managed. Hypothetically, if we put each member of the JPP session in a different room and asked them to develop the project WBS, they might all come back with a different rendition. That's all right! There is no single best answer. In practice we have tried to follow one approach only to find that it was making the project work more confusing rather than simpler. In such cases our advice is simply to throw away the work you have done and start all over again with a fresh approach.

We have seen each of the seven approaches described in the following in practice. There are *noun-type* approaches (physical components, functional components), *verb-type* approaches (design-build-test-implement project objectives), and *organizational* approaches (department, process, geographic location).

Noun-Type Approaches

Physical Decomposition

Projects that involve building products can usually follow this approach. Take a bicycle, for example. Its physical components are a frame, wheels, seat, fork, rims, gears, brakes, and so on. If each is to be manufactured, this approach may produce a simple WBS that is easily understood by all concerned parties.

The noun-types approaches lend themselves to summary reporting much better than the other approaches we will learn. In fact, the federal government has developed a rather intricate scheme of WBSs exactly for that purpose.

Functional Decomposition

Using the bicycle example, we can build the WBS using the functional components of the bicycle. The functional components are steering system, gear shifting system, braking system, pedaling system, and so on.

Verb-Type Approaches

Design-Build-Test-Implement

This approach is usually used in those projects that involve a methodology. Application systems development is an obvious situation. The systems development life cycle has a number of points of similarity with the project management life cycle. The chronology of major steps in the methodology becomes the first-level breakdown of the project work. For those who think in chronological order this approach is straightforward.

Verb-type approaches lend themselves very well to summary reporting of schedule information. In fact, the WBS, at the lowest levels of granularity, will be expressed in verb form. After all, we are talking about work, and that implies action—and that implies verbs!

Objectives

This approach is used when progress reports at various stages of project completion are prepared for senior management. Reporting project completion by objectives gives a good indication of the deliverables that have been produced by the project team. Objectives will almost always relate to business value and will be well received by senior management and the customer as well. There is a caveat, however. This approach can cause some difficulty as objectives often overlap. Their boundaries can be fuzzy. More attention will need to be given to eliminate redundancies and discovering gaps in the defined work.

Other Approaches

The deployment of project work across geographic or organizational boundaries will often suggest a WBS that parallels the organization.

Geographic Approach

If project work is geographically dispersed (our space program, for example), it may make sense from a coordination and communications aspect to partition the project work first by geographic location and then by some other approach at each location.

Business Function Approach

Finally, breaking the project down first by business process and then by some other method for each process may make sense. This has the same advantages and disadvantages as the departmental approach, with the added complication that integration of the deliverables from each process may be more difficult than in the former case. Again, no single approach can be judged to be best for a given project. Our advice is to consider each at the outset of the JPP session and pick the one that seems to bring clarity to defining the project work.

Departmental Approach

On the other hand, departmental boundaries and politics being what they are, we may benefit from partitioning the project first by department and then within department by whatever approach makes sense. We benefit from this structure in that a major portion of the project work is under the organizational control of a single manager. Resource

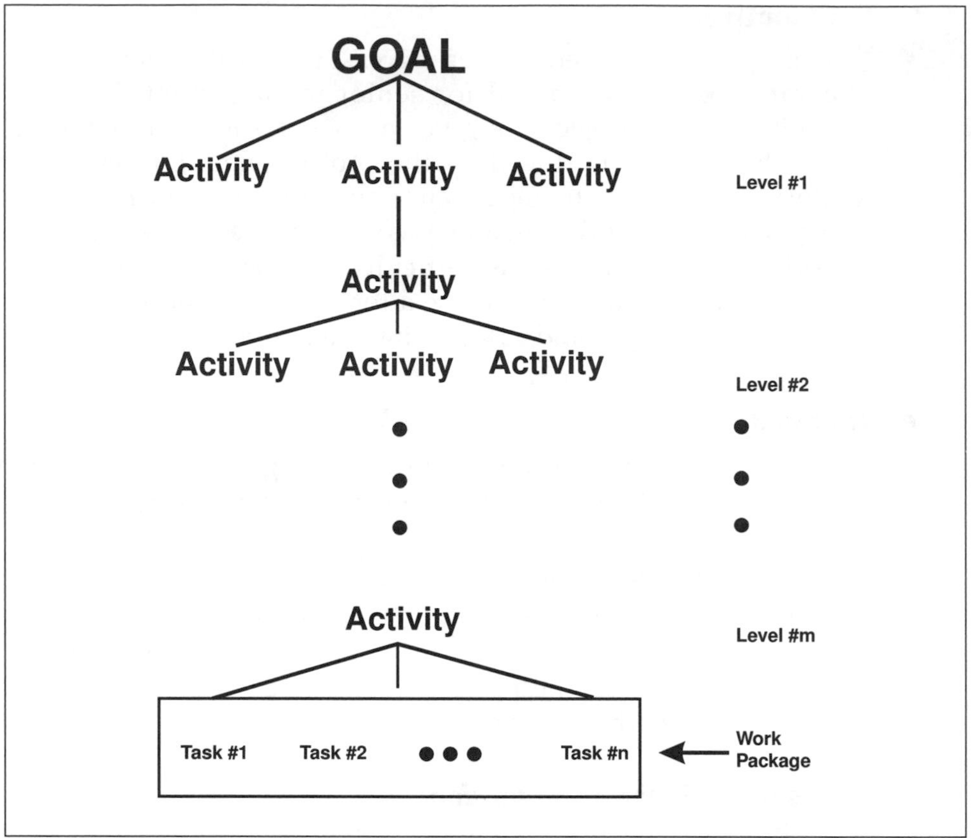

Figure 8.1 Hierarchial visualization of the Work Breakdown Structure.

allocation may be simplified this way. On the other hand, we add additional needs for communication and coordination across organizational boundaries in this approach.

Whatever approach is used the WBS can be generically represented, as shown in Figure 8.1. We introduce this hierarchy here in order to develop some terminology. The goal statement represents the reason for doing the project. The Level 1 partitioning into some number of activities (a.k.a. chunks of work) is a necessary and sufficient set of activities. That is, when each of these first-level activities is complete, the project is complete. For any activity that does not possess the six characteristics, we partition it into a set of necessary and sufficient activities at Level 2. The process continues until all activities have met the six criteria. This defines a set of activities that will each have an activity manager, someone who is responsible for completing the activity.

The lowest-level activities are defined by a work package. A work package is simply the list of things to do to complete the activity. The work package may be very simple, for example, getting management sign-off on a deliverable. On the other hand, a work package may be a miniproject and consist of all the properties of any other project, except that the activity defining this project possesses the six criteria and need not be further partitioned. We will return to the work package later in the course.

Some examples will help clarify. Figure 8.2 is a partial WBS for building a house and Figure 8.3 is the indented outline version (for those of you who prefer an outline format to a hierarchical graph). Both convey exactly the same information.

Figure 8.4 shows the WBS for the traditional waterfall systems development methodology. For our systems readers this format could become a template for all your systems development projects. It is a good way to introduce some standardization into your systems development methodology.

Six Criteria to Test for Completeness in the WBS

Developing the WBS is the most critical part of the JPP. If we do this part right, the rest is comparatively easy. For that reason we spend some pages discussing the completion test and its use in developing the WBS.

In this section we present a simple decomposition process that shows you how to identify the activities that must be done from the beginning to the completion of the project. It is these activities that will be the lowest level of managed work for the project manager. At this point in the planning process we have completed the Project Overview Statement. Further planning activities may cause us to go back and reconsider the Project Overview Statement, but for now we proceed on the assumption that it is complete. Our technique for generating the WBS will reduce even the most complex project to a set of clearly defined activities. The WBS will be the document that guides the remainder of the planning activities.

The completion rule is applied by asking, for each activity: Does it possess these six characteristics? If not, decompose the activity and ask

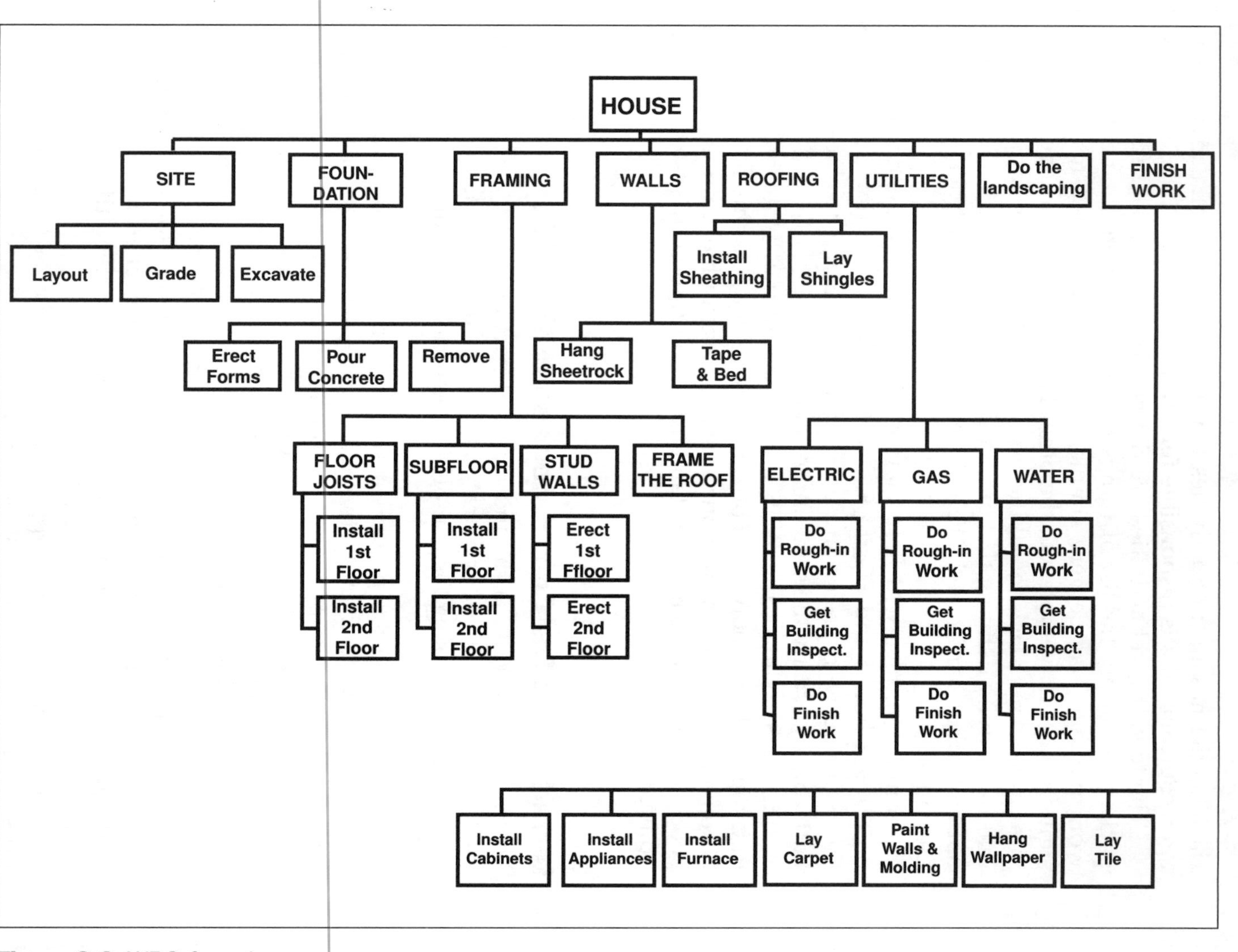

Figure 8.2 WBS for a house.

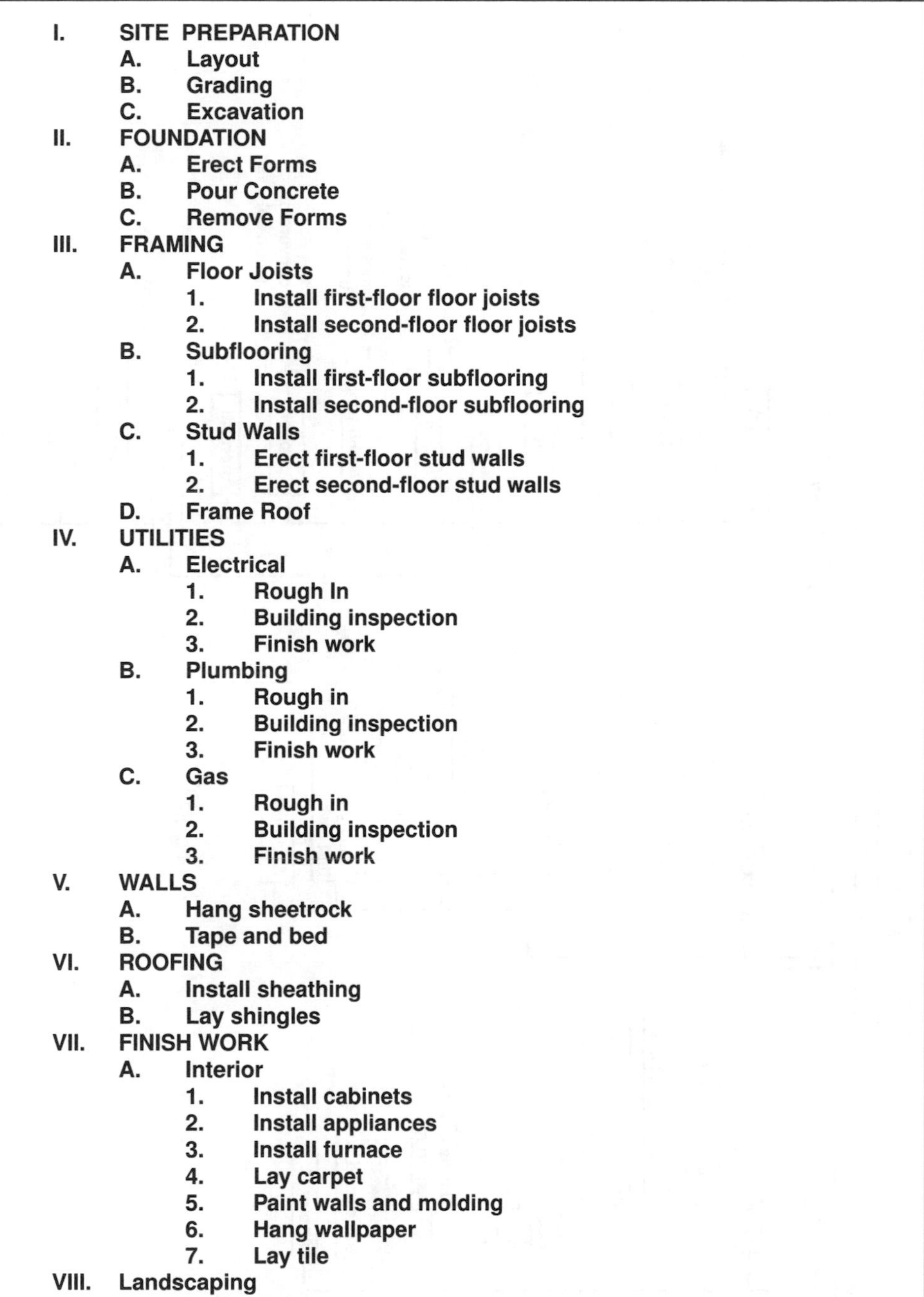

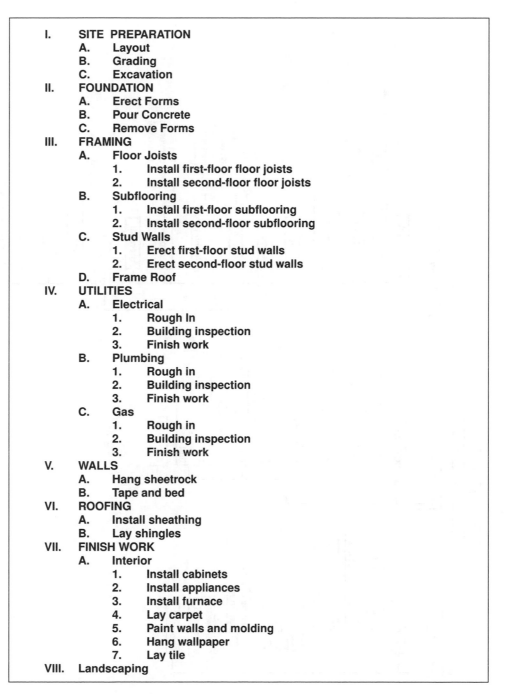

I. SITE PREPARATION
    A. Layout
    B. Grading
    C. Excavation
II. FOUNDATION
    A. Erect Forms
    B. Pour Concrete
    C. Remove Forms
III. FRAMING
    A. Floor Joists
        1. Install first-floor floor joists
        2. Install second-floor floor joists
    B. Subflooring
        1. Install first-floor subflooring
        2. Install second-floor subflooring
    C. Stud Walls
        1. Erect first-floor stud walls
        2. Erect second-floor stud walls
    D. Frame Roof
IV. UTILITIES
    A. Electrical
        1. Rough In
        2. Building inspection
        3. Finish work
    B. Plumbing
        1. Rough in
        2. Building inspection
        3. Finish work
    C. Gas
        1. Rough in
        2. Building inspection
        3. Finish work
V. WALLS
    A. Hang sheetrock
    B. Tape and bed
VI. ROOFING
    A. Install sheathing
    B. Lay shingles
VII. FINISH WORK
    A. Interior
        1. Install cabinets
        2. Install appliances
        3. Install furnace
        4. Lay carpet
        5. Paint walls and molding
        6. Hang wallpaper
        7. Lay tile
VIII. Landscaping

Figure 8.3 Indented outline WBS for a house.

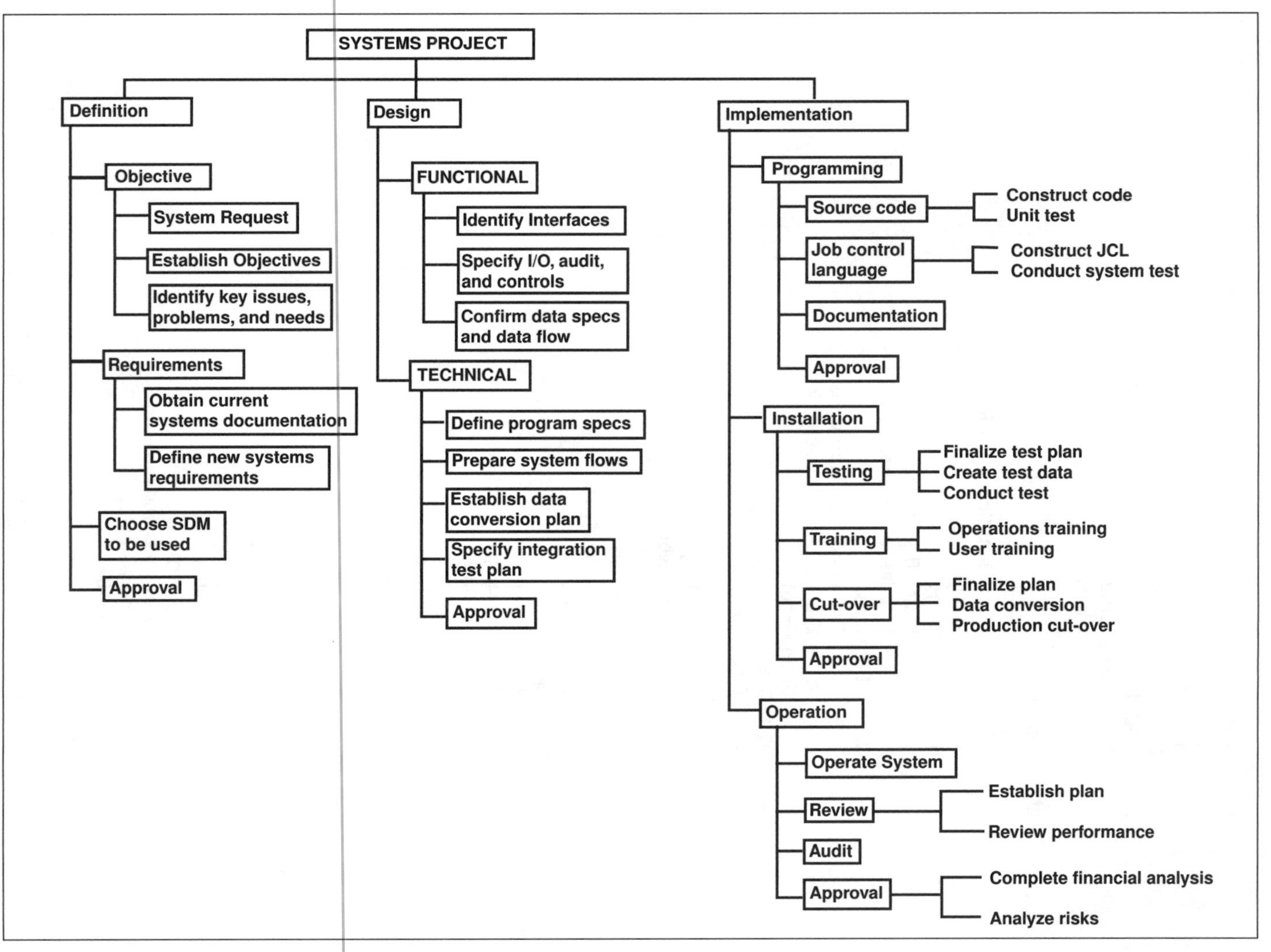

Figure 8.4 WBS for a system development methodology.

- **Status/completion are measurable.**
- **Clearly defined start/end events.**
- **Activity has a deliverable.**
- **Time/cost *easily* estimated.**
- **Activity duration within acceptable limits.**
- **Work assignments are independent.**

Figure 8.5 WBS completion test.

the questions again. As soon as an activity possesses the six characteristics, there is no need to further decompose it. As soon as every activity in the WBS possesses these six characteristics, the WBS is defined as complete.

We define a complete WBS as one in which each activity possesses the six characteristics given in Figure 8.5. An earlier four-criteria version of this completion test was introduced by Weiss and Wysocki.[1] We have continued to refine the criteria and present an updated version here.

Measurable Status

At any point in time during the project the project manager might need to know the status of an activity. If the activity has been defined properly, that question is easily answered. For example, it has been estimated that the systems documentation will be about 300 pages in length and require approximately four months of full-time work to write. Here are some possible reports that your activity manager might give in response to What is the status of...?

1. Let's see, the activity is supposed to take four months full time. I've been working on it for two months full time. I guess I must be 50 percent complete.

1. Weiss, Joseph W., and Robert K. Wysocki. *5-Phase Project Management: A Practical Planning and Implementation Guide.*

2. I've written 150 pages, so I guess I am 50 percent complete.
3. I've written and had approved 150 pages and estimate that the remaining work will require two more months. I am 50 percent complete.

No one would buy the first answer, but how many times is that the information we get? What is even worse, we accept it as a valid statement of progress! While the second answer is a little better, it doesn't say anything about the quality of the 150 pages that have been written and it says nothing about the reestimate of the remaining work. So we see that an acceptable answer must state what has been actually completed (approved, not just written in our example) and what remains to be done, along with an estimate to completion. Remember, we will know more tomorrow than we do today. After having worked through about half of the activity, the activity manager should be able to give a very accurate estimate of the time required to complete the remaining work.

A simple metric that has met with some success is to compute the proportion of tasks completed as a percentage of all the tasks that comprise the activity. This is certainly a very objective measure. While it may seem somewhat inaccurate, it is a good technique. Best of all it is quick. The project manager and activity manager do not have to sit around mired in detail about the percentage completed.

Bounded

The activity should have a clearly defined starting and ending event. Once the beginning event has occurred, work may begin on this activity. The production of the deliverable will most likely be the ending event that signals work is closed on the activity.

Deliverable

The result of completing the work that comprises the activity is the production of a deliverable. A visible sign that the activity is complete. That could be an approving manager's signature, the deliverable of a physical product or document, the authorization to proceed to the next activity, or some other sign of completion.

Cost/Time Estimable

Here we are concerned with our ability to estimate the time and or cost of completing the activity. Being able to do this at a low level in the

WBS allows us to aggregate to higher levels and estimate the total project cost and completion date. By successively decomposing activities to finer levels of granularity we are likely to encounter primitive activities that we have done before. Having experience at these lower levels of definition gives us a stronger base on which to estimate activity cost and duration for similar activities. We will have more to say on activity duration estimation in the next chapter.

Acceptable Duration Limits

While there is no fixed rule we recommend activities that are less than two calendar weeks duration. There will of course be exceptions, especially for those activities whose work is repetitive and simple. There is no need to break down the activity further. If we can estimate the time to check one document, then it does not make much difference if the activity requires two months to check 400 documents or four two-week periods to check 100 documents per period. The danger we are trying to avoid is to have longer duration activities whose delays can create serious project scheduling problems.

Activity Independence

This characteristic is very important. If an activity has this characteristic, it means that once work has begun on the activity it may continue without interruption or the need to get additional input or information until the activity is complete. We may choose to schedule it in parts because of resource availability, but we could have scheduled it as one continuous stream of work.

Use of the WBS

The WBS is both a planning tool and a reporting tool. In the planning phase the WBS gives the project team a detailed representation of the project as a collection of activities that must be completed in order for the project to be completed. It is at this activity level that we will estimate effort, elapsed time, and resource requirements; build a schedule of when the work will be completed; and estimate deliverable dates and project completion.

The WBS is also used as a structure for reporting project status. As work is completed activities will be completed. Completion of lower-level activities causes higher-level activities to be complete. Some of these higher-level activities may represent significant progress, whose completion will be milestone events in the course of the project. Thus the WBS defines milestone events that can be reported to senior management and to the customer.

How to Use a JPP Session to Identify Project Activities

The best way to generate the WBS is as part of the JPP session. Noting that there may be as many as 20 to 30 participants, gathering around a computer screen won't do the job. Neither will projecting the screen on an overhead projector. The only way we have found that works consistently is to use sticker notes, marking pens, and plenty of whiteboard space. In the absence of whiteboard space you might wallpaper the planning room with flip-chart or butcher paper. You cannot have too much writing space.

Figure 8.6 lists the steps to follow in building the WBS within the JPP session. Note that the entire planning team decides on the approach for the first-level breakdown. After that the group is partitioned into teams, with each team having some expertise for part of the WBS. Hopefully they will have all the expertise they need to develop the remainder of their part of the WBS. If not, outside help may be

1. **The planning team agrees on the approach to building the first level of the Work Breakdown Structure.**
2. **The planning team creates the Level 1 activities.**
3. **Divide the planning team into groups, one for each Level 1 activity.**
4. **Each group agrees on the approach to building the remaining Work Breakdown Structures.**
5. **Each group reports their Work Breakdown Structure to the team.**
6. **The planning team critiques and discusses the group presentations and completes the Work Breakdown Structure.**

Figure 8.6 Steps to building a Work Breakdown Structure.

brought in as needed. Be careful not to clutter the team with too many people.

After sufficient time has been allotted for each team to derive its part of the WBS, presentations are made by a spokesperson from each team. They will describe how the team developed its part of the WBS and what is and is not contained in each project activity. It is at this time that the participants will begin to see that there are overlaps or missing activities, because one team thought another team would include that activity but did not. Do not worry; that is natural. The important thing is to pay close attention to each presentation and ask yourself if there is something in their WBS that you did not expect to see or, conversely, is there something not there that you expected to see. The issue here is to strive for a complete WBS. Unless a report structure is to be defined by the WBS it does not matter where an activity appears in the WBS. The important consideration is that it does appear.

As the discussion continues and activities are added and deleted from the WBS, there will be questions about agreement between the WBS and the POS. Throughout the exercise the POS should be posted on flip-chart paper and hung on the walls of the planning room. Each participant should compare the scope of the project as, described in the POS, with the scope as presented in the WBS. If something in the WBS appears out of scope, challenge it. Either expand the scope or discard the appropriate WBS activities. Similarly, look for complete coverage of the scope, as described in the WBS with the POS. This is the time to be critical and carefully define the scope and work to accomplish it. Mistakes found now, before any work is done, are far less costly and disruptive than if found late in the project.

The dynamic at work here is one of changing project boundaries. The edges of the project envelope are never clearly defined at the outset. There will always be reason to question what is in and what is not in the project. That is all right! Just remember that the project boundaries have not yet been set. That will happen once the project has been approved to begin. Until then we are still in the planning mode and nothing is set in concrete.

Alternative Way to Build the WBS

The approach that we have used to this point is the top-down approach. We have seen others use a bottom-up approach and describe it here for completeness. Unless there is some reason to use the bottom-up approach, we recommend the top-down approach. In our experience there is less danger of missing part of the project work using the top-down approach.

The bottom-up approach works as follows: The first steps are the same as the top-down approach. Namely, the entire planning team agrees to the first-level breakdown. The planning team is then divided into as many groups as there are first-level activities. Each group then makes a list of the activities that must be completed in order to complete the first-level activity. To do this they proceed as follows: Someone in the group identifies an activity, and tells it to the group. If the group agrees, then it is written on a slip of paper and put in the middle of the table. The process repeats itself until no new ideas are forthcoming. The group then sorts the slips into activities that seem to be related to one another. This grouping activity will hopefully help the planning team add missing activities or remove redundant ones. Once the group is satisfied they have completed the activity list for their first-level breakdown, they are finished. Each group then reports to the entire planning team the results of its work. Final critiques are given, missing activities added, and redundant activities removed.

While this has worked well in many cases, there is the danger of not defining all activities, or defining activities at too high or low a level of granularity. The completeness criteria that we defined is not assured through this process. Our caution then is that you may not have as manageable a project as when you follow the top-down approach.

Round numbers are always false.

Samuel Johnson
English critic

Figures are not always facts.

Aesop
Greek fabulist

You get more control over estimation by learning from evolutionary early and frequent result deliveries than you will if you try to estimate in advance for a whole large project.

Tom Gilb
Principles of Software Engineering Management

CHAPTER 9

ESTIMATE ACTIVITY DURATION

CHAPTER LEARNING OBJECTIVES

As a result of participating in the learning experiences in this chapter you will be able to:

1. Understand the difference between effort and duration.
2. Know how to use any one of five activity duration estimation methods.
3. Know when to use a particular estimation technique.

Causes of Variation in Activity Duration

Activity duration is a random variable. Because we cannot know what factors will be operative when work is underway on an activity, we cannot know exactly how long it will take. There will of course be varying estimates with varying precision for each activity. One of our goals in estimating activity duration is to have defined the activity to a level of granularity so that our estimates have a narrow variance; that is, the estimate is as precise as we can make it at the planning stages of the project. As project work is completed we will be able to improve the earlier estimates. There are several causes of variation in the actual activity duration, as discussed in the following.

Varying Skill Levels

Our strategy is to estimate activity duration based on the typically skilled people resources being assigned to work on the activity. In actuality this may not happen. We may get a higher- or lower-skilled person assigned, thus causing actual duration to vary from planned duration. It is these varying skill levels that will be both a help and a hindrance to us.

Unexpected Events

Murphy lives in the next cubicle and will surely make his presence known, but in what way and at what time we do not know. Such things as random acts of nature, vendor delays, incorrect shipments of materials, traffic jams, power failures, sabotage, and so on, are but a few of the possibilities.

Efficiency of Work Time

Every time a worker is interrupted it takes more time to get up to the level of productivity at the time of the interruption. We cannot control the frequency or time of interruptions but we do know that they will happen. As to their effect on staff productivity, we can only guess. Some will be more affected than others.

Mistakes and Misunderstandings

Despite all of our efforts to be complete and clear in describing the work to be done, we simply will miss a few times. This will take its toll in reworks or scrapping semicompleted work.

Elapsed Time vs. Labor Time vs. Productive Time

It is also important to understand the difference between labor time and clock time. They are not the same. For example, let us say that an estimate has been provided that a certain task requires ten hours of perfectly efficient and uninterrupted labor to complete. Under normal working conditions, how many hours do you think it will really take? Something more than ten for sure. To see why this is so let us consider the data shown in Figure 9.1.

If a person could work at perfect efficiency, he or she could accomplish ten hours of work in ten hours. Such a person would be truly unique, for what is more likely is daydreaming, learning time, a change of approach, rework, and so on. Several estimates for how efficient a person is have been put forward. They typically range from 66 to 75 percent. Using the 75 percent estimate means that a 10-hour task will require about 13 hours and 20 minutes to complete. That is without interruptions, which we know always happen.

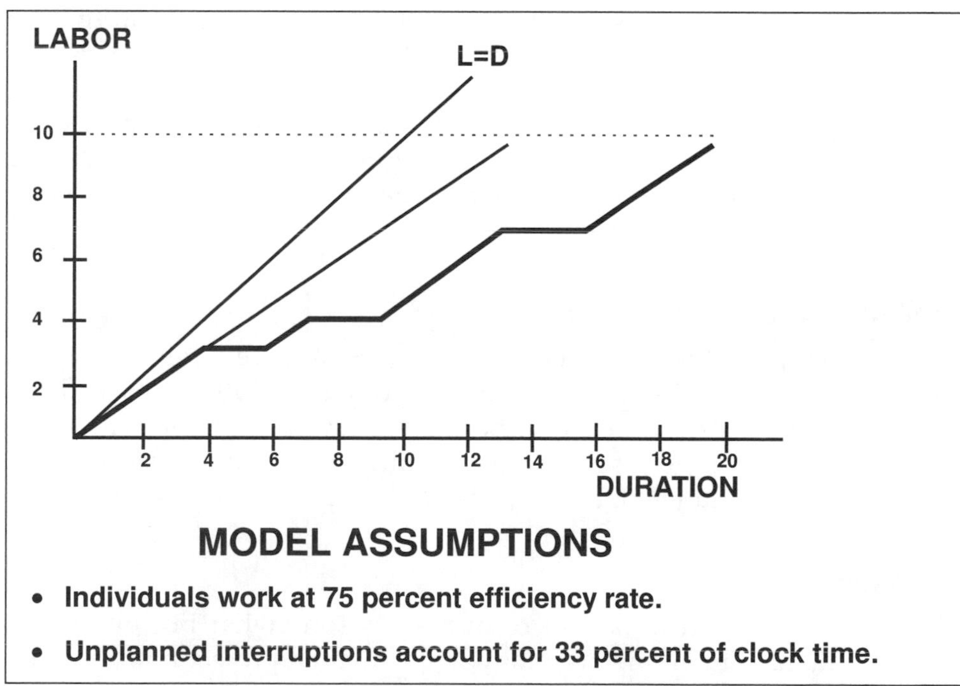

Figure 9.1 Elapsed time vs. labor time vs. productive time.

For some professionals interruptions are frequent (technical support, for example), while for others interruptions are infrequent. We polled the Technical Support Unit of a midsize Information Services Department and found that about one-third of their time was spent on unplanned activities. Unplanned activities might include a phone call with a question to be answered, a systems crash, power interrupts, random events of nature, the boss stops in to visit on an unrelated matter, a phone call from your golfing buddies, and so on. Using the 75 percent efficiency figure and the 33 percent unplanned activities figure means that a 10-hour task will take approximately 20 hours to complete. It is this elapsed time that we are interested in estimating for each activity in the project. For costing purposes, we are interested in the labor time actually spent on an activity.

Five Methods for Estimating Activity Duration

Estimating activity duration is challenging. We may be on familiar ground for some and totally unfamiliar ground for others. Whatever the case, we must produce an estimate. It is important that senior management understand that the estimate may be little more than a WAG. In many projects the estimate will be improved as we learn more about the deliverables from having completed some of the project work. Reestimation and replanning are common. In our consulting practice we have found the five techniques described in Figure 9.2 to be quite suitable for planning estimates.

Similarity to Other Activities

Some of the activities in your WBS may be similar to activities completed in other projects. Yours or others' recollections of those activities and their durations may be used to estimate the present activity's duration. In some cases this may require extrapolating from the other activity to this one, but in any case it does provide an estimate.

Historical Data

This is getting ahead of ourselves somewhat but every good project management methodology will contain a project notebook. In this notebook you will have recorded the estimated and actual durations of activities. It is this historical record that can now be used on the current

- **Similarity to other activities**
- **Historical data**
- **Expert advice**
- **Delphi technique**
- **Three-point technique**

Figure 9.2 Activity duration estimation techniques.

project. The recorded data becomes your knowledge base for estimating activity duration. This differs from the previous technique in that a record has been kept.

Historical data can be used in quite sophisticated ways. One of our clients has built an extensive database of activity duration history. They have recorded not only estimated and actual durations but also the characteristics of the activity, the skill set of the people working on it, and other variables that may be useful. When a new activity duration is needed they are able to go to their database with a complete definition of the activity, and with some rather sophisticated regression models estimate the activity duration. They build product for market and it is very important to them to be able to estimate as accurately as possible. Again, our advice is that if there is value added for a particular tool or technique, use it. We know that this client has asked that question and the answer is obvious.

Expert Advice

When the project involves a breakthrough technology or a technology that is being used for the first time in the organization, there may not be any local experience or even professionals skilled in the technology within the organization. In these cases you will have to appeal to outside authorities. Vendors may be a good source, as will noncompetitors who are using that technology.

Delphi Technique

In the absence of expert advice the Delphi method can produce good estimates. This is a group technique that extracts and summarizes the knowledge of the group to arrive at an estimate. After being briefed on the project and the nature of the activity, each individual in the group is asked to make a best guess as to the activity duration. The results are tabulated and presented (see Figure 9.3) to the group in a histogram (First Pass). Those whose estimates fall in the outer quartiles are asked to share the reason for their guess. After listening to the arguments, each group member is asked to guess again. The results are presented as a histogram (Second Pass) and again the outer quartile estimates are defended. A third guess is made and the histogram plotted (Third Pass). Final adjustments are allowed and then the average of the third guess is used as the group's estimate. While the technique seems rather simplistic it has been shown to be effective in the absence of expert advice.

Three-Point Technique

Activity duration is a random variable. If it were possible to repeat the activity several times under identical circumstances, we would experience a variation in duration times. That variation may be tightly

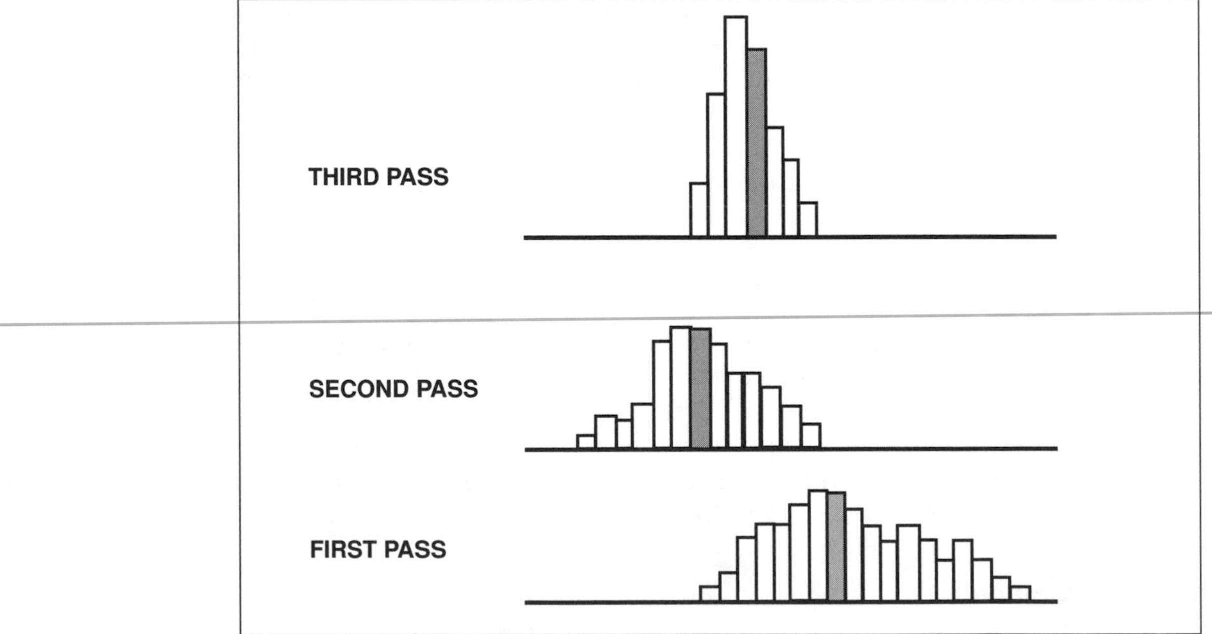

Figure 9.3 The Delphi technique.

grouped around a central value or it might be widely dispersed. In the first case, we would have considerable information on that activity's duration, as compared to the latter case in which we would have very little or none. In any given instance of the activity we would not know at which extreme the duration would likely fall, but we can make probabilistic statements about their likelihood in any case.

This method gives us a framework for doing just that. In order to use the method we will need three estimates of activity duration: optimistic, pessimistic, and most likely. The optimistic time is defined as the shortest duration one has had or might expect to experience given that everything happens as was expected. The pessimistic time is that duration that would be experienced (or has been experienced) if everything that could go wrong did go wrong and yet the activity was completed. Finally, the most likely time is that time usually experienced. For this method you are calling on the collective memory of professionals who have worked on similar activities but for which there is no recorded history. Figure 9.4 is a graphical representation of the three-point method.

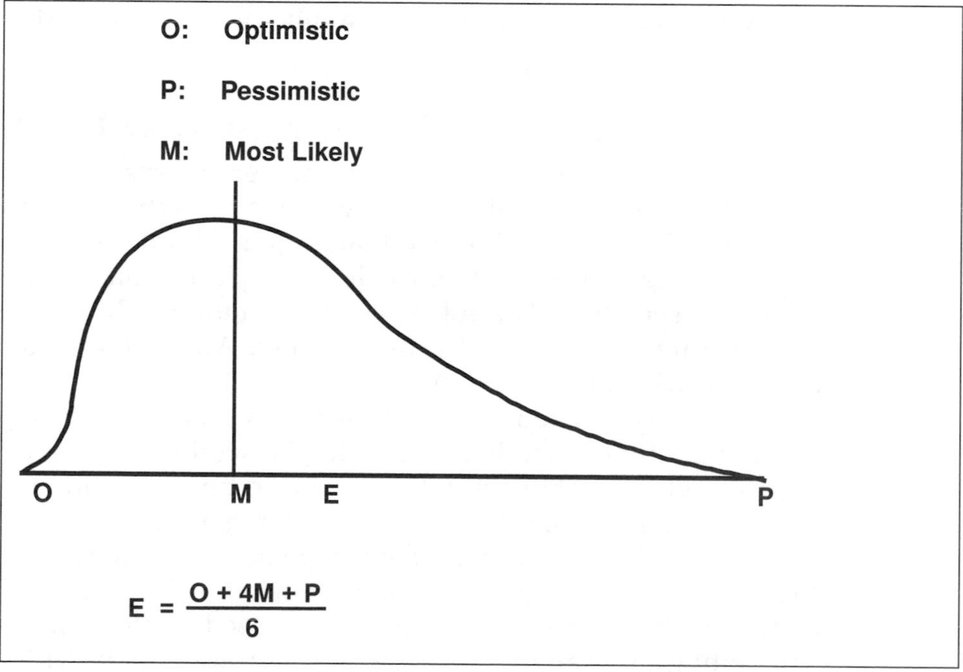

Figure 9.4 The three-point method.

A sixth method can be developed by combining the Delphi and three-point methods. This method is called the Wide-Band Delphi technique. It involves a panel, as in the Delphi technique. The panel is asked to give optimistic, pessimistic, and most likely estimates for an activity duration. The results are compiled and any extreme estimates are removed. Averages are computed for each of the three estimates and the averages are used as the optimistic, pessimistic, and most likely durations.

Estimation Precision

Systems development methodologies generally follow a phased approach wherein knowledge gained in an early phase is used for decision making and to improve estimates of activities in later phases of the project. In our top-down project planning model we start out with *roughly right* estimates with the intention of improving the precision of these estimates later in the project. Management and the customer must be aware of this approach. Most of us have the habit of assuming that a number, once written, is inviolate and absolutely correct regardless of the circumstances under which the number was determined.

How to Use a JPP Session to Estimate Activity Duration

Since you have assembled the subject matter experts on your planning team, you have all the information you need to estimate activity duration in the JPP session. The methodology is simple. During the WBS exercise ask each subteam to provide activity duration estimates as part of their presentation. The subteam's presentation will then include the activity duration estimates it determined. Any disagreement can be resolved during the presentation.

We have conducted many JPP sessions and offer some advice on estimating activity duration during the JPP session.

First, get it roughly right. Do not waste time deciding whether the duration is nine or ten days. By the time the activity is open for work the team will have a lot more knowledge about the activity and will be able to provide an improved estimate—rendering the debate time a waste of time. As one of our authors expressed it after some frustration with getting the planning team to move ahead quickly with estimates: Are you 70 percent sure you are 80 percent right? Good; let's move on.

Second, spend more effort on front-end activities than on back-end activities. As project work commences back-end activities may undergo change. In fact, some may be removed from the project altogether.

Third, consensus is all that is needed. If you have no serious objections to the estimate, let it stand. It is so easy to get bogged down in minutiae. The JPP session is trying enough on the participants. Let's not make it any more painful than needed. Save your energy for the really important parts of the plan—like the WBS!

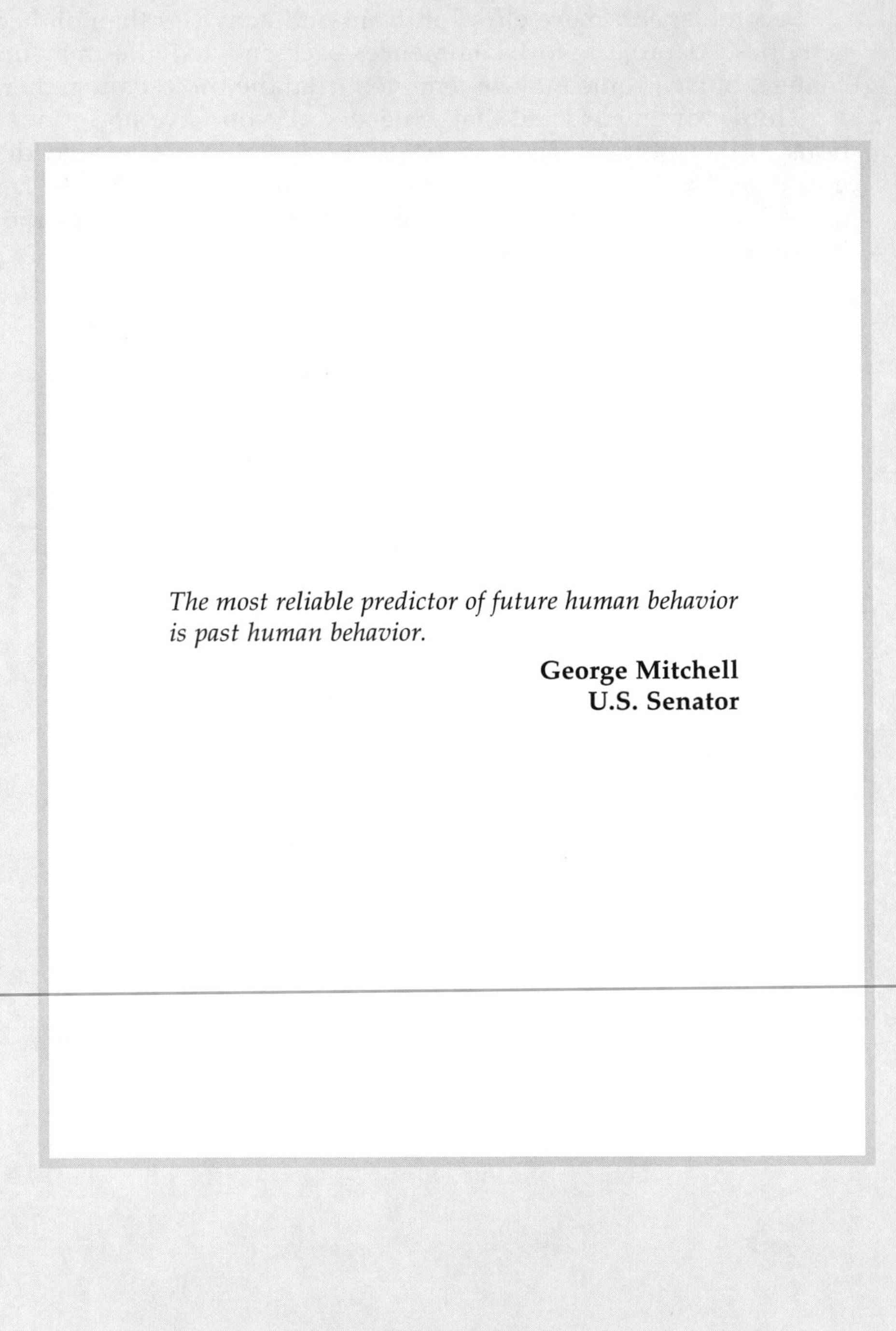

The most reliable predictor of future human behavior is past human behavior.

George Mitchell
U.S. Senator

CHAPTER 10

DETERMINE RESOURCE REQUIREMENTS

CHAPTER LEARNING OBJECTIVES

As a result of participating in the learning experiences in this chapter you will be able to:

1. Understand the relationship between resource allocation and activity duration.
2. Know three ways to assign resources to meet project schedules.
3. Use a skills matrix to schedule people to project activities.

The Resource/Activity Problem

There are two fundamental approaches to project management that require explanation here. The first approach is the market-driven approach, which treats time-to-market as a given and plans resource utilization around time to market constraints. In other words, resources can expand in order to meet time to market requirements. The second approach is the resource-driven approach, which involves the effective use of resources. Here the goal is to keep all resources productively engaged. Obviously the two are not compatible. We cannot minimize time to market while simultaneously optimizing resource utilization.

Figure 10.1 is a graphic portrayal of the resource scheduling problem. The pipeline represents a resource. Its diameter is the current level of the resource available for any project. Activities can be forced into the pipeline until the rate at which they are forced exceeds the rate at which work can be completed. While we may try to force more into the

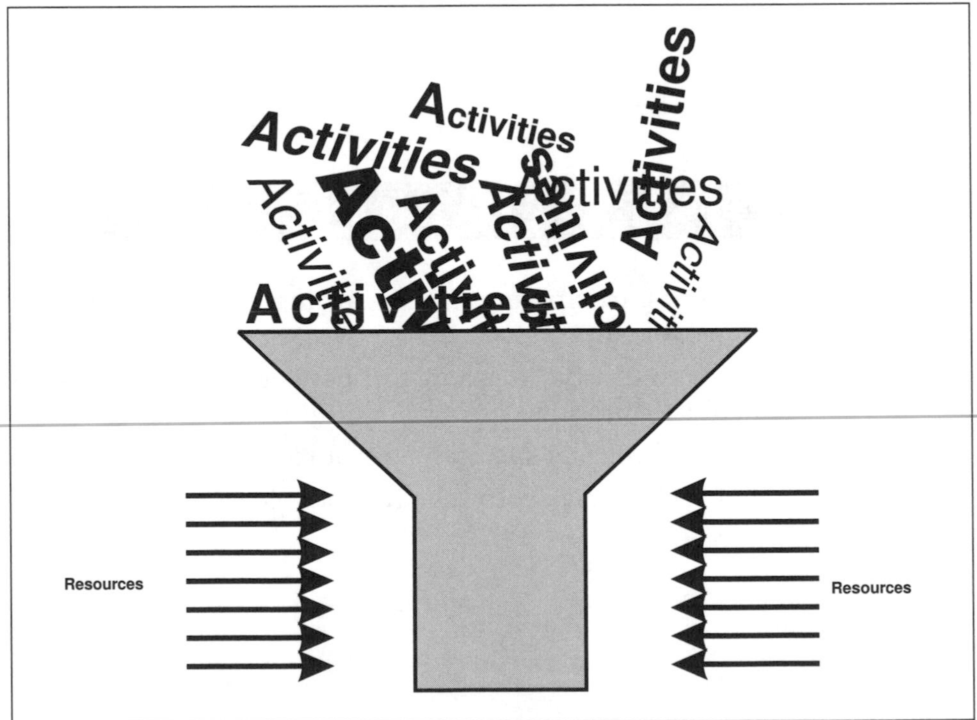

Figure 10.1 The resource scheduling problem.

pipeline than it can accommodate all that happens is that we create turbulence in the pipeline, and the system becomes unstable even to the point at which it ruptures due to overload (weekend and long hours are the root causes of the rupture.)

Activity flow through the pipeline is smoothest at the center, which is where we have allocated the core team work. Along the boundary of the pipeline we have assigned the work to be done by the contract team. There is more turbulence at the walls of the structure.

The deliverables from this visualization are completed activity work. Due to the constriction on the diameter, only so much completed work can flow from the pipe. Too many organizations think that by simply adding more into the top, more will come out of the bottom. The rationale is that people will work harder and more efficiently knowing that more is expected. While this may be true in a limited sense, it is not in the best interest of the project. Mistakes will be made.

Resource Needs

There are three ways to assign a resource to an activity (see Figure 10.2). Market-driven and resource-driven projects will have different options. The choice is driven more by resource availability than by any other factor.

Assign at a Constant Rate

If the activity is scheduled to take, say, 40 hours of clock time to complete and requires 20 hours of effort to complete, and we assign work at a constant rate, the team member will work half-time over a period of 40 clock hours in order to log in 20 hours of effort to complete the work.

- **Assigning as a rate (prorated)**
- **Assigning as a total amount**
- **Assigning as a profile**

Figure 10.2 Estimating resource assignments.

Assign as a Total Amount

Alternatively we may assign the worker to the activity until the work is completed.

Assign as a Profile

There will be cases in which the person cannot work at a constant rate because of other commitments. In such cases we may assign the work to be done at different rates over the 40 window. For example, we might assign the worker three-quarter time for 20 hours and half-time for 20 hours. Other variations are also possible. In many cases the start of work will be delayed until the person is available, and then they will work full time to the completion of the activity.

Types of Resources

People

In most cases the resources you will have to schedule are people resources. This is also the most difficult to schedule, so we devote considerable space in this chapter to people resources. The difficulty arises because we plan the project by specifying the types of skills we need, when we need them, and in what amounts. Note that we do not specify by name the resource we need, and this is where problems arise.

Skills Matrices

We find more and more of our clients are developing skills inventory matrices for staff, and skills needs matrices for tasks. The two matrices are used to assign staff to tasks. The assignment might be based on task characteristics, such as risk, business value, criticality, or skills development.

Skills Categories

This part of the skills matrix is developed by looking at each task that the unit must perform and describing the skills needed to perform the task. Since skills may appear in unrelated tasks, the list of possible skills must be standardized across the enterprise.

Skill Levels

While a binary assessment (that is, you either have the skill or you don't) is certainly easier to administer, it isn't sufficient for project management. Skills must be qualified with a statement of how much of the skill the person possesses. Various methods are available and companies often develop their own skill-level system. We prefer to use Bloom's Taxonomy, as described in Chapter 2.

Facilities

Project work takes place in locations. Planning rooms, conference rooms, presentation rooms, auditoriums, and so on are but a few examples of facilities that projects require. The exact specifications as well as the precise time at which they are needed are some of the variables that must be taken into account. The project plan can provide the detail required. The facility specification will also drive the project schedule because of availability.

Equipment

Equipment is treated exactly the same as facilities. What is needed and when drive the activity schedule because of availability.

Money

Accountants would tell us that everything is eventually reduced to dollars, and that is true. For the project manager those dollars must be expressed in a form that can help them manage project work. Project expenses typically include travel, room and meals, supplies, and so on.

Materials

Parts to be used in the fabrication of products and other physical deliverables are often part of the project work, too.

Resource Loading vs. Activity Duration

The duration of an activity is affected by the amount of a resource we schedule to work on the activity. Recall that when we estimated activity duration it was under the assumption that the typically skilled resources and typically allocated amounts would be used. In practice that will generally not happen. Instead we will have a higher or lower (usually lower) skill level assigned. In those cases we may wish to add more resources in order to constrain the activity duration within the planning limits. This is called *Crashing the Activity* and it works as described in the following.

By way of example, suppose you are asked to pick up the chair and take it out of the room into the hallway. You might try to do it without any help, in which case you would pick up the chair and carry it to the door, set it down, open the door and hold it open with your foot as you pick up the chair, carry it through the door, and set it down in the hallway.

Suppose you could get someone to help you by opening the door and holding it open while you pick up the chair and carry it out to the hallway. With one person helping you would be willing to say that it reduced the time to complete the task. Suppose you could add a third person. With one holding the door open the other two could each grab a side of the chair and carry it out to the hallway. Would you be willing to say that three people could complete the task in less time than two, and certainly less than one? Maybe, maybe not. The point of this simple example is to show that there are diminishing returns for adding more resources. You would probably agree that there is a maximum loading of resources onto a task to minimize the activity duration, and that by adding another resource you will actually begin to increase the duration. There will be occasions on which the project manager will have to consider the maximum loading of a resource onto a task to minimize activity duration.

A second consideration for the project manager is the amount of reduction in duration for adding resources. The relationship is not linear. Consider the chair example again. Does doubling the resource halve the duration? Can two people dig a hole twice as fast as one? Probably not. The explanation is simple. By adding the nth person to an activity you create the need for n more communication links. Who is going to do what? How can the work of several persons be coordinated? There may be other considerations that actually add work. To assume that the amount of work remains constant as you add resources is simply not correct. New kinds of work will emerge from the addition of a resource to an activity.

A third aspect for the project manager to consider is the impact on risk from having added another resource. If we limit the resource to people, we must consider the possibility that two people will prefer to approach the activity in different ways, with different work habits, and different levels of commitment. The more people working on an activity the more likely one will be absent; the higher the likelihood of a mistake being made, the more likely they will get in each other's way. Consider the hole-digging project if you need an example.

How to Use a JPP Session to Determine Resource Requirements

The planning team includes resource managers or their representatives. At the time the planning team is defining the WBS and estimating activity duration, estimates of resource requirements will be made.

We have found the following practice effective: First, create a list of all the resources required for the project. For people resources give only position title or skill level. Do not name specific people even if there is only one person with the requisite skills. Envision a person with the typical skill set and loading on the project activity. Activity duration estimates are based on typically skilled workers as should resource requirements. You will worry about changing this relationship later in the planning session. Second, when presentations are made of the WBS, resource requirements can be reported, too.

Structure is not organization.

Robert H. Waterman
Management consultant

The man who goes alone can start today, but he who travels with another must wait til that other is ready.

Henry David Thoreau
American naturalist

In every affair consider what precedes and what follows, and then undertake it.

Epictetus
Greek philosopher

Every moment spent planning saves three or four in execution.

Crawford Greenwalt
President, DuPont

CHAPTER 11

CONSTRUCT/ANALYZE THE PROJECT NETWORK

CHAPTER LEARNING OBJECTIVES

As a result of participating in the learning experiences in this chapter you will be able to:

1. Construct a network representation of the project activities.
2. Compute the Earliest Start (ES), Earliest Finish (EF), Latest Start (LS), and Latest Finish (LF) times for every activity in the network.
3. Identify the critical path in the project.
4. Use advanced network dependency relationships for improving the project schedule.
5. Analyze the network for possible schedule compression.
6. Use the critical path for planning, implementation, and control of the project activities.

Network Representation of a Project

One of the first thoughts that come to mind is: Why use network-based scheduling? Surely a Gantt Chart is easier to build and does not require use of an automated tool. There are at least two reasons that we put forward.

First, the network provides a visual layout of the sequence in which project work will flow. The Gantt Chart reflects only the order imposed by the manager and in fact hides much of that information. You see, the Gantt Chart does not contain all of the sequencing information that exists. Unless you are intimately familiar with the project activities you cannot tell from the Gantt Chart what comes before and after what. The network representation shows that information explicitly.

Second, the network representation allows one to compute the earliest time at which the project can be completed. That information does not follow from a Gantt Chart. The Gantt Chart reflects only when the manager would like to have the work done.

The WBS identifies the set of activities whose work must be scheduled. The next task for the planning team is to determine the sequence in which these activities can be done. You could, of course, do them one at a time until they are all done. That is a simple approach and in all but the most trivial projects that approach would not give us an acceptable completion date.

Alternatively, one might examine each activity and determine which must be completed before others can begin. Through this analysis, a sequence will emerge. Begin with the WBS to define a sequence of activities that will represent the project. Simply recognizing that some activities may be worked on in parallel with other activities, and others cannot begin until certain other activities have been completed, is enough to grasp the complication involved. The first step is to examine each activity and ask what other activity or activities must be complete before this activity may begin. These other activities are called *immediate predecessors*. An activity that may be started after all its predecessor activities have been completed is called a *successor activity*.

A project is a sequence of interconnected activities. As such it can be represented by a diagram called a *project network*. The type of network we will use defines the project in terms of nodes and connecting arcs. The nodes represent the activities that comprise the project. The connecting arcs represent the predecessor/successor relationship between the activities. This representation is called a *precedence diagram* and is constructed as defined in the following.

Activity on the Arrow

One of the early methods for representing project activities as a network dates back to the early 1950s and the Polaris Missile Program. It is called the Activity on the Arrow (AOA) method. As Figure 11.1 shows, each activity is represented by an arrow. The node at the left edge of the arrow is the event *begin the activity* while the node at the right edge of the arrow is the event *end the activity*. Every activity is represented by this configuration. Nodes are numbered sequentially and the sequential ordering had to be preserved at least in the early versions. Due to the limitations of the AOA method, ghost activities had to be added to preserve network integrity. Only the simplest of dependency relationships could be used. This technique proved to be quite cumbersome as networking techniques progressed. One seldom sees this approach used today.

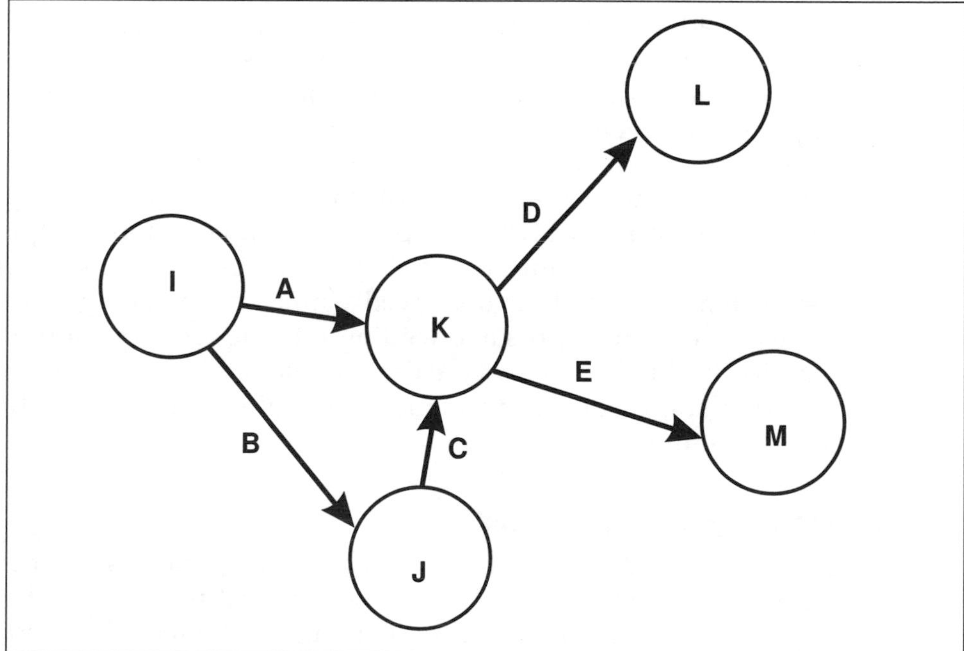

Figure 11.1 Activity on the arrow.

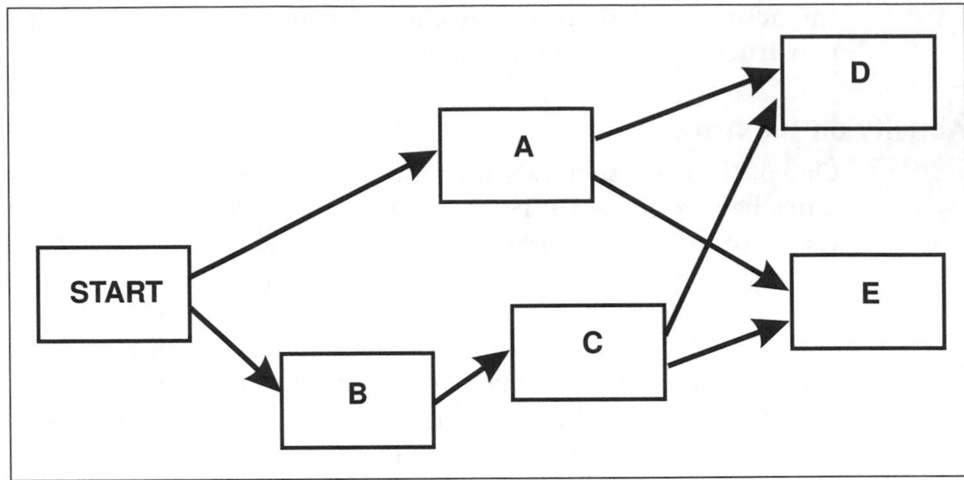

Figure 11.2 Activity on the node.

Activity on the Node

With the advent of the computer the AOA method lost its appeal and a new method replaced it. Figure 11.2 shows the Activity on the Node (AON) method. The term more commonly used to describe this approach is Precedence Diagramming Method (PDM). The PDM represents each activity as a node, with the connecting arcs representing the relationship between activities. In this format an activity begins when its predecessors have been completed. However, more complex dependencies are also possible, as we shall see presently. The simplest dependency, Finish to Start, is displayed with arcs emanating from the right edge of the predecessors and leading into the left edge of the successor activity. In this format every activity must have at least one predecessor and one successor except for the beginning activity and the ending activity of the project.

Precedence Diagramming Method

First we must determine the predecessors and successors of each activity. For each activity ask: What activities must be complete before I can begin this activity? Here we are looking for the technical dependencies between activities. Once an activity is complete it will have produced an output, a deliverable, which becomes input to its successor activities.

Work on the successor activities requires only the output from its predecessor activities. Later we will incorporate management constraints that may alter these dependency relationships. For now we prefer to delay consideration of the management constraints; they will only complicate the planning at this point.

What is the next step? While the list of predecessors and successors to each activity contains all the information we need to proceed with the project, it does not represent the information in a format that tells the story of our project. Our goal will be to provide a graphical picture of the project, but in order to do that we need to spell out a few rules first. Once we know the rules we can create the graphical image of the project. In this section we will teach you the few simple rules for constructing a project network.

The basic *unit of analysis* in a sequenced network is the activity. Activities on the network will be represented by a rectangle that we call an *activity node* shown in Figure 11.3. Every activity in the project will have its own activity node. The entries in the activity node describe the time-related properties of the activity. Some of the entries describe characteristics of the activity, such as its expected duration (E), while others describe calculated values (ES, EF, LS, LF) associated with that activity. We will define these calculated values shortly.

Figure 11.3 Activity node.

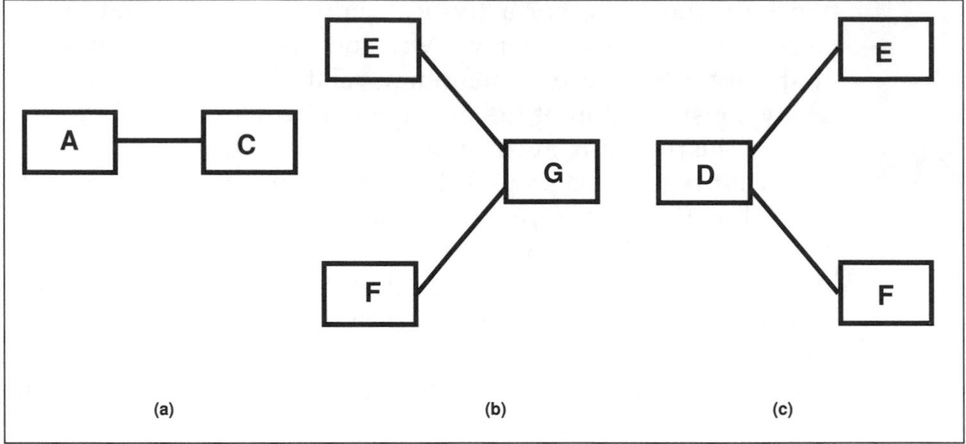

Figure 11.4 Diagramming conventions.

Network Diagramming Conventions

The network will comprise activity nodes and connecting lines that describe the precedence relationships among the activities. The network diagram is time sequenced to be read from left to right. Every activity in the network, except the start and end activities, must have at least one activity that comes before it (its predecessor) and one activity that comes after it (its successor). The start activity has no predecessor and the end activity has no successor. Such networks are called *connected*. Figure 11.4 gives examples of how the variety of relationships that might exist between two or more activities can be diagrammed.

Types of Activity Dependencies

There are four types of activity dependencies, as described in the following and illustrated in Figure 11.5.

Finish to Start

The Finish to Start (FS) dependency simply says that Activity A must be complete before Activity B can begin. It is the simplest and most risk-averse of the four types. It is the type we recommend be used in the initial project planning session.

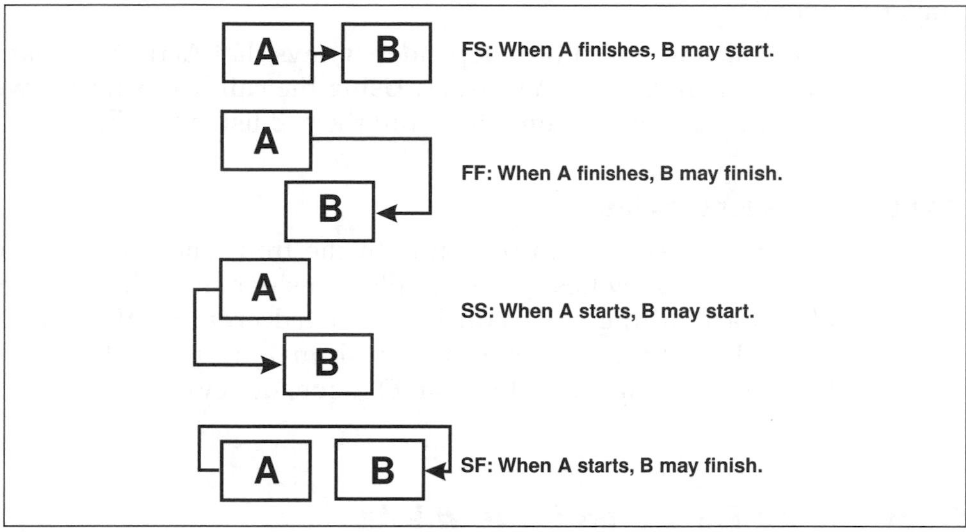

Figure 11.5 Dependency relationships.

Start to Start

The Start to Start (SS) dependency says that Activity B may begin once Activity A has begun. Note that there is a no-sooner-than relationship between Activities A and B. Activity B may begin no sooner than Activity A. As a simple example, consider the assembling of a call list and the act of calling. If Activity A is to assemble the call list and Activity B is to place the calls, then we may begin placing the calls once we have begun to assemble the call list. In other words, we do not have to wait until the entire call list is assembled before we begin placing the calls. You should see that SS dependencies reduce the total time to do both activities as compared to a FS dependency. We will use this fact in the section dealing with schedule compression strategies.

Start to Finish

The Start to Finish (SF) dependency is a little more complex than the previous two cases. Here Activity B may be finished no sooner than Activity A has started. As an example, consider the beating of a person's natural heart (Activity A) and the beating of an artificial heart (Activity B). In the operating procedure the artificial heart may be turned off no sooner than the person's natural heart has started beating.

Finish to Finish

The Finish to Finish (FF) dependency says that Activity B may finish no sooner than Activity A finishes. Using the call list example, we see that the calls cannot be completed until the call list is finished.

Composite Dependencies

Dependencies can be used on both the front end and the back end of two related activities. For example, consider the call list example. You may start calling once you have started creating the call list (an SS dependency) but you may not finish making the calls until you have finished creating the call list (an FF dependency).

Sequencing Based on Constraints

In this chapter we are concerned only with the technical dependency between activities. We will talk about another kind, managerial dependencies, later.

Technical Constraints

Technical dependencies between activities are those that arise because one activity (the successor) requires output from another (the predecessor) before work can begin on it. In the simplest case the predecessor must be completed before the successor can begin. We advise using FS relationships in the initial construction of the network. SS and FF will be used later as we analyze the network for schedule improvements.

Discretionary Constraints

Choices made here are often risk-aversion strategies. Through the sequencing activities the project manager gains a modicum of comfort with the project work.

Best Practices

The practices in place in an industry can be a powerful influencer here, especially in dealing with bleeding-edge technologies. In some cases the dependencies added by the project manager may be part of a risk-aversion strategy following the experiences of others.

Unique Requirements

These arise in situations where a critical resource, say an irreplaceable expert or one-of-a-kind piece of equipment, will be involved on several project activities. Apart from any technical constraints, the project manager may impose dependencies that accommodate the scarce resources.

Management Constraints

A second type of dependency is a management-imposed dependency. We shall see how these arise when we conduct an analysis of the resulting network of technical dependencies, and as part of the scheduling decisions we will make as project manager. For now it is sufficient to know that they exist. They differ from technical dependencies in that they can be reversed, while technical dependencies cannot.

Interproject Dependencies

Here we are dealing with activities in separate projects. The dependencies are technical but exist between projects rather than within a project. These can arise when a very large project was decomposed into smaller, more manageable projects. This will allow project subteams to focus on just their area of work. Occasionally large projects are defined along organizational or geographic boundaries. Although we would prefer to avoid such decomposition, it may be necessary at times.

It is becoming quite common today for organizations to develop technology in one project, which another project will need to meet its goal.

Date Constraints

Date constraints are used to force an activity to occur on a particular schedule. In our date-driven world it is a continual temptation to put the date requested as the required delivery date. These constraints generally conflict with the calculated schedule driven by the dependency relationships between activities. Date constraints generally create negative float situations and hence unneeded complication in interpreting the project schedule.

Date constraints come in three types: *no earlier than*, *no later than*, and *on this date*. They may be used on either the start or finish side of an activity. The most troublesome is the *on this date* constraint. It firmly sets a date and affects all activities that follow it. The next most troublesome is the *no later than* constraint. It will not allow an acitivy to occur beyond the specified date. Both types can result in negative float. If at all possible, do not use them. There are alternatives that we discuss in the next chapter. The least troublesome is the *no earlier than*. At worst it simply delays an activity's schedule and hence by itself cannot cause negative float.

The Use of Lag Variables

We may also introduce pauses or delays between activities through the use of *lag variables*. For example, in the call list example, suppose for some reason we wished to delay the placing of calls until we had some minimal number of names on the call list. We estimate that it will take two days to reach that minimal number. In order to represent this requirement using dependency relationships, consider: Once we have started to build the call list (Activity A) we can begin placing calls (Activity B) but only after we have spent two days building the call list. In other words we have an SS relationship between A and B, with a lag of two days.

Build the Project Network

Early Schedule

In order to establish the project schedule, we will compute two schedules: the Early Schedule and the Late Schedule. The combination of these two schedules will give us the information we need to identify a sequence of activities within the project, which control the completion date of the project. This sequence is known as the *critical path*.

The earliest start (ES) time for an activity is the earliest time at which all predecessor activities of that activity have been completed and the subject activity can begin. The ES time of an activity having no predecessor activities is arbitrarily set to 1, the first day on which the project is open for work. The ES time of activities having one predecessor activity is determined from the EF time of the predecessor activity. The ES time of activities having two or more predecessor activities is determined from the maximum of the EF times of the predecessor activities. The early schedule is shown in Figure 11.6.

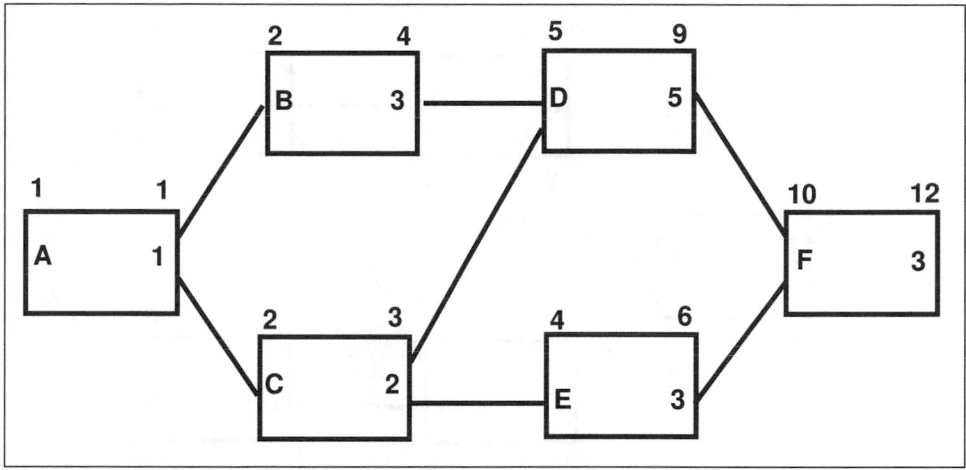

Figure 11.6 Forward-pass calculations.

Late Schedule

The latest start (LS) and latest finish (LF) times of an activity are the latest times at which an activity can start or be completed without causing a delay in the completion of the project. To calculate these times we will work backward in the network. First set the LF time of the last activity on the network to the EF time of that activity. The LF time of all immediate predecessor activities is determined by the minimum of the LS times of all activities for which it is the predecessor. The late schedule is shown in Figure 11.7.

Network Characteristics

The convention we adopt in this book is that all activities in the network have at least one predecessor and one successor activity with the exception of the start and end activities. If this convention is followed, then the critical path is relatively straightforward to identify. If, however, the convention is not followed, or there are date constraints imposed on some activities, or the resources follow different calendars, then the critical path may be rather elusive.

Critical Path

The critical path is defined as the longest path (in terms of activity duration) through the network. It drives the completion date of the pro-

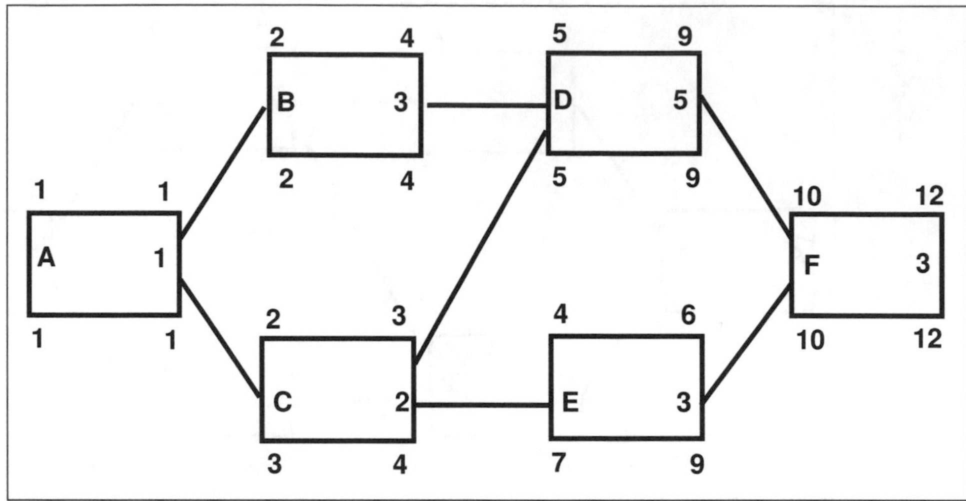

Figure 11.7 Backward-pass calculations.

ject. The sequence of activities that define the critical path are such that any delay in the completion of any one of them will delay the completion of the project. Obviously the project manager will be paying particular attention to critical path activities. The critical path for our example problem is shown in Figure 11.8.

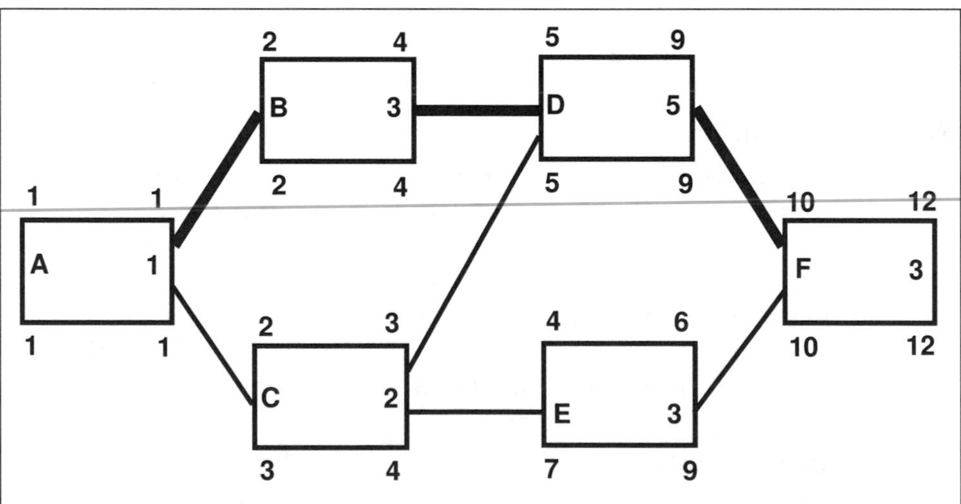

Figure 11.8 Critical path.

One way to find the critical path in the network is to enumerate all possible paths. For projects of any size this method is not feasible and we have to resort to the second method of finding the critical path. First we compute a quantity known as the activity slack time. Slack time (a.k.a. float) is the amount of delay that could be tolerated in the starting time or completion time of an activity without causing a delay in the completion of the project. Slack time is mathematically the difference (LF – EF). Based on the method we used to compute the early and late schedules, the sequence of activities having zero slack is defined as the critical path. In the general case, the critical path is the path that has minimum slack.

Near-Critical Path

While we are tempted to rivet attention on critical path activities, there are other activities that require equal attention. We call these *near-critical* paths and introduce the concept by way of a simple example. Suppose the critical path activities are activities in which the project team has considerable experience, then duration estimates are based on historical data and are quite accurate in that the estimated duration will be very close to the actual duration. On the other hand, there is a sequence of activities not on the critical path for which the team has little experience. Duration estimates have large estimation errors. Suppose further that such activities lie on a path that has little total float. It is very likely that this near-critical path may actually drive the project completion date even though the total path length is less than the critical path length. Obviously this path cannot be ignored.

Float

Float (also known as slack) is defined with reference to an activity. It is a property that all activities have and is expressed in units of time. It defines a window of time within which an activity must be completed. Consider, for example, an activity that has a duration of three days. The window of time within which this activity must be completed is the difference (LF – ES). If LF – ES = duration, then the activity has zero float. In other words, activities with zero float must be completed on schedule or they will delay completion of the project. When this difference is not zero but some positive number, it defines a window that is wider than the duration of the activity. Figure 11.9 diagrams this situation.

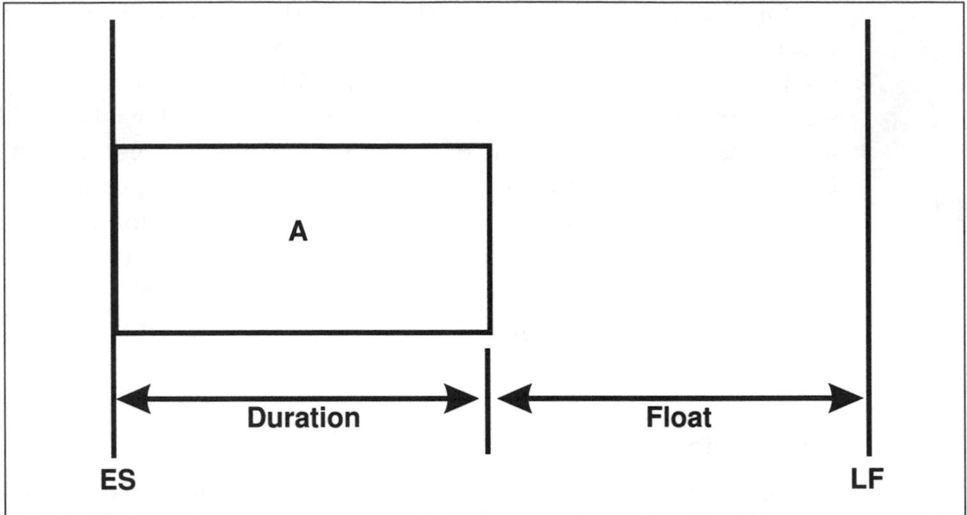

Figure 11.9 ES to LF window of an activity.

To schedule Activity A we must pick a start time greater than or equal to ES but less than or equal to LF — duration. The actual choice will often depend on the availability of the resources that are required for the activity. In some cases it may be necessary to schedule the activity work in discrete parts. That is, resource availability may require that work on Activity A may have to be interrupted. Recall that one of the completeness criteria, independence, assures that work on Activity A can be scheduled in one continuous interval of time. Several examples of scheduling alternatives are shown in Figure 11.10.

Free Float

Free float is the amount of delay that can be scheduled in an activity's start time without causing a delay in the early schedule of any activities that are its immediate successors.

Total Float

Total float is the amount of delay that can be scheduled in an activity's finish time without delaying the completion date of the project.

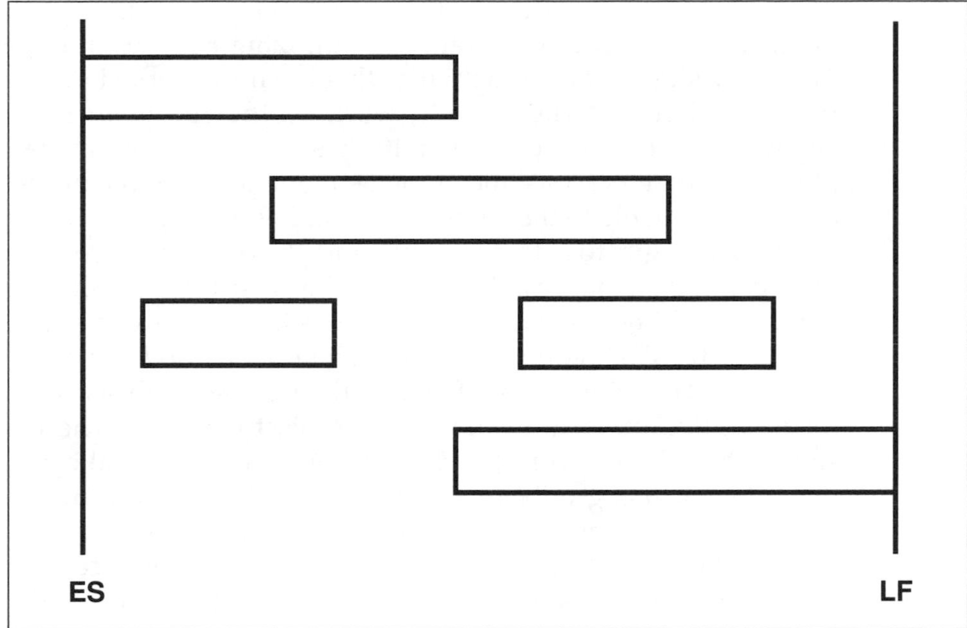

Figure 11.10 Scheduling alternatives.

Analyze the Project Network

Schedule Compression

At this point in the JPP we have created the initial project network and now begin the task of analyzing it in relation to the project constraints of time, cost, and resources. There are two types of questions yet to be answered: Who does what, and when? In this section we look at the problem of compressing the project schedule to meet deadlines that the current project completion data does not meet.

Bottleneck Analysis

Once we have completed the network calculations we will begin an analysis of the network. Almost without exception the initial calculations result in a project duration beyond the expected completion date.

At this point we will begin to analyze the network to see where we might compress project duration by utilizing SS and FF dependencies. This allows us to convert activities that are now worked on in series into more parallel patterns. That is, work on the successor activity might begin once the predecessor activity has reached a certain stage of completion. In many cases some of the deliverables from the predecessor can be made available to the successor so that work might begin on it.

As we begin to adjust the network through replacement of series with parallel sequences of activities, the critical path will move. Generally there will be a sequence of activities that will always remain on the critical path. This sequence will be called a *bottleneck*.

Figure 11.11 illustrates a few iterations of the analysis you might perform in attempting to compress the project duration. The top diagram shows the original critical path resulting from the initial construction of the network using only FS dependencies. The middle diagram shows the results of changing the FS dependency between activities A and B. Note that the critical path has changed to a new sequence of activities in the lower parallel sequence. A further change of the FS dependency between activities C and D again moves the critical path to the lower sequence at the start of the project. Note, however, that the sequence EFG remained on the critical path through both iterations. While further compression may cause that to change, it does identify a sequence of activities deserving particular attention as the project commences.

Use of Networks

Networks can be used for detailed project planning, during implementation as a tool for analyzing scheduling alternatives, and as a control tool.

Planning

Even for large projects, the project network gives a clear graphical picture of the relationship between project activities. It is at the same time a high-level and detailed-level view of the project. During the planning phase we have found it very beneficial to have the network displayed on whiteboards or flip charts so that all members of the planning team can use it for scheduling decisions. We explore this in more detail in the sections that present the JPP details.

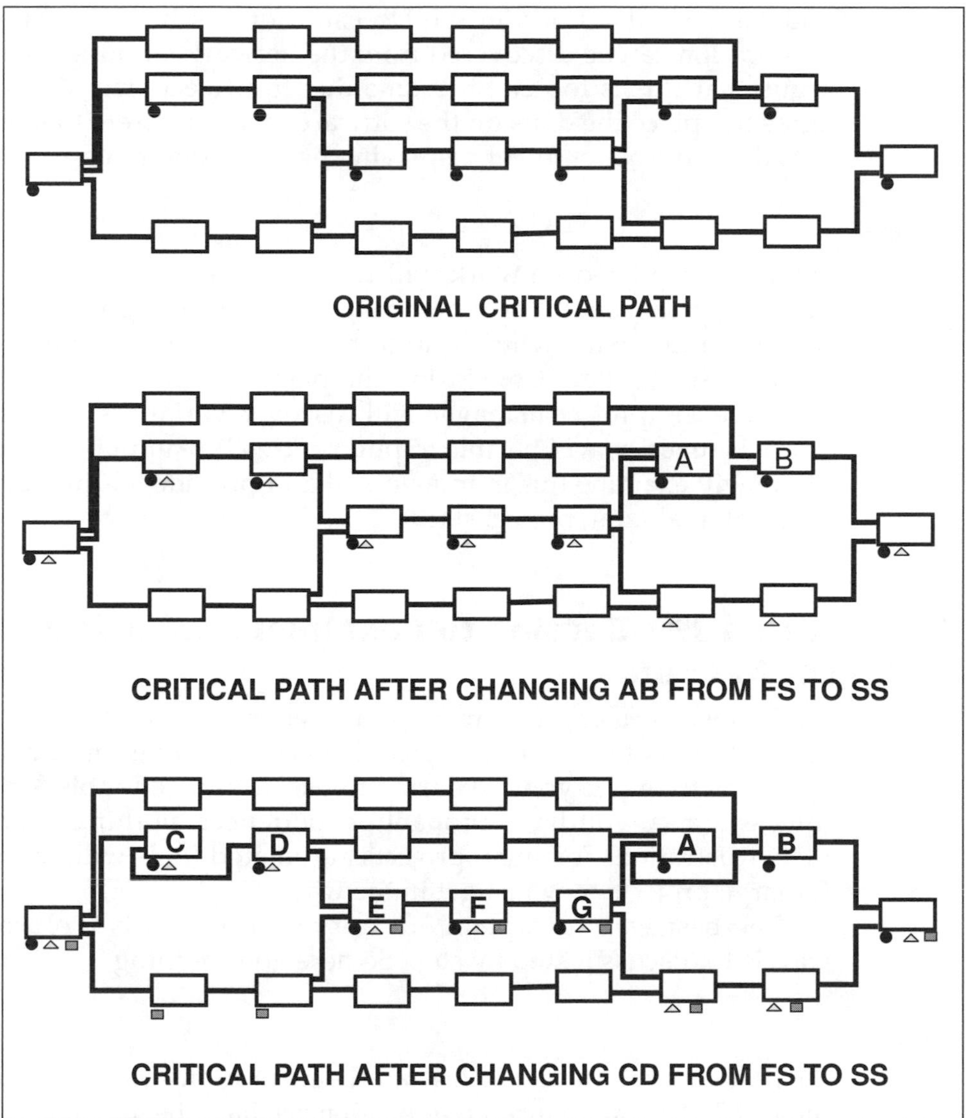

Figure 11.11 Schedule compression iterations.

Implementation

For those project managers using automated project management software tools, they will update the project file with activity status and estimate-to-completion data. The network is then automatically updated and can be printed or viewed. Decisions on rescheduling and resource reallocation can be discovered from the network, although some would argue that this is too cumbersome due to project size. We cannot disagree but place the onus on the software manufacturers to market products that do a better job of displaying network diagrams.

Control

While the updated network will retain the status of all activities, the best graphical report for monitoring and controlling project work will be the Gantt Chart, which cannot be produced unless you have done network scheduling. Comparing the planned schedule with the actual schedule the project manager will discover variances and, depending on their severity, will be able to put a get-well plan in place. In Chapter 16 we will examine this in more detail and provide additional reporting tools for analyzing project status.

How to Use a JPP Session to Construct and Analyze a Project Network

We believe in using the appropriate technology and nowhere is that more obvious than in our approach to constructing and analyzing the project network. If you have tried to use automated tools for this planning exercise, you have probably experienced nothing short of complete frustration. For small projects automated tools will do the job, but for large projects they just get in the way.

The best way to explain our approach, which is foolproof by the way, is to discuss it step by step. So here goes nothing.

Step 1

We first enter all the activities and their durations into MS Project. Print the PERT diagram. Since no dependencies have been entered, the PERT diagram is a columnar report with one activity per row—not a very informative PERT diagram but it serves our purposes.

Step 2

Cut out each activity node and scotch tape it to a sticker note. (Don't forget to create start- and end-node milestones.) We use the 3″ by 3″ size because it allows you to put the node at the top and write in large numbers the task ID number, so that the project planning team will be able to see the task ID from anyplace in the planning room.

Step 3

Affix each sticker note to the whiteboard. Placing them at the rightmost edge of the white board space will facilitate your work. Ordering them by task ID number and/or WBS major category will make it easier to find them later on.

Step 4

Place the start node at the left edge of the whiteboard. Ask the planning group to identify all tasks that have no predecessors. As they are called out, the planning group should listen and voice any objections. If there are none, then place the tasks on the whiteboard and connect them to the start node with a black, erasable marker pen. At each step the facilitator calls out the task numbers, any predecessors, and the dependency relation. The technographer, on hearing this, records the information in MS Project. This exchange is important, for errors can occur if the technographer tries to listen to the planning group's conversation. The technographer should cue off only the facilitator's commands. Continue until no new tasks having no predecessors are identified.

Step 5

Next have the planning group identify tasks that can be done, given those that have been posted on the whiteboard. Again, if there are no objections, affix these sticker notes to the whiteboard and draw the appropriate connecting arcs. The facilitator calls out the additions, and the technographer records them. The process continues until all tasks have been posted on the whiteboard.

Step 6

The technographer reviews the predecessor and successor data to make sure the network is connected. Any discrepancies are noted and corrected.

Step 7

It's now time to find out if the first draft of the network meets the project delivery dates. This rarely happens and some analysis of the network is needed. Start by identifying the critical path by placing a large, red dot on the sequence of tasks that identify the critical path. The real value of the whiteboard and sticker note approach becomes obvious as the planning group tries to identify ways to reduce the time on the critical path. To compress the project schedule look for opportunities to change FS relationships to SS relationships, with perhaps some lag time introduced. Be careful not to get carried away with schedule compression, because it will aggravate the resource scheduling problem. Remember, you are cramming the project work into a shorter window of time, and that tends to increase the probability of creating scheduling conflicts.

At each iteration check to see if the critical path has moved to a different sequence of activities. When all of these types of schedule compression possibilities are exhausted, look for places to add resources to reduce duration times. Be careful here because project risk may increase due to additional needs for communication and coordination between project team members working on the same activity. With each schedule compression, check the critical path, because it can move and create other compression possibilities.

This report, by its very length, defends itself against the risk of being read.

Winston Churchill
English Prime Minister

Learn to write well, or not to write at all.

John Dryden
English poet

If you don't get the reader's attention in the first paragraph, the rest of your message is lost.

Public Relations maxim

CHAPTER 12

Prepare the Project Proposal

CHAPTER LEARNING OBJECTIVES

As a result of participating in the learning experiences in this chapter you will be able to:

1. Understand the purpose of the project proposal.
2. Know what constitutes a good proposal.
3. Write an effective project proposal.

Purpose of The Project Proposal

The *project proposal* is the deliverable from the detailed planning phase. As such it states the complete business case for the project. This includes expected business value as well as cost and time estimates. In addition to this information for senior management there are details on what is to be done, who is going to do it, when it is going to be done, and how it is going to be done. In other words, it is the roadmap for the project.

Contents of The Project Proposal

Following is the Table of Contents for a typical project proposal. You will see a remarkable resemblance to the topics we have covered in Chapters 7 through 12. Rightly so, for the project proposal is a restatement of all the planning work that has been done so far. It is presented here in a clear and concise form. Spare the reader!

Background

This page-or-less description details the situation that led to this project proposal. It often states the business conditions, opportunities, and/or problems giving rise to the project. It sets the stage for later sections and puts the project in the context of the business.

Objective

Another short section that gives a very general statement of what you hope to accomplish through this project. Avoid jargon because you don't know who might have reason to read this section. Use the language of the business, not the technical language of your department. The objective should be clearly stated so that there is no doubt as to what is to be done and what constitutes attainment of the objective.

Overview of Approach to Be Taken

For those who might not be interested in the details of how you are going to reach your objective, this section provides a high-level outline of your approach. Again, avoid jargon whenever possible. Give a brief statement of each step and a few sentences of supporting narrative. Brevity and clarity are important.

Detailed Statement of Work

Here is where you can give the details of your approach. Include what will be done, when it will be done, who will do it, how much time will be required of them, and what criteria will be used to measure completeness. This is the roadmap of all the project work.

Time and Cost Summary

It is our practice to include a summary page of time and cost data. This usually works best if done in a Gantt Chart format. Often it will have been stated over several pages and is brought together here for easy review and comment by the customer.

Appendixes

We reserve the appendix for all supporting data and details that are not germane to the body of the proposal. Anticipate questions your customer might have and include answers here. Remember that this is detail beyond the basic description of the project work. Supporting information is generally found here.

Format of the Project Proposal

There are no hard and fast rules as to format. You will surely be able to find examples of successful proposals in your department to be used as guides. Once you have your ideas layed out, share them with a trusted colleague. Their advice may be the most valuable you can get.

Detailed Statement of Work

PREVIEW

The implementation phase begins with management's approval of the project proposal.

In Chapter 13 we discuss the final details of assembling the project team and establishing the rules and procedures governing how the team will work together. As soon as the specific resources are committed to the project, a final *tuning* of the project schedule is done (Chapter 14), the work assignments are defined (Chapter 15), and the work commences.

Despite the best efforts to plan and document the project work, things seldom go according to plan. In Chapter 16 we introduce a number of monitoring and control tools for analyzing and reporting project progress. These tools include procedures for managing change and resolving problems.

Finally, when the project work has been completed and accepted by the requestor, a series of closing activities begins. These are discussed in Chapter 17.

PART 4

OVERVIEW

Implementation

OVERVIEW

PART 4

The productivity of a work-group seems to depend on how the group members see their own goals in relation to the goals of the organization.

Paul Hersey and Kenneth H. Blanchard

When the best leader's work is done the people say, We did it ourselves.

Lao-Tzu
Chinese philosopher

Leadership is the manager's ability to get subordinates to develop their capabilities by inspiring them to achieve.

John A. Reinecke and William F. Schoell

CHAPTER 13

RECRUIT AND ORGANIZE THE PROJECT TEAM

CHAPTER LEARNING OBJECTIVES

As a result of participating in the learning experiences in this chapter you will be able to:

1. Define the three components of a project team.
2. Describe the characteristics of an effective project manager.
3. Describe the characteristics of an effective project team member.
4. Understand the differences in roles and responsibilities of core vs. contracted team members.
5. Help contracted team members become part of the team.
6. Understand the tools of an effective team.

Recruit the Project Team

We like to think of the project team as having three separate components, as shown in Figure 13.1.

Project plans and their execution are only as successful as the manager and team who implement them. Building effective teams is as much an art as it is a science. Some would in fact call it a craft. In building an effective team, consideration must be given not only to the technical skills, but also to the critical roles and chemistry that must exist between and among the project manager and the team members. The selection of project manager and team members will not be perfect—there are always risks with any personnel decision. In this module we will create an awareness of the important characteristics that should be part of an effective project manager and project team, provide a checklist to assist you in your selection process, and suggest guidelines for organizing the project in an organization.

The Project Manager

Ideally the project manager is assigned to the project from cradle to grave. There may be some cases where the project manager is not identified until the project has been approved for implementation. That is, the project manager will not have participated in the scoping and definition phases. The assignment as project manager will usually not be full time. In many cases the project manager will have simultaneous responsibility for more than one project. Figure 13.2 lists the qualifications and skills required to be an effective project manager.

The project managers are the leaders of projects. In them is vested the responsibility of completing projects on time, within budget, and accord-

THE PROJECT TEAM

- **Project Manager**
- **Core Team**
- **Contracted Team**

Figure 13.1 The project team.

PROJECT MANAGER

- **Background and experience**
- **Leadership and strategic expertise**
- **Technical expertise**
- **Interpersonal competence**
- **Proven managerial ability**

Figure 13.2 The project manager.

ing to specifications, and the authority to get the job done. They represent projects to the organization and to external groups. Harold Kerzner states that since the roles and responsibilities of the project manager are so important, his or her selection should be general management's responsibility.[1] If you are working in a large organization, a group or committee is usually assigned to help screen project manager candidates.

Timing

The timing in selecting a project manager varies. Ideally we would want the project manager in the chair at the very beginning of the project. In contemporary organizations we are seeing the project manager assigned after the proposal has been approved by senior management. This has led to a number of problems, of which short schedules are the most significant. Short schedules arise in projects that are defined generally between the account representative and the customer (whether internal or external). These agreements usually constrain all sides of the triangle as well as the scope. All too often the project manager will have been put in a no-win situation. One rule that we all learned a long time ago is: The sooner the project manager and team are involved in planning the project, the more committed they will be to its implementation. (This is also true for other members in the organization, whose expertise and resources are required to implement the project.)

1. Kerzner, Harold. *Project Management: A Systems Approach to Planning, Scheduling, and Controlling*. New York, NY: Van Nostrand Reinhold.

Selection Criteria

Select a project manager who is experienced, capable, and competent in getting the project done on time, within budget, and according to specifications. Easier said than done. Recall Figure 2.1 which categorized project manager skills as visible and able to be developed, while competencies were largely not visible and difficult to develop in the individual. We do not intend to repeat the discussion from Chapter 2 but offer a few general comments in the following.

Background and Experience

This is difficult to find in many organizations. The problem is the demand for experienced project managers outstrips the supply. The solution for many organizations is to create a learning laboratory for wanna-be project managers and those who are acquiring project management skills and competencies. A hierarchy is commonly put in place. That hierarchy might start at team member, activity manager, milestone manager, and project manager (working up the scale from Type D to Type A projects). Refer to the section in Chapter 4, "Classification of Project Types," if you don't remember the taxonomy of project types. As an adjunct to on-the-job experience acquisition, there are several training alternatives available to *build your own* project managers. These can take various forms but the most common are reviewing project documentation, attending and later supporting JPP sessions, observing project status meetings, and maintaining project documentation, which is assigned to the role of technographer in a JPP session.

The Core Team

The project team is comprised of two categories of team members: *core* and *contracted*. Core team members are with the project from cradle to grave. Just as in the case of the project manager, this assignment is usually not full time. In matrix organizations it is a practice to have professional staff assigned to more than one project at a time. This is especially true when the staff member possesses a skill not commonly found in the staff. Core team members will have some portion of their time allocated to the project, say, 25 percent full-time equivalent persons. The core team is usually identified at the beginning of the scoping phase. This means that they can participate in the early definition and planning of the project. Figure 13.3 lists the qualifications and skills required to be an effective core team member.

- **Commitment**
- **Shared responsibility**
- **Flexible**
- **Task oriented**
- **Work within schedule and constraints**
- **Trust and mutual support**
- **Team oriented**
- **Open minded**
- **Work across structure and authorities**
- **Able to use project management tools**

Figure 13.3 The core team.

Selection Criteria

Because of the downsizing, rightsizing, and capsizing going on in corporate America, much of the option of choosing core team members has been lost to the project manager. While the situation differs, depending on the organizational structure (see Part V, "Enterprise Considerations," for more details on this hot topic), the project manager may have little or no latitude. To drive the point home consider a situation in which you have choices between the A Team and the B Team. Pick your battles carefully because you may want to consider the A Team for critical path activities, high-risk activities, and high-business-value projects. Be ready to horse-trade between projects, too! Give the resource managers an opportunity to use noncritical path activities as on-the-job training for their staff. Remember, they have as many staff development and deployment problems as you have project planning and scheduling problems. Trading a favor of staff development for an A Team member may be a good strategy.

Since you may be expecting specific criteria we offer a list. In our project management consulting work, we have compiled a list of characteristics that high-technology engineers, in particular, have offered as successful characteristics in their project teams. These are born out of experience. Figure 13.3 lists the characteristics you might want to consider in selecting team members, regardless of the nature of the project.

The Contracted Team

The contracted team members are available only for short periods of time on the project (see Figure 13.4). They possess a skill that is needed for only a brief time on the project. They are assigned to the project when it is time for them to contribute the skills. As soon as they have completed their assigned task they leave the project. Contracted team members present the project manager with a number of problems. In most systems development efforts, it is unlikely that professionals would be assigned full time to the project team. Rather, people will join the project team only for the period of time during which their particular expertise is needed. The project manager must be aware of the implications to the project when contracted professionals are used.

Implications of Contracted Team Members

- There may be little or no variance in the time contracted team members are available, so the activities on which they will work must remain on schedule.
- They must be briefed on their role in the project and how their activity relates to other activities in the project.
- Commitment of contracted members is always a problem, since their priorities probably lie elsewhere.

- **Window of availability**
- **Project orientation**
- **Commitment to a problem**
- **Quality is a problem**
- **Level of supervision**

Figure 13.4 The contracted team.

- Quality of work may be an issue for some of the same reasons just given.
- Contracted team members will often require more supervision than core team members.

Organize the Project Team

Authority

Authority and responsibility go hand in hand. To have one and not the other makes no sense. How often have we been in situations where we were responsible for making a certain thing happen but had no authority over the resources needed to make it happen, or no authority to make and carry out a decision? In order to be effective the project manager must have authority over the project. It is his or her job to get the project done on time, within budget, and according to specification. That authority is often delegated but it is the project manager who is ultimately responsible.

The major difficulty that project managers have is that the project team is not their line responsibility. Team members are assigned based on their expertise but they report to another manager. This means that the project manager will have to exercise the best leadership skills and diplomacy to get the job done. The key is in the project-planning activities that schedule resources to windows of time. It is here that the commitment of people resources is made by the resource manager. Honoring that commitment within the time allotted reduces the incidence of problems. If the project manager would remember to keep the resource managers involved and aware of all project changes, negotiations will proceed much better when circumstances warrant.

Responsibility

There is no question where the responsibility lies. This cannot be delegated. The project manager typically assigns activity management responsibility to team members. They are then responsible for completing their assigned activity within its scheduled window of time and for producing the activity deliverables on time according to specification, but it is the project manager who is ultimately responsible for completing the project as expected.

Establish Team Operating Rules

One of the major failings of project teams is the definition and agreement as to what the team operating rules will be. There are several areas to consider in drafting such rules. These are briefly discussed in the sections that follow.

Decision Making

There are three major types of decision-making models: *directive, participative,* and *consultative*. Each has its advantages and disadvantages, as described in the following.

Directive

In this model the person with the authority—the project manager for the project, and the activity manager for the activity—makes the decision for all. While this is certainly expedient, it has obvious drawbacks. The only information available is the decision maker's information, which may or may not be correct or complete. An added danger is that those who disagree or were left out of the decision may not carry it out.

Participative

At the other extreme is the participative approach. Everyone on the team probably has something to contribute, so there will be a synergy created as the best decision is sought. Because all had a chance to participate, commitment will be much stronger than in the directive approach. Obviously there are additional benefits to team building—empowerment of the team. Whenever possible we recommend a participative approach.

Consultative

This middle ground approach combines the best of the other two types. While the person of authority makes the decision, it is done only after having consulted with everyone to get input and ideas. Thus this approach is participative at the input stage but directive at the point of decision. In some cases, in which expediency is required, this approach is a good one to take.

Conflict Resolution

There are three styles that are commonly used to resolve conflicts: *avoidance, combative,* and *collaborative*. These are briefly described in the following.

Avoidance

Some people will do anything to avoid a direct confrontation. They agree even though they are opposed to the outcome. This style cannot be tolerated on the project team. Each person's input and opinion must be sought. It is the responsibility of the project manager to make sure that this happens. A simple device is to ask each team member in turn what they think about the situation and what they would suggest be done about it. Often this will diffuse any direct confrontation between two individuals on the team.

Combative

While some avoid confrontation at all costs, others seem to seek it out. Some team members play devil's advocate at the drop of a hat. There are times when this is advantageous—testing the team's thinking before the decision is rendered. At other times it tends to raise the level of stress and tension when many view it as a waste of time and not productive. The project manager will know who these team members are and must act to mitigate the chances of these situations arising. One technique we have used with success is to put such individuals in charge of forming a recommendation for the team to consider. With such an approach there is less opportunity for combative discussion, since the combative team member is sharing recommendations before others give reason for disagreement.

Collaborative

In this approach the team will look for win-win opportunities. There will always be some common ground, and the approach seeks out that common ground as the basis for moving ahead to a solution. The approach encourages each team member to put opinions on the table and not avoid the conflict that may result. At the same time they do not seek to create conflict unnecessarily. The approach is constructive, not destructive.

Consensus Building

This is an excellent tool to have in the project team tool kit. In all but a few cases there will be a legitimate difference of opinion as to how a problem or issue should be addressed. There will be no clearcut action that all can agree upon. In such situations the team must fashion an action or decision that none have serious disagreement with even though they may not agree in total with the chosen action. To use the method successfully make sure that everyone on the team is heard from. Talk through the issue until an acceptable action is identified. Conflict is good but try to be creative as you search for a compromise action. As soon as no one has serious objections to the defined action, you have reached a consensus. Once a decision is reached, all team members must support it.

Brainstorming

Try it you'll like it! When you have exhausted all other avenues to solve a problem, try brainstorming. You may find it to be a diamond in the rough! The method is simple and quick too! A typical brainstorming approach goes something like this: Assemble together those individuals that may have some knowledge of the problem area. They need not be experts. In fact, it may be better that they are not. You need people to think creatively and *outside the box*. Experts tend to think inside the box. The session starts with everyone throwing any idea out on the table. No discussion (except clarification) is permitted. This continues until no new ideas are forthcoming. Silence and pauses are okay. There then begins a discussion of items on the list. Look to combine ideas or revise ideas based on each members perspective. In time some solutions will begin to emerge. Don't rush the process, and by all means test each idea with an open mind. Remember, you are looking for a solution that no individual could identify but hopefully the group will be able to identify. This is a creative process and must be approached with an open mind. Convention and *We've always done it that way* have no place in a true brainstorming session.

Team Meetings

Team meetings are held for a variety of reasons including problem definition and resolution, scheduling work, planning, discussing situations that affect team performance, and decision making. There are several procedural matters that the team will need to decide upon. These include: meeting frequency; agenda preparation; meeting coordinator; how decisions will be reached; how problems will be presented, defined, and solved; and who records and distributes meeting minutes. That's right, minutes are kept. They are an important part of project documentation, as you will see.

The hammer must be swung in cadence, when more than one is hammering the iron.

Giordano Bruno
Italian philosopher

Behind an able man there are always other able men.

Chinese proverb

CHAPTER 14

Level Project Resources

CHAPTER LEARNING OBJECTIVES

As a result of participating in the learning experiences in this chapter you will be able to:

1. Understand why resources should be leveled.
2. Utilize various approaches to leveling resources.
3. Determine the appropriate use of substitute resources.
4. Properly define and use management reserve.
5. Use a variety of techniques to schedule work.

The Need to Level Resources

Ideally the project manager wants the number of resources (people, in most cases) to follow a logical pattern throughout the life of the project. In other words, it would not be advisable to have the number of people working on the project fluctuating wildly from day to day or week to week. This would impose too many management and coordination problems that can otherwise be avoided with a little resource leveling planning. The ideal project would have the number of people resources relatively level over the planning phases, building gradually to a maximum during the project work phases, and decreasing through the closing phases. Such increase and decrease is manageable and expected in the life of a well-planned project. Such is our goal in this chapter.

Scheduling Activities

Recall that one of the six characteristics of a complete WBS was activity independence. That means that once work has begun on an activity, work can continue without interruption until the activity is done. We will generally not schedule the work to be continuous for a number of reasons but we could if we wanted to. That property allows the following discussion to take place.

Splitting Activities

Resource availability, or rather the lack of it, may require some rather creative scheduling on the part of the project manager. For example, let us say that an activity requires one person for three days within a five-day window. In other words, there are two days of slack in the schedule for that activity. The project manager would prefer to have the activity scheduled for its early start date but the unavailability of the resource for three consecutive days will require scheduling the activity work over a longer period of time. One solution would be to have the resource work for three nonconsecutive days as early as possible in the five-day window.

Stretching Activities

Another alternative that preserves the continuity of the activity work is to stretch the work over a longer period by having the resource work on the activity less than full time. Using the same example as the previous one, the project manager may request the resource on some percentage basis for five days in order to get in the required three days of work. This percentage could be constant over the five days or follow some profile. Resource availability may be the determining factor as to exactly how the activity can be stretched.

Assigning Substitute Resources

We have estimated activity duration on the assumption that a typically skilled resource will be available to work on the activity. That may not be possible and the project manager may find that some other strategy is needed. One approach would be to use lesser-skilled resources but add to the total number of hours requested. Here the thinking is that a lesser-skilled resource would require a longer period of time to complete the activity work. Be careful in using this tactic, however. Activity duration can be adversely affected by using more than one resource. By adding a second resource there is a need for communication and coordination that did not exist when only one resource was working on the activity. This will obviously add to the duration time for the activity.

The same effect is present when we add resources to reduce activity duration. This is called *crashing the activity*. In some cases it may actually result in crash and burn. Let us try to understand the dynamics involved here. In order to consider adding resources to reduce activity duration, the activity must be *partitionable*, which means that the work can be divided in some manner. Painting a room is clearly partitionable. Pregnancy is not partitionable. Writing a computer program may or may not be partitionable. If it is partitionable, then consideration must be given to such issues as logic, design, programming style, variable naming, bridge coding, test data, communications, and so on. All of these tend to increase activity duration, thus offsetting gains that result from adding resources. In fact, adding resources will generally reduce duration up to a point. Further addition of resources will cause duration to begin increasing. While the calculation of the optimal resource loading may not be possible, to know that such a model is operative is sufficient.

Management Reserve

There is a strong temptation on the part of the project manager to pad the activity estimates to give a little *cushion* in case of problems. While this may seem perfectly innocent on the surface, it is really fraught with problems. First, the project manager has to remember where all the *cookie jars* are hidden. This is no small task especially in larger projects. Second, Parkinson's Law says that work will expand to fill the available space—and it will. We recommend another approach—one that keeps the management reserve visible, one that helps the project manager manage the project and the reserve, too!

First, let us talk about this notion of creating management reserve. In every budget there is always a line item called *contingency*. This is an amount in the budget that is not allocated to any specific expense but is available to handle those many unforeseen situations that arise. The good manager will watch the balance in the contingency line and try not to spend it unless there is no alternative. The same notion makes sense for project managers. We recommend creating a small management reserve line in the project plan. Our management reserve is not dollars but time. The amount of time is not important, but for the sake of an example let us say it is 4 percent of the total of the durations for all the project activities. Rather than hide it in each of the activities, we are going to place it at the end of the project as an activity with a duration equal to the management reserve we just computed.

In the project plan, we will have computed the start date for the management reserve activity. Any delay in project activities will cause the start date of the management reserve activity to slip proportionately. Management reserve can then be decremented to bring the activity back on schedule. A good project manager will want to manage the management reserve so as to not spend it unnecessarily. Whenever the management reserve start date slips, the project will come in late by the

- **Leveling, allowing end date to move**
- **Leveling using float**
- **Smoothing**
- **Splitting activities**
- **Assigning replacement resources**

Figure 14.1 Strategies for resource scheduling.

amount of the slippage. This is a good tool for the project manager, as it is somehow a barometer of the general health of the project.

Scheduling Work

Once we have an activity schedule in place we must consider the actual scheduling of work within the ES and LF of each activity. That is the topic of this section. There are several situations to consider, as shown in Figure 14.1.

Leveling with Variable End Dates

Within the ES and LF of each activity we can adjust the start and end dates to level resource loading. By moving the dates to stretch the activity, we can reduce the amount of work required on any given day and hence reduce the percent of effort required of any resource. Be careful not to delay activities beyond their ES data unless it is unavoidable. Float is your resource and you may want to spend it only when there are no other alternatives.

Leveling Using Float

This strategy is related to the previous one in that it utilizes float to level resources. Here the work is continuous and only its start date is adjusted within the limits of the float (free or total) assigned to the activity.

Smoothing

When the project work is initially scheduled it will usually result in erratic changes in the staffing levels on the project. Management would rather have staffing levels remain somewhat fixed, or level, across the life of the project. This helps reduce problems associated with work space and facilities. By displaying a resource histogram the project manager can graphically show the changes in staffing levels across the project. Given that there is slack in some of the activity schedules, the project manager may be able to reschedule activities so as to level the head count across the project.

Rather than allowing them [subordinates] the autonomy to get involved and do the work in their own ways, what happens all too often is the manager wants the workers to do it the manager's way.

Edward L. Deci
University of Rochester

Work smarter, not harder.

Anonymous

CHAPTER

Schedule and Document Work Packages

Chapter Learning Objectives

As a result of participating in the learning experiences in this chapter you will be able to:

1. Define a work package and its purpose.
2. Describe the format and explain the contents of a work package.
3. Know when to require work package descriptions.
4. Know how to use Gantt Chart scheduling of work packages.

Definition of a Work Package

At this point you have essentially completed all JPP session activities. The project work has been defined as a list of activities; activity duration and resource requirements are specified, the project network is built; and the activity schedule is done. The JPP session attendees have reached a consensus! Whew, that's a lot and you probably wondered if it would ever be finished. There is one more step to go before project work can commence: Get the work defined at the task level. Recall from Figure 8.1 that a work package contains a description of the tasks that comprise an activity. We like to think of work packages as insurance policies or disaster plans.

Let us turn now to defining the work package and see the role that it has in your project plans.

Purpose of a Work Package

The work package will become the bedrock for all project work. It describes in detail the tasks to be done in completing the work for an activity. In addition to the task descriptions the package includes start and end dates for the activity. At the discretion of the work package manager, the start and end dates for each task in the work package might also be given. We stress again the need for prudence in adopting this level of detail. There is always a trade-off between the need for detail and the need to spend work time accomplishing work and not shuffling papers. We also point out that the work package description is an insurance policy. If for some reason the work package manager is unable to continue with the project, will someone know the status of the work package, what has yet to be completed, and how it is to be completed?

The work package can also be adapted to status reporting. Tasks comprise the work to be done and if the tasks are checked off as complete, there is a measure of what percent of the activity is complete. Some organizations simply use the percent of tasks completed as the percent of activity completion. This simple yet effective metric is not open to disagreement. A task is either complete or not.

Format of a Work Package

Work Package Assignment Sheet

This is the first of two reports we will discuss. The Work Package Assignment Sheet (Figure 15.1) is a report for the project manager only. As you can see, it gives the Earliest Start and Latest Finish times for each activity. Activity managers should not have this information (except in self-directed work teams).

Float is one of the few resources available to the project manager and should not be made available to anyone other than the project manager. The project manager is unlikely to tell an activity manager that their activity is scheduled for completion on, say, July 15, but they really have until August 15 because of the float. Activity managers should be given the scheduled start and end dates for their activities.

The Work Package Assignment Sheet will have limited value in smaller projects but can be invaluable in larger ones. One of the authors was personally involved in a project that consisted of over 4,000 activities. That means as many as 4,000 activity managers at any point in time. In fact, over the seven-year life of the project there were more than 10,000 activity managers. This report became a phone directory that needed constant updating as team members came and went.

Work Package Description Report

A work package (a.k.a. statement of work) is shown in Figure 15.2. A work package may consist of one or several tasks. They may be nothing more than a *to-do list*, which can be completed in any order. On the other hand, the work package can consist of tasks that take the form of a miniproject, with a network to describe it. Work packages are assigned to a single individual, whom we call an *activity manager* or *work package manager*. They are responsible for completing the activity on time, within budget, and according to specification. They have the authority and the access to the resources needed to complete the assignment. Sounds like a project manager doesn't it?

Once the project plan has been approved, it is the activity manager's responsibility to generate the work package documentation.

WORK PACKAGE ASSIGNMENT SHEET	Project Name MKTG.MIS		Project No. 91.01	Project Manager PAUL BEARER	
Work Package		Schedule		Manager	Phone
Number	Name	Earliest Start	Latest Finish		
A	DESIGN	03/01/91	04/01/91	ANNA LYST	
B	PROD.EVAL	04/02/91	07/02/91	HY ROWLER	
C1	PLACE.LOCATE.PT1	04/02/91	03/04/92	SY YONARA	
C2	PLACE.LOCATE.PT2	07/03/91	03/04/92	HY ROWLER	
D	PROD.FCAST	07/03/91	03/04/92	SY YONARA	
E	PROD.DELETE	03/05/92	06/02/92	HY ROWLER	
F	PROMO.REGION	03/05/92	07/06/92	TERRI TORY	
H	PRICE	08/04/92	02/05/93	HY ROWLER	
I	PLACE.DESIGN	06/05/92	08/03/93	HY ROWLER	
J	PROMO.SALES.LEAD	07/07/92	11/05/92	TERRI TORY	
G	PROMO.MEDIA	07/07/92	02/05/93	SY YONARA	
K	PROMO.SALES.RPT	10/07/92	02/05/93	TERRI TORY	
L	SYSTEM.TEST	02/08/93	05/10/93	ANNA LYST	
M	SYSTEM.ACCEPT	05/10/93	06/10/93	ANNA LYST	
Prepared by PAUL BEARER	Date 03/01/91	Approved by SAL VATION		Date 03/01/91	Sheet 1 of 1

Figure 15.1 Work Package Assignment Sheet.

WORK PACKAGE DESCRIPTION	Project Name: MKTG.MIS	Project No.: 91.01	Project Manager: PAUL BEARER
Work Package Name: PROD.DELETE	Work Package No.: 91.01.1.3	Work Package Manager: HY ROWLER	Phone: 3410 / Date: 3 - 1 - 91
Sch Start: 3 - 5 - 92 / Sch End: 6 - 2 - 92	Critical Path: Y (N)	Predecessor Work Package(s): 91.01.1.2	Successor Work Package(s): 91.01.2.2

TASK					
No.	**NAME**	**DESCRIPTION**	**TIME (days)**	**RESPONSIBILITY**	**PHONE**
1.3.1	CRITERAI	Identify deletion criteria	12	Product Managers	
1.3.2	OUT.INFO	Identify output info requirements	5	Product Managers	
1.3.3	IN.DATA	Identify input data requirements	4	Programmer/Analyst	
1.3.4	PGM.DOC	Prepare program documentation	5	Programmer	
1.3.5	CODE.PGM	Code program	16	Programmer	
1.3.6	TEST.PGM	Test Program	10	Programmer	
1.3.7	APPR.PGM	Approve program performance	7	Product Manager & VP Mktg	
1.3.8	IMPL.PGM	Implement the model	7	Operations	

Prepared By	Date	Approved By	Date	
HY ROWLER	3-1/91	PAUL BEARER	3-1/91	Sheet 1 of 1

Figure 15.2 Work package description report.

Before we inundate you with more planning documentation, let us assure you that not all activities will require or should require work-package documentation. Limit your choices to critical path activities, near-critical path activities, and high-risk activities. The work-package documentation contains a work-package description report that describes in detail each task in the activity.

The descriptions of tasks given in the work package must be complete so that anyone could pick it up, read it, and understand what has to be done to complete the activity. Furthermore, each task must be described so that the status of the work package is easily determined. Ideally, the task list is a check-off list. Once all the tasks have been checked off as being completed the activity is complete. Each task will also have a duration estimate attached to it. In some project Joint Project Planning sessions these estimates may have been supplied as a bottom-up method of estimating activity duration.

Scheduling Work Packages

Once the network has been constructed and analyzed as to feasibility of completing the project on time, within budget, and according to specification, it is time for the project manager to determine the scheduled start and end date for each activity in the project. At this point the resource available to the project manager is the slack time associated with each activity. This is a resource that should not be shared with anyone, even the project team members (except for self-directed work teams). By way of an assignment with the MKTG.MIS project we will see just how the project manager can proceed.

Gantt Charts are flexible and simple-to-understand tools. As such we recommend their use in planning and reporting. We discuss their use here as a planning tool and leave for Chapter 16 the discussion of their use as reporting tools.

There are two Gantt Chart formats that we like to use. The first is organized by activity start date. This is a useful format for status reporting but has little value as a planning tool. The second format organizes activities by activity manager. This is a useful format for planning but has little value in status reporting.

The first Gantt Chart format is produced directly from the initial project network. It arranges activities according to their ES times. The resulting Gantt Chart is given in Figure 15.3. Each activity is repre-

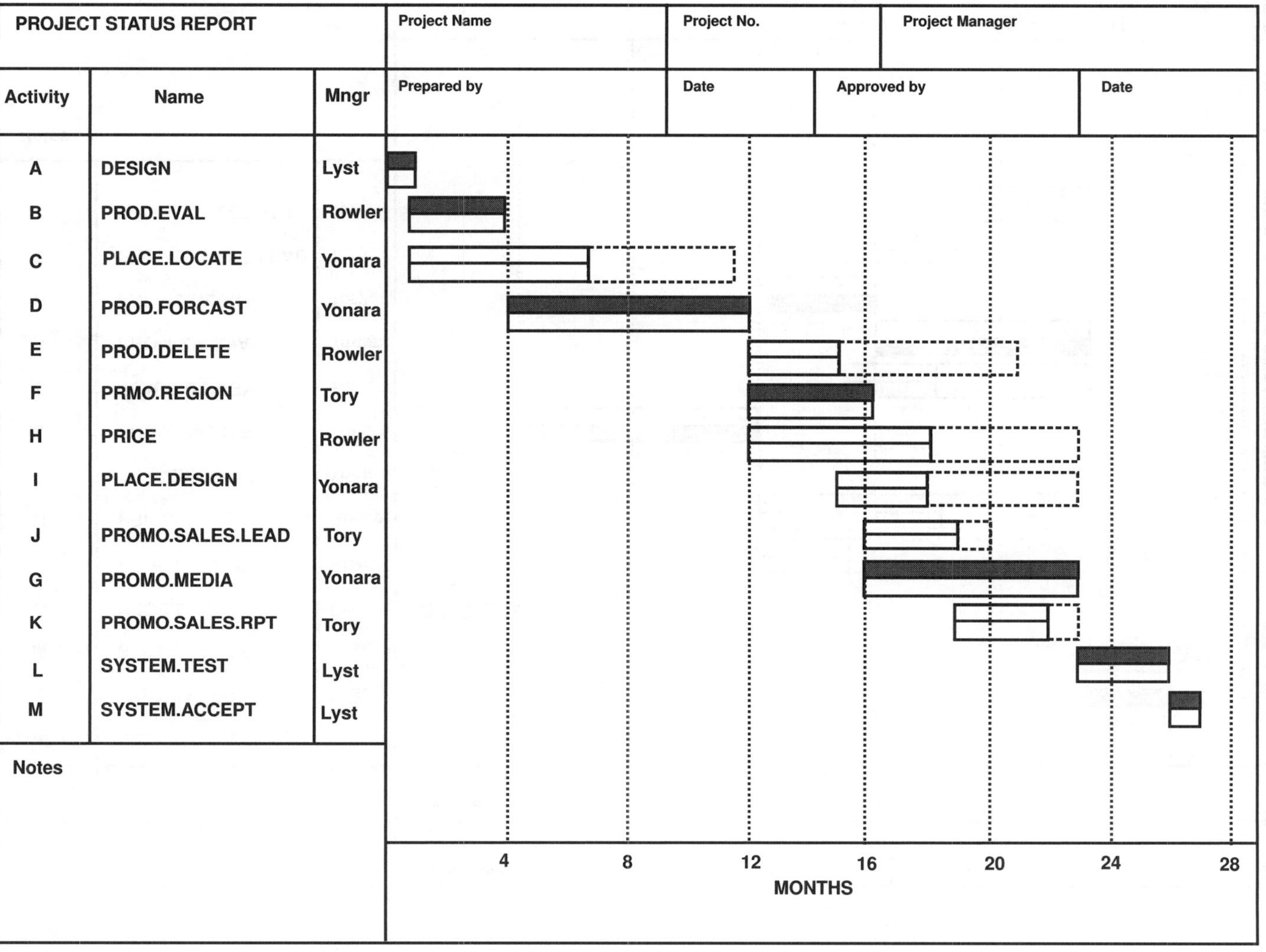

Figure 15.3 Gantt chart by ES times.

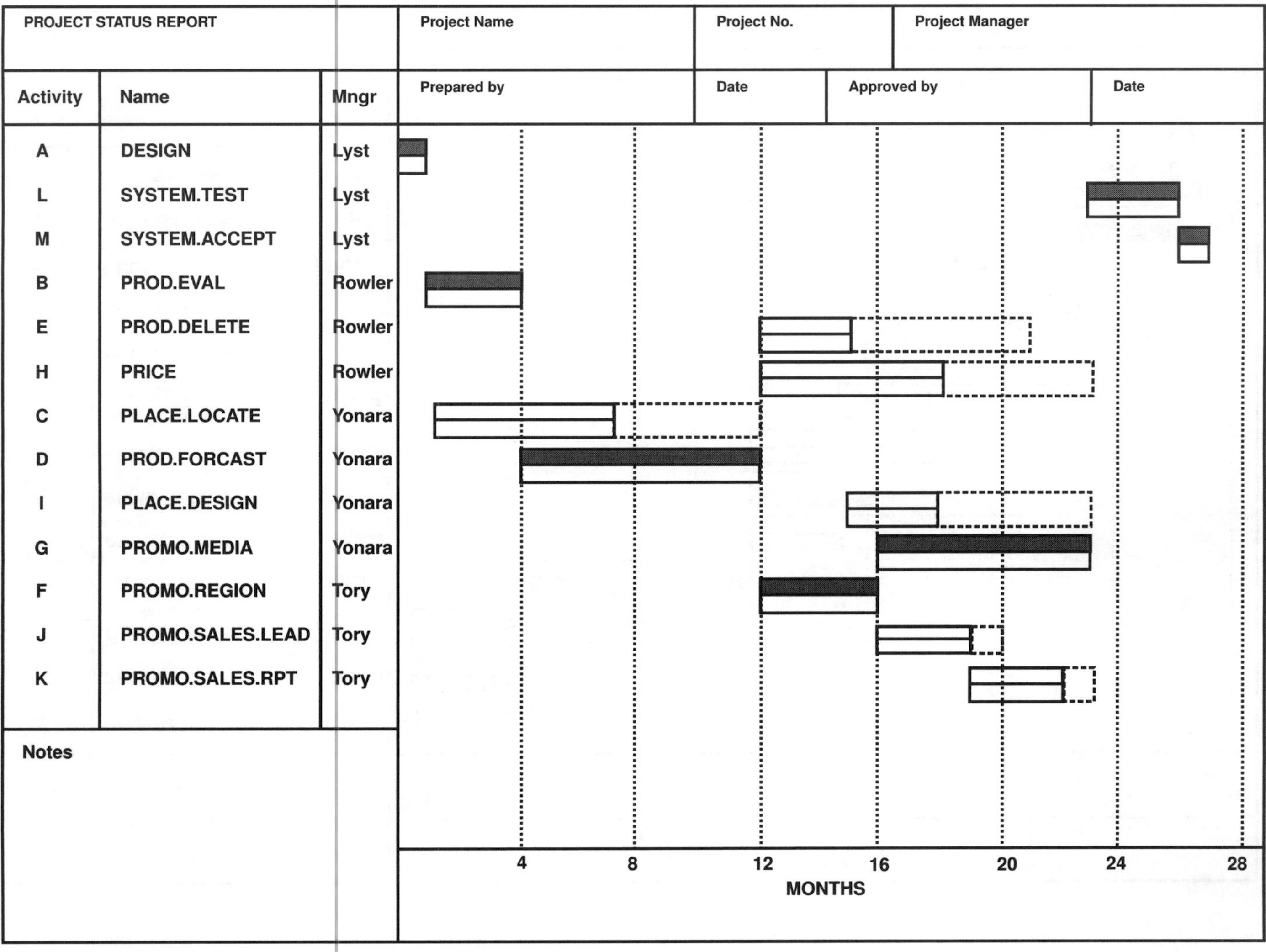

Figure 15.4 Gantt Chart by activity manager.

sented by a double bar. The upper bar is shaded for those activities that are on the critical path. The lower bar will be used to report activity status. Noncritical path activities have their float shown as a dashed bar. The left edge of the bar is aligned with the ES time. The right edge of the bar is aligned with the LF time of the activity. We note here, and will reinforce this point later, that float is never shown in a project status report except for those reports that are for the project manager's eyes only.

The second format, which is more useful for planning and not at all useful for reporting outside the project team, is shown in Figure 15.4. Here we have sorted the activities by activity manager. This allows us to quickly spot any schedule conflicts and resolve them.

When you are drowning in numbers you need a system to separate the wheat from the chaff.

Anthony Adams
Vice President, Campbell Soup Co.

If two lines on a graph cross, it must be important.

Ernest F. Cooke
University of Baltimore

CHAPTER 16

MONITOR AND CONTROL PROGRESS

CHAPTER LEARNING OBJECTIVES

As a result of participating in the learning experiences in this chapter you will be able to:

1. Understand the reasons for implementing controls on the project.
2. Track the progress of a project.
3. Measure and analyze variances from the project plan.
4. Determine the appropriate corrective actions to restore a project to its planned schedule.
5. Use Gantt Charts to track project progress and identify warning signs of schedule problems.
6. Reallocate resources to maintain the project schedule.
7. Report project status with graphical tools.
8. Establish trend charts for early warning signals.
9. Properly identify corrective measures and problem escalation strategies.

Control vs. Risk in Project Management

In this chapter you will learn about a variety of control tools. Most can be used in numeric and tabular form but we suggest the use of graphics wherever possible. This approach is particularly effective, especially as part of a project status report to management. In general, senior managers aren't interested in reading long reports only to find out that everything is on schedule. They are surely pleased that your project is on schedule but would rather spend their time on other pursuits. On the other hand, if projects are not on schedule, they want to know it right away and they want to know what corrective action you plan to take. This module will prepare you for that eventuality.

Purpose of Controls

We put controls in place to draw our attention to certain aspects or characteristics of the project as work is underway. We typically track performance levels, costs, and time schedules. The three major reasons for putting controls in place are discussed in the following (Weiss and Wysocki).[1]

To Track Progress

To track progress the project manager will want to have in place a periodic (at least biweekly but weekly is best) reporting system that identifies the status of every activity scheduled for work since the last progress report. These reports should summarize progress for the current period as well as cumulative for the entire project.

To Detect Variance from Plan

To detect variance from plan, a comparison of budget to actual is needed. In larger projects (say, 50 or more activities) reports that simply say everything is on schedule and on budget are certainly music to the ears of the project manager, but are otherwise too long and boring to be read and synthesized. Exception reports, variance reports, and graphical reports provide information for management decision making—and provide it in a concise format. These are discussed in the following.

---

1. Weiss, Joselph W., and Robert K. Wysocki. 1991. *5-Phase Project Management: A Practical Planning and Implementation Guide*. Reading, MA: Addison-Wesley.

The project plan is a system. As such it can get out of balance and a get-well plan must be put in place to restore the system to equilibrium. The longer the project manager waits to put the fix in place, the longer it will take for the system to return to equilibrium.

To Take Corrective Action

To take corrective action it is necessary to know where the problem is and to have that information in time to do something about it. Once a significant variance from plan occurs, the next step is to determine whether corrective action is needed and then act appropriately. In complex projects this will require examining a number of *what ifs*. When problems occur in the project, delays result and the project falls behind schedule. For the project to get back on schedule, resources will have to be reallocated. In larger projects the computer will be needed to examine a number of resource reallocation alternatives and pick the best.

High Control–Low Risk

Project risk can be reduced to a point by simply exerting more controls. However, as Figure 16.1 shows, there is a point of diminishing returns. Cost aside there is another impact to consider. In order to comply with

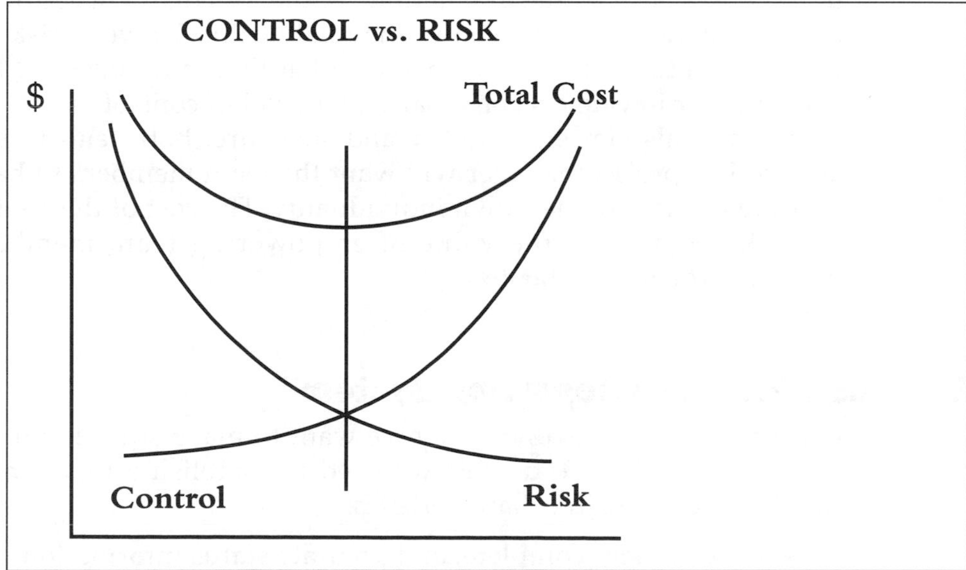

Figure 16.1 The total cost of control and risk.

the controls in place, project team members will have to spend time preparing and defending progress reports. This subtracts from the time spent doing project work.

Low Control–High Risk

At the extreme, having no controls in place and just assuming that the project work will get done according to the plan is foolish. Knowing that the project is sick in time to formulate and implement a get-well plan is critical to project success. Answering the question: How long am I willing to wait before I find out that there is a problem? may provide the clue to how much control to put in place. We will analyze these situations with the Milestone Trend Charts presented later in this chapter.

Achieving Balance

It is very easy to get carried away with controls and the accompanying reports. Certainly the more controls that are put in place, the less likely it will be for the project to get in trouble. The reverse is also true. The fewer the controls, the higher the risk of serious problems being detected too late to be resolved. The project manager will need to strike a balance between the extent of the control system and the risk of unfavorable outcomes. Just as in the insurance industry—compare the cost of the policy against the dollar value of the loss that will result from the consequences. Figure 8.1 shows the relationship between risk and control. Conceptually there is a balance point that minimizes the total cost exposure for having chosen a particular level of control.

Control also implies rigidity and structure. Both tend to stifle creativity. The project manager will want the team members to have some latitude to exercise their own individuality. The cost of the control must be weighed against the value of empowering team members to be proactive (hence risk takers).

Establish Progress Reporting System

Once project work is underway we want to make sure that it proceeds according to plan. To do this we need to establish a reporting system that has the following characteristics:

- Gives timely, complete, and accurate status information.
- Doesn't add so much overhead time as to be counterproductive.

- Is readily acceptable to the project team and senior management.
- Gives warning of pending problems in time to take action.
- Is easily understood by those who have a need to know.

Purpose, Contents, and Frequency of Reports

Types of Project Status Reports

There are four types of reports we can discuss. They are given in the following.

Current Period

These reports cover only the most recently completed period. They report progress on those activities that were open or scheduled for work during the period. Reports might highlight activities completed, and the variance between scheduled completion date and actual completion date. For any activities whose progress was not according to plan there should be some discussion of the reason for the variance, and appropriate corrective measures put in place to correct the schedule slippages.

Cumulative

These reports contain the history of the project from the beginning to the end of the current report period. They are more informative than the current period reports since they show trends in project progress. For example, a schedule variance might be tracked over several successive periods to show improvement. Reports can be at the activity or project level.

Exception

Reports that are produced for senior management merit special consideration. Senior managers do not have a lot of time to read reports that tell them that everything is on schedule and there are no problems serious enough to warrant senior manager attention. In such cases generally a one-page, high-level summary report that says everything is okay is sufficient. It might also be appropriate to include a more detailed report as an attachment for those who might wish to read more detail.

Green, Yellow, Red Reports

We believe in parsimony in all reporting. Here is a technique you might want to try. When the project is on schedule and everything seems to be moving along as planned put a *green* symbol on the first page of the project status report. When the project has encountered a problem, schedule slippage for example, you might put a *yellow* symbol on the report. That is a signal to upper management that the project is not moving along as scheduled but you have a get-well plan in place. *Red* reports are to be avoided at all costs. This means that the project is out of control and you don't have a get-well plan in place or even a recommendation for upper management. If this should occur, our advice is to find an empty box, and pack your belongings in it; your days as project manager are numbered. On a more serious note, the red condition may be beyond your control. For example, the World Trade Center is bombed and a number of companies have lost their computing systems. The hot site is overburdened with companies looking for computing power. Your company is one of them and the loss of computing power has put your project seriously behind in final system testing. There is little you can do to avoid such acts of nature.

Variance Reporting Tools

Most of us are familiar with variance reports. Simply put, the report has three columns: the planned number, the actual number, and the difference between the two. The impact of departures from plan are signified by larger values of these difference (the variance). Typical variance reports are snapshots in time (the current period) of the status of the entity being tracked. Most variance reports do not include data points that report how the project reached that status.

Project variance reports may be used to report project as well as activity variances. For the sake of the managers that will have to read these reports, we recommend that one report format be used regardless of the variable being tracked. Top management will quickly become comfortable with a reporting format that is consistent across all projects or activities within a project. It will make life a bit easier for the project manager, too. Figure 16.2 lists the reasons why we would want to measure duration and cost variances.

Early detection of out-of-control situations is also important. As Figure 16.3 illustrates, the longer we have to wait to discover a problem, the longer it will take for our solution to bring the project back to a stable condition.

- **Catch deviations from curve early.**
- **Dampen oscillation.**
- **Allow early corrective action.**
- **Weekly schedule variance.**
- **Weekly effort (personhours/day) variance.**

Figure 16.2 Why measure variance?

As to what we should record, refer to Figure 16.4. Recall that our planning estimates of activity duration and cost were often based on little or no information. Now that we have completed some work on the activity, we should be able to provide a better estimate of the duration and cost exposure. This will reflect itself in a reestimate of the work remaining to complete the activity.

Positive Variances

Given the alternative, the project manager would rather hear that the project is ahead of schedule or under budget. As we will soon see, positive variances bring their own set of problems, which can be as serious as negative variances. Positive variances may allow for rescheduling to bring the project to completion early, under budget, or both. Resources

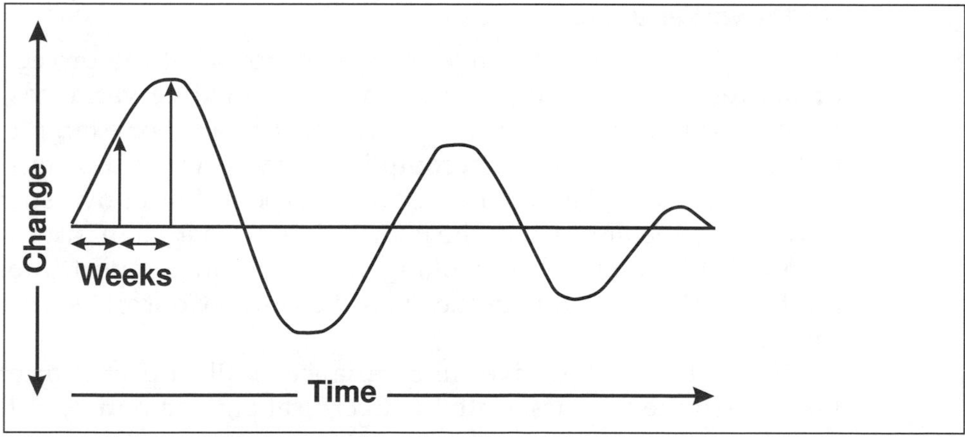

Figure 16.3 Magnitude of change increases with time.

- **Determine a set period of time and day of week.**
- **Everything prior is historical—after is future.**
- **Actual work accomplished during this period.**
- **Record historical and reestimate remaining (in progress work only).**
- **Start and finish dates.**
- **Days worked—remaining (in progress work only).**
- **Resource effort (hours/day) spent—remaining (in progress work only).**

Figure 16.4 How and what to record.

may be reallocated away from ahead-of-schedule projects to behind-schedule projects.

Not all the news is good news, however. Positive variances may also result from schedule slippages, too! Consider budget. Being under budget means that not all dollars were expended, which may be the direct result of not having completed work that was scheduled for completion during the report period. We return to this situation later in the "Cost Schedule Control" section of this chapter.

Negative Variances

Being behind schedule or over budget is not what the project manager or his reporting manager wants to hear. Negative variances, just like positive variances, are not necessarily bad news. For example, we may be overspent because we accomplished more work during the report period than was planned; hence we overspent. But in overspending we may have accomplished the work at less cost than was originally planned. We can't tell by looking at the variance report. More details are forthcoming on this in the "Cost Schedule Control" section later in this chapter.

In most cases negative time variances will impact project completion only if they are associated with critical path activities, or the schedule slippage on noncritical path activities exceeds the activity's total float. It should be clear to our readers that variances use up the float time for that activity; more serious ones will cause a change in the critical path.

Negative cost variances may result from uncontrollable factors, such as cost increases from suppliers, unexpected equipment malfunctions, and so on. Some may be the result of inefficiencies or error. We discuss a problem escalation strategy to resolve such situations later in this chapter.

Graphical Reporting Tools

We believe in parsimony in every project report, which means graphics rather than columnar reports. Respect senior managers' time. They have only a few minutes of uninterrupted time to digest your report. They won't be able to do that if they have to read 15 pages before they get any useful information. Having to read several pages only to find out that the project is on schedule is frustrating and a waste of valuable time, too! Perhaps you could fashion an exception report that highlights cases in which performance is outside the nominal or exhibits some condition for a certain number of successive report periods.

Gantt Charts

One picture, a Gantt Chart, will convey a thousand words and do so intuitively, too! What more could a project manager ask for in this hurried work world?

A Gantt Chart is one of the most convenient, most used, and easiest-to-grasp depictions of project activities that we have encountered in our practice. The format is a two-dimensional representation of the project schedule, with activities down the rows and time across the horizontal axis. It can be used during planning, for resource scheduling, and for status reporting. The only downside to the use of Gantt Charts is that they do not contain dependency relationships. In some cases they can be guessed from the Gantt Chart but in most cases they are lost.

Figure 16.5 shows a representation of the MKTG.MIS project as a Gantt Chart using a format that we prefer. As originally reported by Weiss and Wysocki, over the years we have adapted the Gantt Chart to embed considerably more information in one graph.[2] The modifications

---

2. Weiss, Joselph W., and Robert K. Wysocki. *5-Phase Project Management: A Practical Planning and Implementation Guide.*

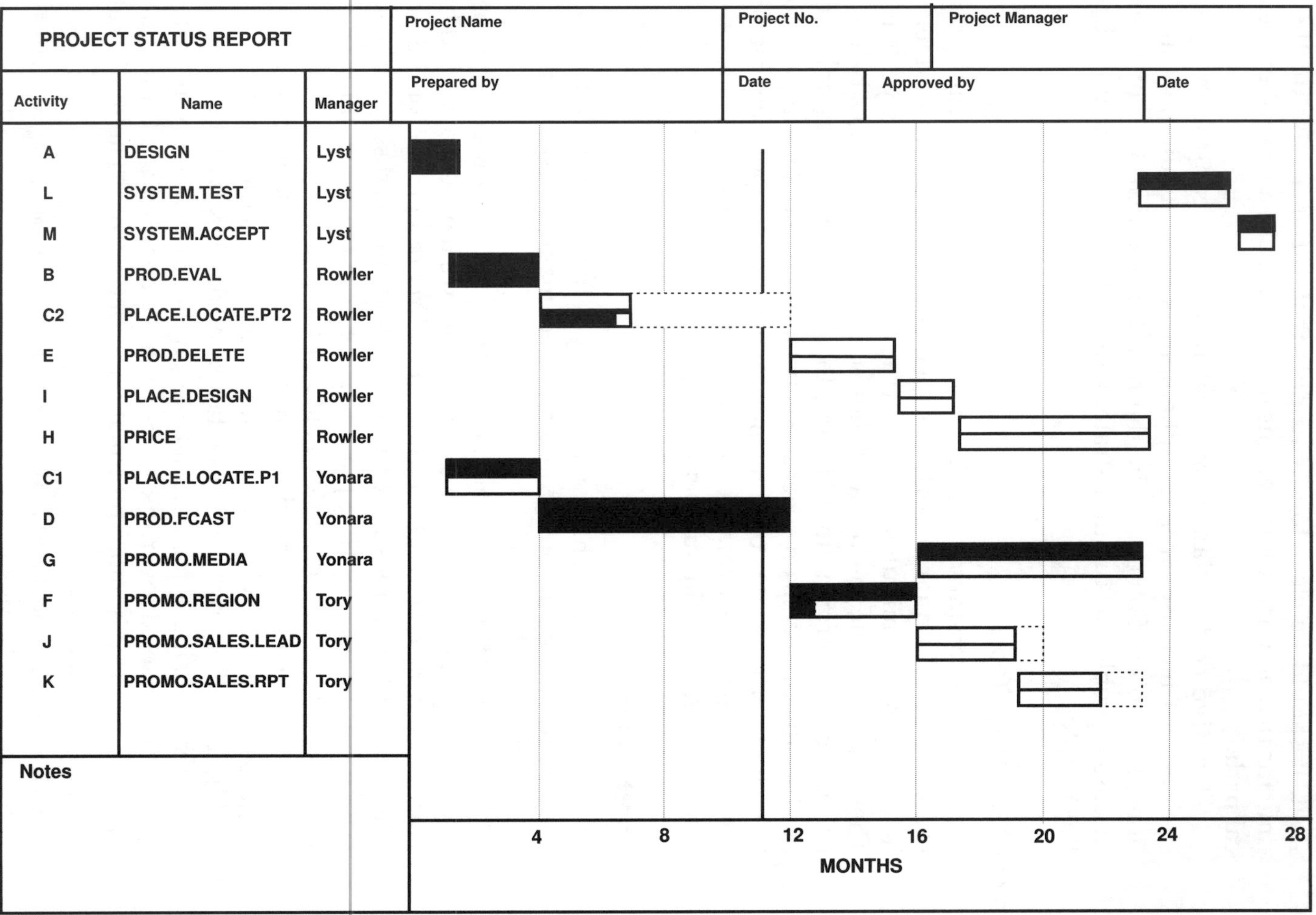

Figure 16.5 Gantt Chart Project Status Report.

remove most of the shortcomings attributed to Gantt Charts, with little increase in complexity (or clutter). In my format each activity is represented by a double bar whose width is the planned time for that activity.

One of the major modifications is to show critical path activities by shading the upper bar. Slack time for noncritical activities is shown with dashed lines (this is another of our variations). The shading shown in the lower part of the activity bars represents the proportion of that activity that is completed. If the project were exactly on schedule, the shading would extend to the vertical line (the time-now line) at the eleventh month. The report was generated using a graphics package but the same content can now be generated from most microcomputer project management software packages.

Milestone Charts

To understand the material in this section you will have to master a few basic concepts in statistics. We have prepared an appendix to this chapter that has all you will need to know. You might want to review that before going on. Milestones are zero-duration activities (the term *events* is also used to define zero-duration activities) that represent significant events in the project. For example, a milestone might signify the completion of all activities associated with an objective or major deliverable in the project. The health of the project can be gauged by tracking changes in the date on which the milestone event is expected to occur. In each project update the estimated start/completion date of each activity and milestone are recomputed. By way of example let us look at a milestone trend chart for a hypothetical project.

The trend chart plots the difference between the planned and estimated date of a project milestone at each project report period. The milestone is planned to occur at the ninth month of the project. That is the last project month on this milestone chart. The dashed lines represent one, two, and three standard deviations above or below the forecasted milestone date. Any activity in the project has an expected completion date that is normally distributed. The mean and variance of its completion date is a function of the longest path to the activity from the time-now line.

In this example, the unit of measurement is one month. For this project. the first project report (at month 1) shows that the new forecast milestone date will be one week later than planned. At the second project report date (month 2 of the project) the milestone date is forecast on target. However, the next three project reports indicate a slippage to two weeks late, then three weeks late, and finally four weeks late (at month 5 of the project). In other words, the milestone is one month late and there are only four more project months in which to recover the slippage. Obviously the project is in trouble. The project would appear to be drifting out of control and in fact it is. Some remedial action is required of the project manager.

There are certain patterns that signal an out-of-control situation. These are given in the following. Figure 16.6 depicts a project that is drifting out of control. Each report period shows additional slippage since the last report period. Four such successive occurrences, however minor they may seem, require special corrective action on the part of the project manager.

Figure 16.7, while it does show the milestone to be ahead of schedule, reports a radical change between report periods. An activity duration may have been grossly overestimated. There may be a data error. In any case, the situation requires further investigation.

Figure 16.8 signals a project that may have encountered a permanent schedule shift. In the example, the milestone date seems to be varying around one month ahead of schedule. Barring any radical shifts

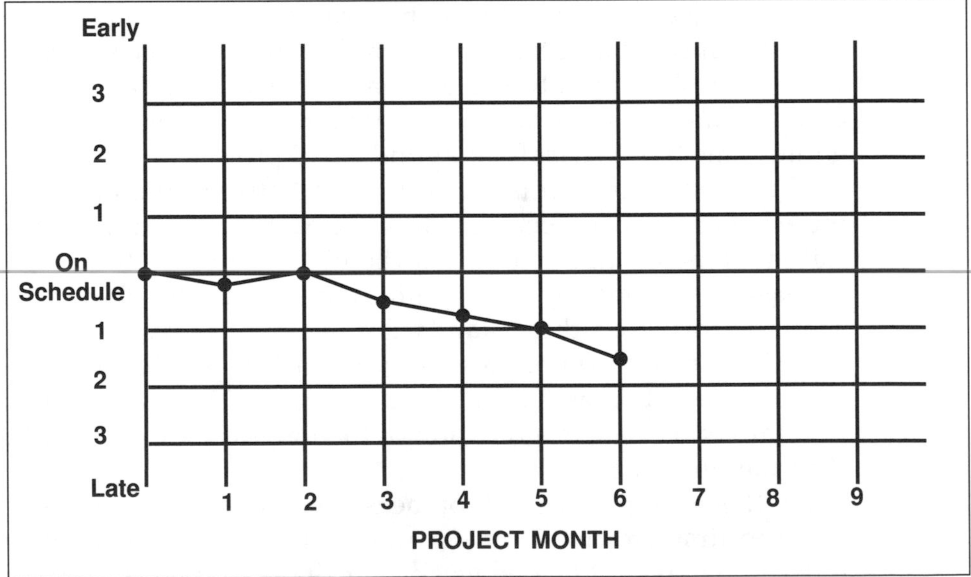

Figure 16.6 A run up or down of four or more successive data points.

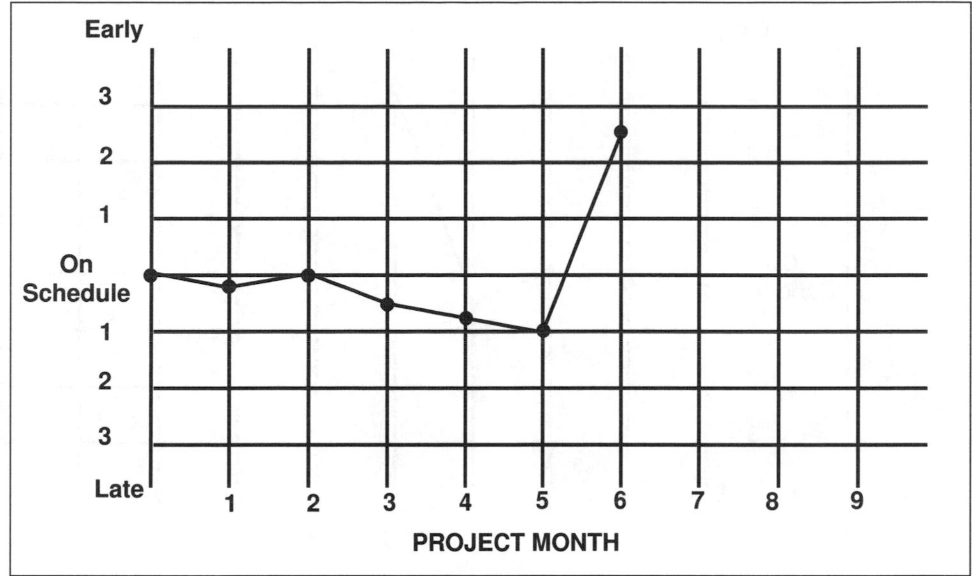

Figure 16.7 A change of more than three standard deviations.

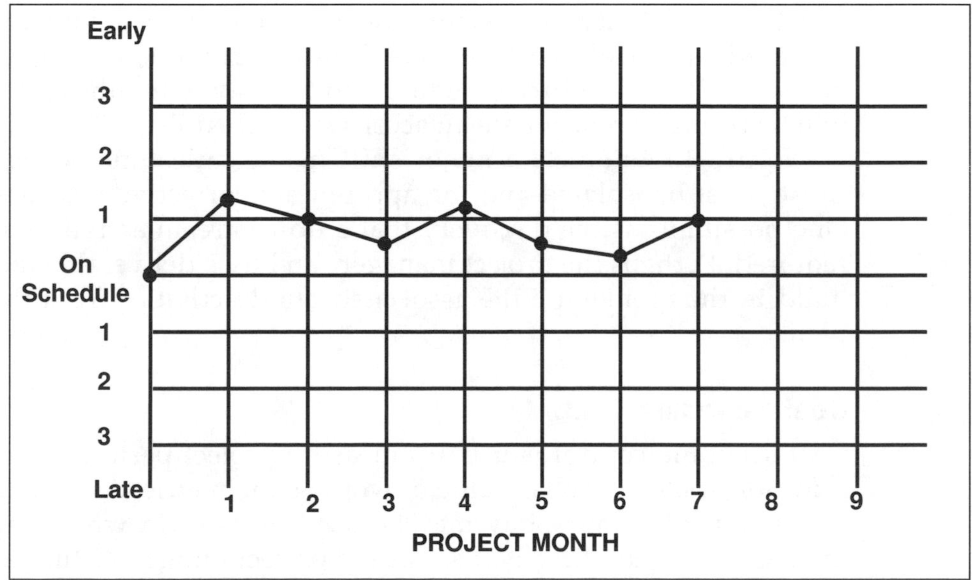

Figure 16.8 Seven or more successive data points above or below the planned milestone date.

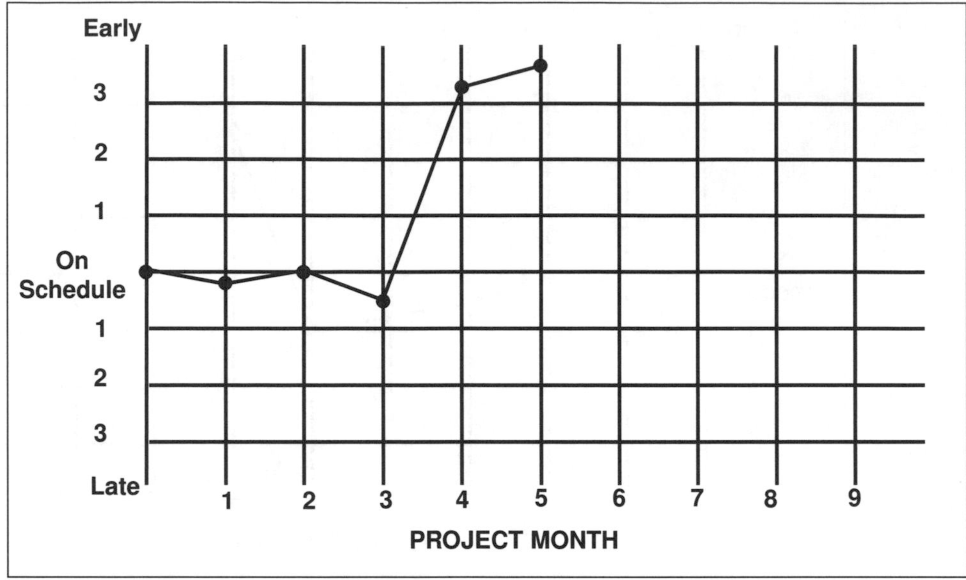

Figure 16.9 Two successive data points outside three standard deviations from the planned milestone date.

and the availability of resources over the next two months, the milestone will probably come in one month early. Remember, you have negotiated for a resource schedule into these two months and now you will be trying to renegotiate an accelerated schedule.

Figure 16.9 depicts a major shift in the milestone schedule. The cause must be isolated and the appropriate corrective measures taken. One possibility is the discovery that a downstream activity will not be required. Perhaps the project manager can buy a deliverable rather than build it, thus removing the associated build activities from the project plan.

Cost Schedule Control

Cost schedule control is used to measure project performance and, by tradition, uses the dollar value of work as the metric. As an alternative, resource personhours/day may be used in cases in which the project manager does not directly manage the project budget. Actual work performed is compared against planned and budgeted work expressed in these equivalents. These metrics are used to determine schedule and cost variances for both the current period and cumulative to date.

The reader is cautioned, however, that cost and resource person-hours/day are not good objective indicators with which to measure performance or progress. While this is true, there is no other good objective indicator. Given this we are left with dollars or person-hours/day, which we are at least used to working with in other contexts. One drawback that these metrics have is that they report history. Although they can be used to make extrapolated predictions for the future, they primarily provide a measure of the general health of the project upon which the project manager will take some action to restore the project to good health.

You will recall the S curve from Chapter 4, reproduced here as Figure 16.10. This represents the baseline progress curve for the original project plan. By using it as a reference we can compare our actual progress to date against the curve, and determine how well we are doing. Again, progress can be expressed as either dollars or person-hours/day.

By adding the actual progress to the baseline curve, we can see where we currently are vs. where we planned to be. Figure 16.11 shows the actual progress curve to be below the planned curve. If this represented dollars, we might be tempted to believe the project is running under budget. Is that really true?

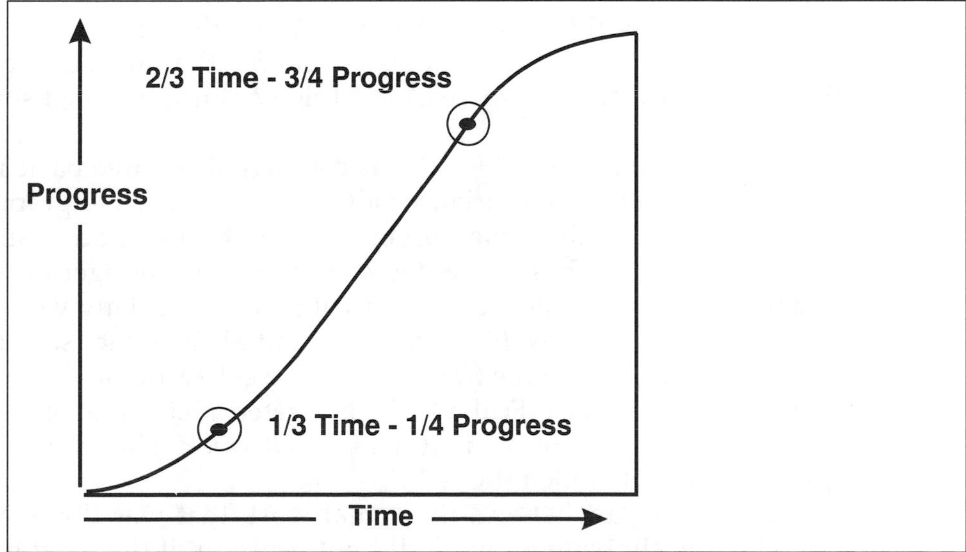

Figure 16.10 The S curve.

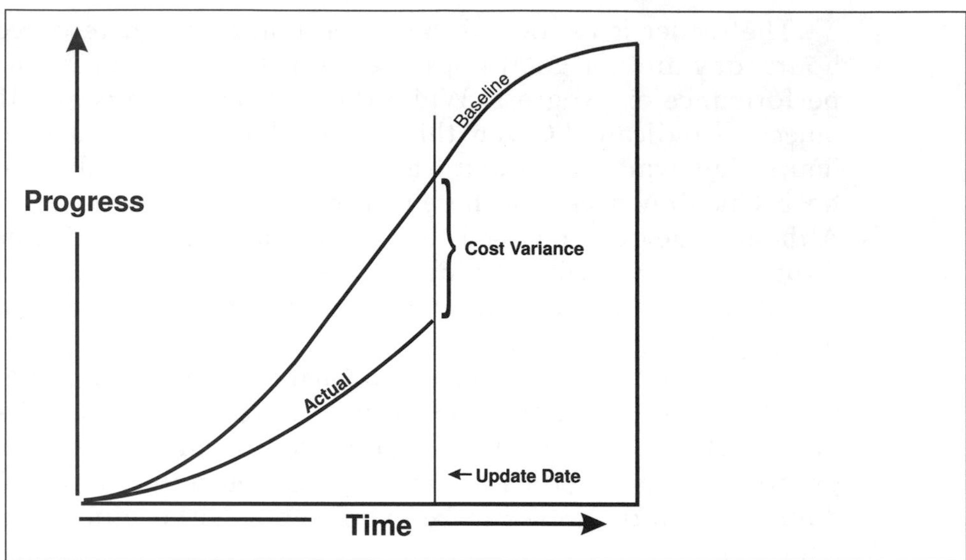

Figure 16.11 Baseline vs. actual cost curve illustrating cost variance.

Rarely do projects run significantly under budget. A more common reason for the actual curve to be below the baseline is that the activities that should have been done have not been and thus the dollars or personhours/day that were planned to be expended have not been. In Figure 16.12 the possible schedule variance is highlighted.

To provide you with the tools to answer the question of whether there has really been a progress schedule variance we need some additional information.

Cost/schedule control (C/SC) is comprised of three basic measurements that result in two variance values. Figure 16.13 is a graphical representation of the three measurements. The figure is an example of a single activity that has a five-day duration and a budget of $500. The budget is prorated over the five days at an average daily value of $100. The left panel of Figure 16.13 shows an initial (baseline) schedule with the activity starting on the first day of the week (Monday) and finishing at the end of the week (Friday). The budgeted $500 value of the work is planned to be accomplished all within that week. This is the Budgeted Cost of Work Scheduled (BCWS).

The center panel shows the actual work that was done. Note that the schedule slipped and work did not begin until the third day of the week. Using an average daily budget of $100 we see that we were able

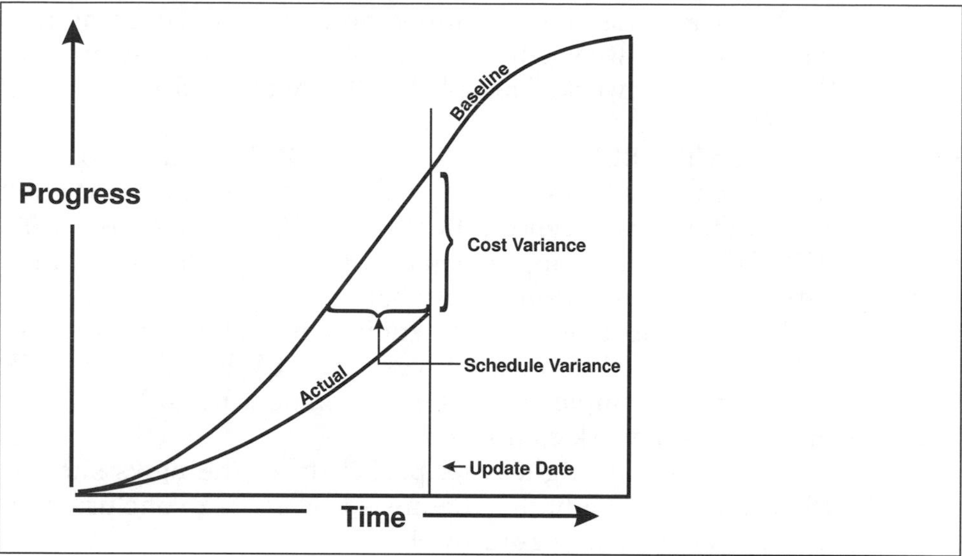

Figure 16.12 Baseline vs. actual cost illustrating schedule variance.

to complete only $300 of the scheduled work. This is the Budgeted Cost of Work Performed (BCWP).

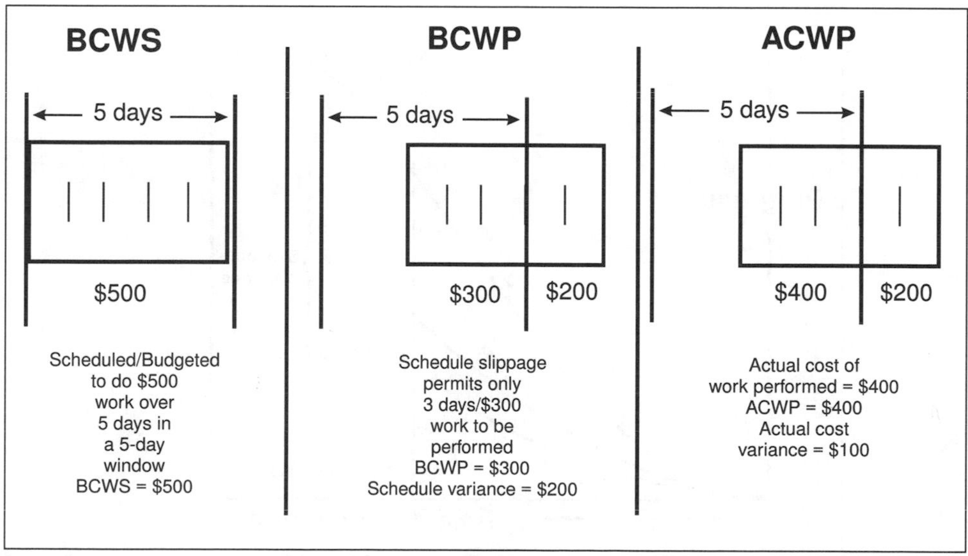

Figure 16.13 Cost/performance indicators.

The rightmost panel shows the actual schedule as in the center panel but now we see the actual dollars that were spent to accomplish the three days work. This $400 is the Actual Cost of Work Performed (ACWP).

Using the BCWS, BCWP, and ACWP there are two variances that can be computed and tracked. The first is schedule variance (SV). SV is the difference between the BCWP and BCWS which is –$200 (BCWP – BCWS) for this example. That is, the SV is the schedule difference between what was done and what was planned to be done, expressed in dollar or personhours/day equivalents. The second is cost variance (CV). CV is the difference between the BCWP and the ACWP, which is $100 in this example. That is, we overspent by $100 (ACWP – BCWP) the cost of the work completed.

Management might react positively to the news shown in Figure 16.11, but they might also be misled by such a conclusion. The reason for this is shown in Figure 16.14.

In order to correctly interpret the data shown in Figure 16.12, we need to add the BCWP as in Figure 16.14. Now comparing the BCWP curve with the BCWS curve we see that we have underspent, because we have not accomplished all of the work that was scheduled. Further, comparing the BCWP curve to the ACWP curve shows that we over-

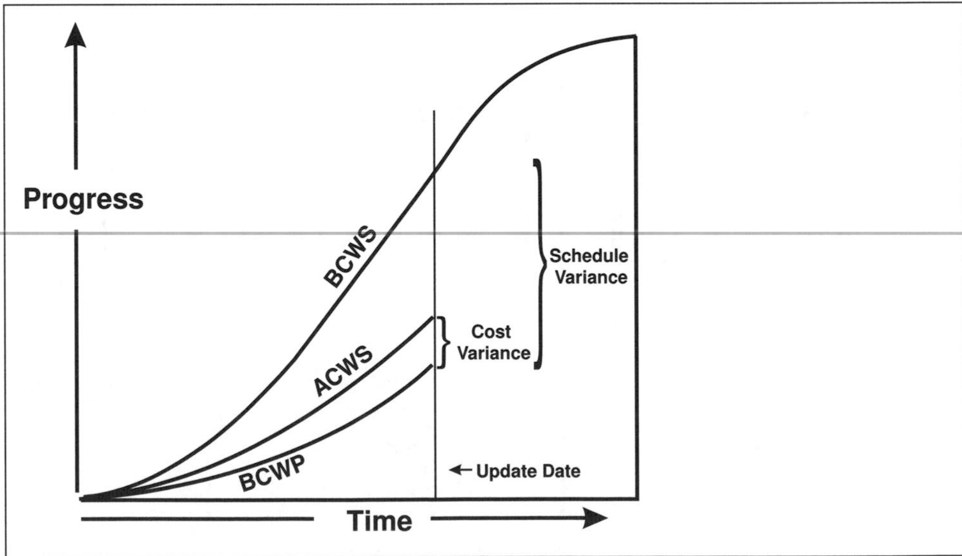

Figure 16.14 The full story.

spent for the work that we did do. Clearly, management would have been misled by Figure 16.11 had they ignored Figure 16.14. The full story is told by comparing both budget variance and schedule variance. Either one by itself may be telling a half-truth.

Earlier we stated that C/SC is a tool for measuring and reporting history. While this is true, Figure 16.15 illustrates that it can be used for achieving a feel for what is in the future.

By the straightforward method of cutting the BCWS curve at the height from the horizontal axis that has been achieved by the BCWP, and then pasting this curve on to the end of the BCWP curve, an extrapolation to the completion of the project can be obtained. Note that this is based on using the original estimates for the remaining work to be completed. We now see that given the rate at which we have been making progress, if we continue at that rate, we will finish beyond the planned completion date. Doing the same thing for the ACWP shows that we will finish over budget. This is the simplest method of attempting to *estimate to completion*, but it clearly illustrates that a significant change needs to occur in the way this project is running.

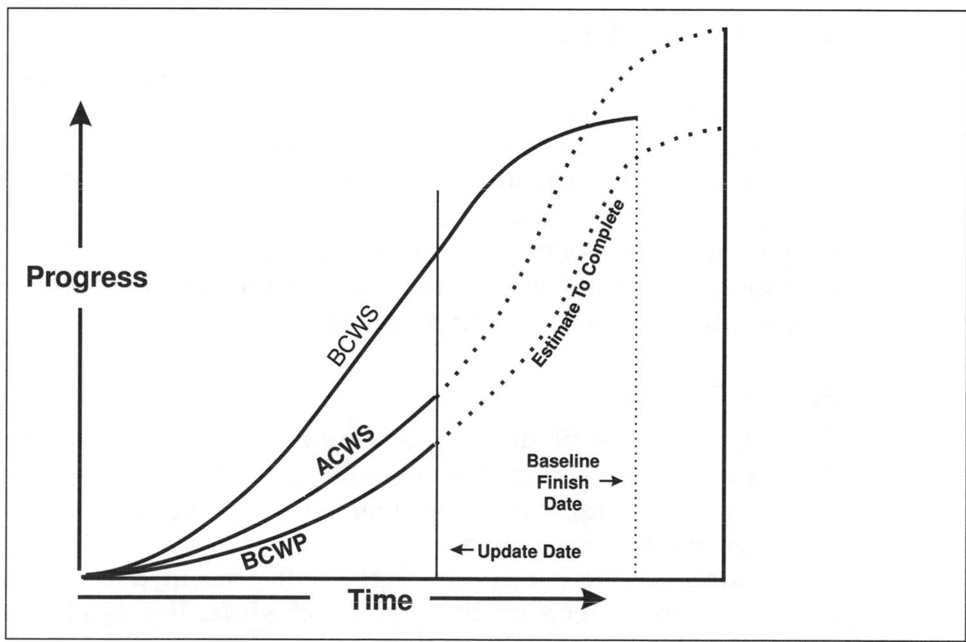

Figure 16.15 BCWS, BCWP, and ACWP curves.

The three basic indicators yield one additional level of analysis for us. Schedule Performance Index (SPI) and Cost Performance Index (CPI) are further refinements. They are computed as follows:

SPI = BCWP/BCWS
CPI = BCWP/ACWP

Some managers will prefer this type of analysis because it is intuitive and quite simple to equate each index to a baseline, which is always 1. Any value less than 1 is undesirable; any value over 1 is good. These indices are usually displayed graphically as trends compared against the baseline value of 1.

Level of Detail

There are always questions about the level of detail and frequency of reporting in project status reports. Our feeling is that the more you report, the more likely it is that someone will take objection or find some reason to micromanage your project. Let us examine this issue in more detail by considering the reporting requirements at the activity, project, and senior manager levels.

Activity Level Manager

Obviously the activity manager will want the most detailed and granular information available. After all, activity managers are directly responsible for getting the work done. Since they manage the resources that are used to complete project work, they will want to know what happened, what was scheduled to happen, who did what (or didn't do what), why it happened as it did, what problems have arisen, what solutions are within reach, and what changes need to be made. These reports are for the use of activity managers.

Project Manager

These reports present status information of all activities open for work during the report period. Just as is the case with activity level reports, there are reports for the project manager, and reports from the project manager to senior management.

Reports for the project manager will present data at the activity level and show effects on the project schedule. If project management software is being used, the posted data from the activity managers will have been used to update the project schedule and produce reports on overall project status. Any slippage at the activity level will have rippled through the successor activities, triggered a new activity schedule, and recomputed project completion dates. These reports will display all scheduling information, including float and resource schedule data. In effect they become working documents for the project manager for schedule adjustments and problem resolution. Since these reports are at a very detailed level, they are not appropriate for distribution beyond the project team. In many cases they may be for the project manager's eyes only.

Senior Management

We recommend a graphical exception report structure. For many projects, reports at the activity level will be appropriate. For large projects either milestone-level or summary task-level reports will be more effective. Remember, senior managers have only a few minutes to review any single project report, so keeping a report to a single page is a good strategy. The best report format, in our experience, is the Gantt Chart. These reports are largely intuitive; that is, they require little explanation. Activities should be listed in the order of scheduled start date, a time-now line shown, and all percent completed displayed.

If the project is sick, a get-well plan should be attached. This will usually be a narrative discussion of the problem, alternative solutions, recommended action, and any other details that are relevant to the issue at hand. This should also be a one-page report.

Using the WBS for a Reporting Structure

Since the WBS shows the hierarchical structure of the work to be done, it can be used for status reporting too. In its simplest form each activity box can be shaded to reflect completion percentages. As lower-level activities are completed, the summary activities above them can be shaded to represent percent complete data. Senior managers will appreciate knowing that major parts of the project are complete. Unfortunately the WBS does not contain scheduling or sequencing information. To the extent that this adds to the value of the report, narrative data or brief tabular data might be added to the report. Figure 16.16 shows a typical status report using the WBS.

While this report is rather intuitive it does not contain much detail. It would have to be accompanied by an explanatory note with schedule and cost detail.

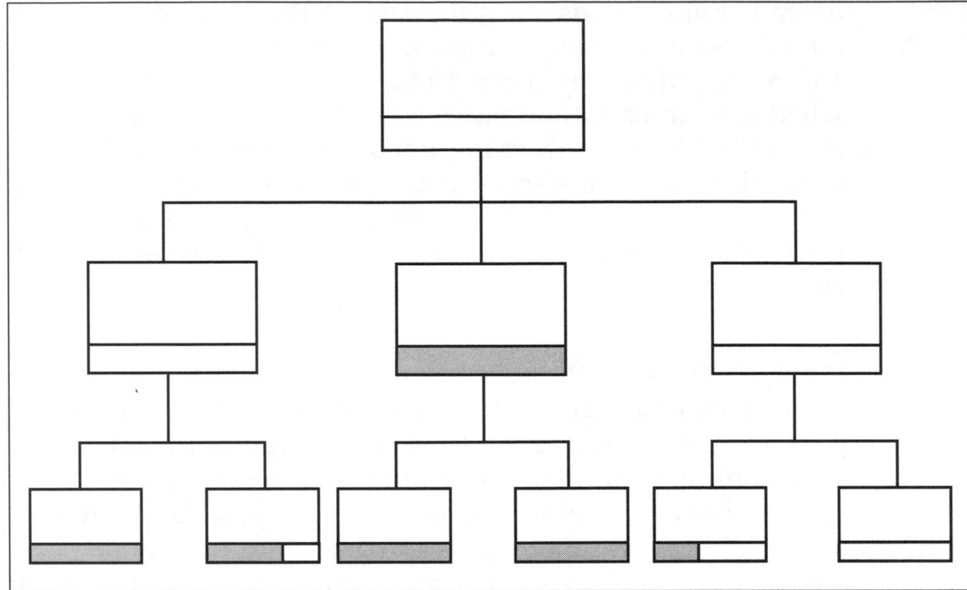

Figure 16.16 Status reporting with the WBS.

Project Status Review Meetings

Project Status Review meetings are just that; they review project status. They are not committee meetings at which problems are solved. They are not discussion groups. They have very specific, timed agendas. They focus on a single project but on occasion it may be useful to have multiple projects included on the agenda. In the sections that follow we discuss specific aspects of the status meeting.

Frequency

Project status is reported weekly by the activity manager to the project manager. Biweekly, the project manager reports to senior management. It therefore makes sense that project status meetings occur biweekly. One of the purposes is to prepare the project manager to report to senior management.

Duration

While project size may be the determining factor, we prefer a one-hour limit. This is the maximum and may not be needed at every project status meeting. Good judgment is needed here. Do not waste people's time!

Format

While the format should be adaptive as project needs dictate, there are certain items that will be part of every status meeting. We recommend that you proceed in a top-down fashion, as follows:

1. The project champion reports any changes that may have a bearing on the future of the project.
2. The customer reports any changes that may have a bearing on the future of the project.
3. The project manager reports on the overall health of the project and the impact of earlier problems, changes, corrective actions, and so on as they impact at the project level.
4. Activity managers report on the health of activities open or scheduled open for work since the last status meeting.
5. Activity managers of future activities report on any changes since the last meeting that will impact project status.
6. The project manager reviews the status of open problems from the last status meeting.
7. Attendees identify new problems and responsibility assigned for their resolution (the only discussion allowed here is for clarification purposes).
8. Closing comments are offered by the project champion, customer, and project manager, as appropriate.
9. The project manager announces the time and place of the next meeting and adjourns the meeting.

Attendees

Expect the list of attendees to vary throughout the life of the project. The project team members will often attend every meeting, but in larger projects it is acceptable to have only those members who now or will in the future contribute to the work to be done. Managers of activities that were open for work, or scheduled for work during the report period, will certainly attend. Those who are involved with successor activities may attend. The customer, or customer representative, will always be present. If any resource managers will be affected by the status (presumed to have departed from the plan), they should be present, too. The project champion will attend every status meeting. Resource managers will attend if a current or future period schedule will be impacted by the resources they command.

Minutes

Minutes are part of the formal project documentation and are taken at each meeting, circulated for comment, revised as appropriate, distributed, and filed in the project notebook (electronic, we hope). Since there is little discussion, the minutes will largely contain any handouts from the meeting, and items assigned for the next meeting. The minutes should also contain the list of attendees, a summary of comments made, and assigned responsibilities made. Ideally, a project administrative support person will be present to take minutes and monitor handouts. The responsibility might also be passed around to the project team members. In some organizations the same person is responsible for distributing the meeting agenda and materials ahead of time for review. This is especially important if decisions will be made during the meeting. People are very uncomfortable if they are seeing important information for the first time, expected to read and understand it, and then make a decision—all at the same time.

Change Control

Change is constant—at least in projects it is. No matter how hard we might try to plan a project, something will happen to necessitate a change in the plan. The most frequent situation starts something like this: Oh, I forgot to tell you that we will also need... or, We have to go to market no later than the third quarter instead of the fourth quarter. How often have you heard sentences that start something like these examples?

Since change is constant, a good project management methodology will have a change management process in place. In effect, the change management process will have us plan the project again. Think of it as a mini-JPP session. There will be a number of outcomes of that planning session, as listed in Figure 16.17.

- **Can be accommodated within the project resources and timelines.**
- **Can be accommodated but will require an extension of the deliverable schedule.**
- **Can be accommodated within the current deliverable schedule but additional resources will be needed.**
- **Can be accommodated but additional resources and an extension of the deliverable schedule will be required.**
- **Can be accomodated with a multiple release strategy and prioritizing of the deliverables across the release dates.**
- **Cannot be accomodated without a significant change to the project.**

Figure 16.17 Possible outcomes of a change request.

Reasons for Project Changes

It is very difficult for anyone, regardless of their skills at predicting and forecasting, to completely and accurately define their needs for a product or service that will be implemented 6, 12, or 18 months in the future. Competition, customer reactions, technology changes, a host of supplier related situations, and many other factors will render a killer application obsolete before it can be implemented. Let's face it—change is a way of life in project management. We might as well face it and be prepared to act accordingly.

Project Change Request

The first principle to ingrain is that every change is a significant change. Adopt that maxim and you will seldom go wrong. What that means is that every change requested by the customer must be documented. That document might be as simple as a memo but might also follow a format provided by the project team. In any case it is the start of another round of establishing conditions of satisfaction. Once the request is clearly understood, then, and only then, can the project team evaluate the impact of the change and whether it can be accommodated.

Project Impact Statement

The response to a change request is a document that we will call a *project impact statement*. It is a response that identifies the alternative courses of action that the project manager is willing to consider. The requestor is then charged with choosing the best alternative. The project impact statement describes the feasible alternatives that the project manager was able to identify, the positive and negative aspects of each, and perhaps a recommendation as to which alternative might be best. The final decision rests with the requestor.

Alternative Strategies

As we can see from Figure 16.17 the alternatives range from honoring the request with no impact on the deliverables; to accommodation with some changes in schedule, resources, or both; to denial.

Some creativity is often called for on the part of the project manager when responding to the requestor. Remember, the requestor has a legitimate reason for the request, and it must be treated with the best of business intentions in mind. Take the multiple release strategy, for example. Here we might ask the requestor to prioritize the original list of features along with those in the change request. Perhaps the change request can be accommodated within the current project plan by postponing some lower-priority features and functions. Alternatively, the project manager might respond as follows: The current plan calls for 100 percent of the functionality to be delivered on July 1. I can give you 80 percent of it on June 1 and the remaining 20 percent, including the change request, on August 1. This will often be a win-win situation. The requestor has something to work with earlier than expected and may find this to be a better situation than originally planned.

Problem Escalation

The resource scheduling problem is intractable. There is no closed form solution. To see how complex the problem really is we have constructed a simple example. Figure 16.18 is a single project with three resources (1, 2, 3) and three activities (A, B, C) already scheduled. Activity D needs to be scheduled and it will require all three resources working at the same time. Unfortunately the window of time within which all three resources are available does not accommodate Activity D.

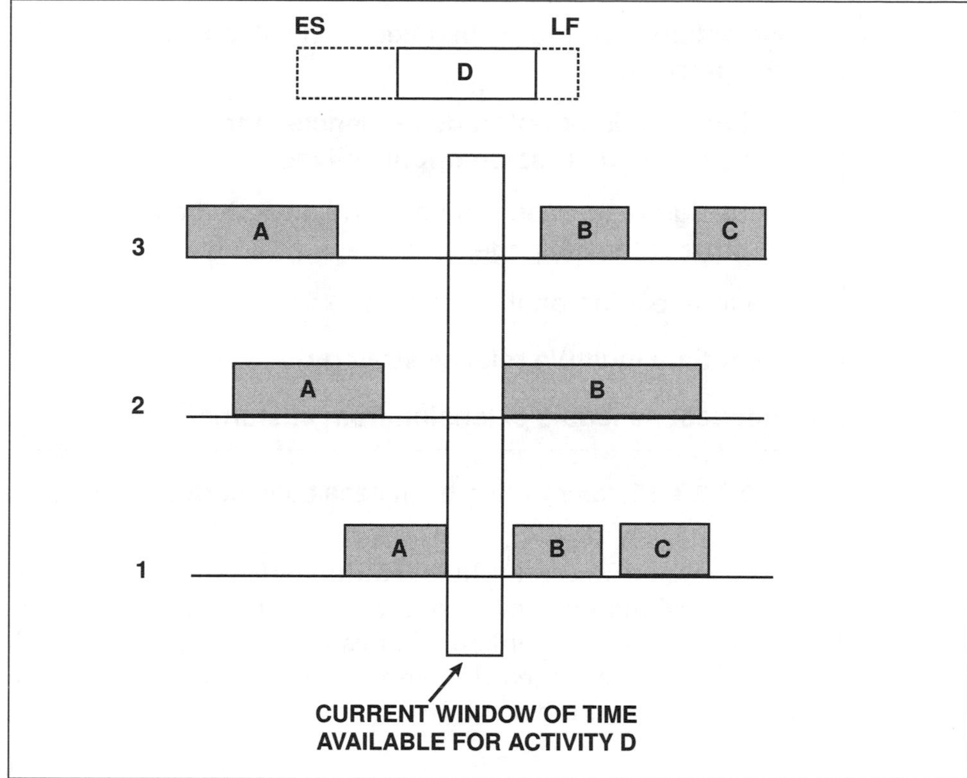

Figure 16.18 The scheduling problem.

Observe also that Activity D is not a critical path activity. What will you do? There are several choices that involve reconsidering the scheduling decisions that have been made on Activities A and B.

When the unplanned happens, the project manager needs to determine the extent of the problem and take the appropriate corrective measures. Minor variations from plan will occur and may not require corrective measures. There are degrees of corrective measures available to the project manager as shown in the following. They are listed in Figure 16.19 in the order in which they should be considered.

Causes

The causes of the problems we discuss in this section arise from the project team. Something has happened that put the project plan at risk.

- **No action required. Scheduled float will correct the problem.**
- **Examine finish-to-start dependencies for schedule compression opportunities.**
- **Reassign resources from noncritical activities to correct the slippage.**
- **Negotiate additional resources.**
- **Negotiate multiple release strategy.**
- **Request schedule extension from customer.**

Figure 16.19 Hierarchy of problem escalation corrective measures.

Late shipments from suppliers, equipment malfunction, sickness, acts of nature, resignations, priority changes, errors, and a host of other factors will give rise to problems that can impact deliverables, deliverable schedules, resource schedules, and so on. The project manager owns the problem and must find a solution.

Escalation Strategies

Project Manager Based

The first three strategies shown in Figure 16.19 are under the control of the project manager and will be the first options pursued. If the problem occurs within a noncritical path activity, it may be resolved by using the free float to resolve the problem. One example might be to reschedule the activity later in its ES to LF window, or extend the duration to use some of the free float. Note that this strategy does not impact any other activities in the project. By using total float we will impact the resource schedule for all activities that have this one as a predecessor. Another approach will be to continue the schedule compression techniques employed in defining the original project plan. This may have an impact on resource schedules just as in the prior case. The last option open to the project manager is to consider the resource pool under his or her control. Are there resources that can be reassigned from noncritical path activities to assist with the problem activity?

Resource Manager Based

Once the project manager has exhausted all the options under his or her control, it is time to turn to the resource managers for additional help. This may take the form of additional resources or rescheduling of already committed resources. Expect to make some trade-offs here. For example, you might be accommodated with this problem but at the sacrifice of later activities in the project. At least you have bought some time to resolve the downstream problem that will be created by solving this upstream problem. If the project manager has other projects underway, there may be some trades across projects that will solve the problem.

Customer Based

When all else fails, the project manager will have to approach the customer. Our first strategy would be to consider any multiple release strategies. Delivering some functionality ahead of schedule and the balance later than planned may be a good starting point. The last resort is to ask for an extension of time. This is not as unpleasant as it may seem, for the customer's schedule may have also slipped and they are relieved to have a delay in your deliverable schedule, too!

Problem Management Meetings

The purpose of these meetings is to provide an oversight function to identify, monitor, and resolve problems that arise during the life of a project. Every project has problems. No matter how well planned or managed, there will always be problems. Many of them arise just as an accident of nature. The World Trade Center is bombed and all the hot sites on Manhattan are overloaded with customer requests for computing time. They can't meet the demand. Customers suffer. But who would have forecast such an extreme disaster and been ready to respond. Should hot sites have hot sites? Nevertheless, the project manager must be ready to take action in such cases. The Problem Management Meeting is one vehicle for addressing all problems that need to be escalated above the individual for definition, solution identification, and resolution.

This is an important function in the management of projects, especially large projects. Problems are often identified in the Project Status Meeting and referred to the appropriate persons for resolution. A group is assembled to work on the problem. Progress reports are presented and discussed at a Problem Management Meeting.

Statistical Concepts for Milestone Trend Charts

In the material that follows we assume that three-point estimates exist for every activity in the project. While that may require some effort on the part of the JPP team and project team, it is information that allows a number of calculations not otherwise possible.

To get started we need some notation. Let an activity be represented by a_i. The longest sequence of activities leading to a_i will be denoted by A_i. Activity a_i has duration d_i and variance v_i. The length of the longest part leading to a_i has duration D_i and variance V_i. These quantities are calculated by simply adding the durations and variances of the activities that define A_i.

The a_i are statistically independent random variables. According to the Central Limit Theorem their sum is normally distributed with mean D_i and variance V_i. Therefore the quantity

$$Z = [X - D_i] / \sqrt{V_i}$$

has a standard normal distribution. This means that we can make probability statements about any sequence of activities in the project network. For example, if Activity a_i. is the finish activity of the project with duration D_i, the probability of completing the project on or before D_i is .5! Are you surprised that you have no better than a fifty-fifty chance of completing the project before its LF date? Observe that D_i is the length of the critical path.

Let us take a little more complicated example. Assume that activity a_i is the milestone activity that represents completion of beta testing and that it is on the critical path. Here is the data:

$$D_i = 120 \text{ days} \qquad V_i = 3 \text{ days}$$

Let us compute the probability that the beta test will be at least two days late. Making the appropriate substitutions gives:

$$\begin{aligned} Pr\{D_i > 122 \text{ days}\} &= Pr\{ Z > (122 - 120)/\sqrt{3}\} = Pr\{Z > 1.155) \\ &= 0.500 - Pr\{Z < 1.155\} \end{aligned}$$

We can read this probability directly from the standard normal table (Figure 16.20). Referring to the table note that the tabled values are the probability from 0 to the computed value of Z. For this example, read

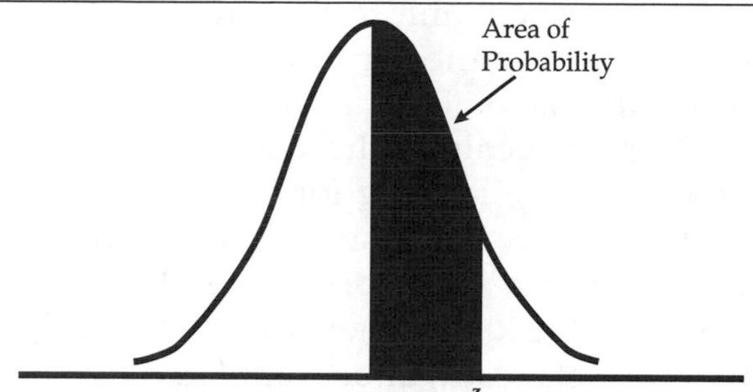

Entries in the table give the area under the curve between the mean and z standard deviations above the mean. For example, for z = 1.25 the area under the curve between the mean and z is 0.3944.

z	0.00	0.01	0.02	0.03	0.04	0.05	0.06	0.07	0.08	0.09
0.0	0.0000	0.0040	0.0080	0.0120	0.0160	0.0199	0.0239	0.0279	0.0319	0.0359
0.1	0.0398	0.0438	0.0478	0.0517	0.0557	0.0596	0.0636	0.0675	0.0714	0.0753
0.2	0.0793	0.0832	0.0871	0.0910	0.0948	0.0987	0.1026	0.1064	0.1103	0.1141
0.3	0.1179	0.1217	0.1255	0.1293	0.1331	0.1368	0.1406	0.1443	0.1480	0.1517
0.4	0.1554	0.1591	0.1628	0.1664	0.1700	0.1736	0.1772	0.1808	0.1844	0.1879
0.5	0.1915	0.1950	0.1985	0.2019	0.2054	0.2088	0.2123	0.2157	0.2190	0.2224
0.6	0.2257	0.2291	0.2324	0.2357	0.2389	0.2422	0.2454	0.2486	0.2518	0.2549
0.7	0.2580	0.2612	0.2642	0.2672	0.2704	0.2734	0.2764	0.2794	0.2823	0.2852
0.8	0.2881	0.2910	0.2939	0.2967	0.2995	0.3023	0.3051	0.3078	0.3106	0.3133
0.9	0.3159	0.3186	0.3212	0.3238	0.3264	0.3289	0.3315	0.3340	0.3365	0.3389
1.0	0.3413	0.3438	0.3461	0.3485	0.3508	0.3531	0.3554	0.3577	0.3599	0.3621
1.1	0.3643	0.3665	0.3686	0.3708	0.3729	0.3749	0.3770	0.3790	0.3810	0.3830
1.2	0.3849	0.3869	0.3888	0.3907	0.3925	0.3944	0.3962	0.3980	0.3997	0.4015
1.3	0.4032	0.4049	0.4066	0.4082	0.4099	0.4115	0.4131	0.4147	0.4162	0.4177
1.4	0.4192	0.4207	0.4222	0.4236	0.4251	0.4265	0.4279	0.4292	0.4306	0.4319
1.5	0.4332	0.4345	0.4357	0.4370	0.4382	0.4394	0.4406	0.4418	0.4429	0.4441
1.6	0.4452	0.4463	0.4474	0.4484	0.4495	0.4505	0.4515	0.4525	0.4535	0.4545
1.7	0.4554	0.4564	0.4573	0.4582	0.4591	0.4599	0.4608	0.4616	0.4625	0.4633
1.8	0.4641	0.4649	0.4656	0.4664	0.4671	0.4678	0.4686	0.4693	0.4699	0.4706
1.9	0.4713	0.4719	0.4726	0.4732	0.4738	0.4744	0.4750	0.4756	0.4761	0.4767
2.0	0.4772	0.4778	0.4783	0.4788	0.4793	0.4798	0.4803	0.4808	0.4812	0.4817
2.1	0.4821	0.4826	0.4830	0.4834	0.4838	0.4842	0.4846	0.4850	0.4854	0.4857
2.2	0.4861	0.4864	0.4868	0.4871	0.4875	0.4878	0.4881	0.4884	0.4887	0.4890
2.3	0.4893	0.4896	0.4898	0.4901	0.4904	0.4906	0.4909	0.4911	0.4913	0.4916
2.4	0.4918	0.4920	0.4922	0.4925	0.4927	0.4929	0.4931	0.4932	0.4934	0.4936
2.5	0.4938	0.4940	0.4941	0.4943	0.4945	0.4946	0.4948	0.4949	0.4951	0.4952
2.6	0.4953	0.4955	0.4956	0.4957	0.4959	0.4960	0.4961	0.4962	0.4963	0.4964
2.7	0.4965	0.4966	0.4967	0.4968	0.4969	0.4970	0.4971	0.4972	0.4973	0.4974
2.8	0.4974	0.4975	0.4976	0.4977	0.4977	0.4978	0.4979	0.4979	0.4980	0.4981
2.9	0.4981	0.4982	0.4982	0.4983	0.4984	0.4984	0.4985	0.4985	0.4986	0.4986
3.0	0.4986	0.4987	0.4987	0.4988	0.4988	0.4989	0.4989	0.4989	0.4990	0.4990

Figure 16.20 Table of the standard normal distribution.

down the leftmost column to find the first two digits of Z (in this case 1.1), then read across the columns for the third digit (in this case to the column headed 0.05). The tabled entry at the intersection of the row headed 1.1 and the column headed 0.05 (namely, 0.3749) is close to the final answer. We are looking for the tabled value corresponding to a Z value of 1.155. This value will lie half way between 1.155 and 1.156 (namely, 0.3760; we interpolate linearly in this table). Hence we get 0.500 – .3760 = 0.1240. In other words there is little better than a chance in ten that the beta test will be completed two or more days late.

Let us try one more that is a little more complicated. Using the same data compute the probability that beta testing will be completed at least four days early. Making the appropriate substitutions gives:

$$\Pr\{D_i < 116 \text{ days}\} = \Pr\{D_i > 124 \text{ days}\}$$

This follows from the symmetry of the normal distribution. Then:

$$\Pr\{D_i > 124\} = \Pr\{Z > (124 - 120) / \sqrt{3}\} = \Pr\{Z > 2.309)$$
$$= 0.500 - \Pr\{Z < 2.309\}$$

From the table of normal variates we see that the probability is about 0.0084—there is little chance of completing beta testing that early.

We can get a little more complex with statements like: What is the probability that beta testing will be completed within one day of the scheduled time? Again because of the symmetry of the normal distribution we can express this as follows:

$$\Pr\{119 < D_i < 121\} = 1 - 2\Pr\{D_i > 121\}$$

The rest is easy! Try it and if you get approximately 0.4362, you understand.

We judge ourselves by what we feel capable of doing, while others judge us by what we have already done.

Henry Wadsworth Longfellow
American poet

We cannot afford to forget any experiences, even the most painful.

Dag Hammerskjold
Secretary General of the United Nations

CHAPTER 17

CLOSE OUT THE PROJECT

CHAPTER LEARNING OBJECTIVES

As a result of participating in the learning experiences in this chapter you will be able to:

1. Understand the steps needed to effectively close a project.
2. Develop a closing strategy.
3. Identify the components of project documentation.
4. Conduct a post implementation audit.
5. Explain the significance of each postimplementation audit question.

Steps in Closing a Project

Closing the project is fairly routine once we have the customer's approval of the deliverables. Figure 17.1 lists the closing steps.

Obtain Client Acceptance

The client decides when the project is done. It is the job of the project manager to demonstrate that the deliverables (whether product or service) meet client specifications. This may be very informal and ceremonial or it may be very formal—involving extensive acceptance testing against the client's performance specifications.

Ceremonial Acceptance

There are two situations that fall under the heading of ceremonial acceptance. The first case involves deadline dates at which the client must accept the project as complete regardless of whether it meets specification. For example, if the project was to plan and conduct a conference, the conference will happen regardless of whether the project work has been satisfactorily completed. The second case involves a project deliverable requiring little or no checking to see if specifications have been met, for example, planning and taking a vacation.

Formal Acceptance

In these cases the client will have written an acceptance procedure that requires the project team to demonstrate compliance with every feature in the client's performance specification. A checklist is often used and requires a feature-by-feature sign-off based on performance tests. These tests should be jointly conducted and administered by the client and appropriate members of the project team.

Install Project Deliverables

This involves going live with the deliverables. This will commonly occur in computer systems work. The installation may in fact be rather involved, being phased, cut-over, or some other rollout strategy. In other cases it will simply involve nothing more than flipping a switch.

1. Ensure all deliverables are installed.
2. Get client acceptance of deliverables.
3. Ensure documentation is in place.
4. Get client sign-off on final.
5. Conduct postimplementation.
6. Celebrate success.

Figure 17.1 Steps in closing a project.

In either case, there will often be some event or activity that turns things over to the customer. This triggers the beginning of a number of close-out activities that mostly relate to documentation and report preparation.

Document the Project

Documentation always seems to be the most difficult part of the project to complete. There is little glamour and no "attaboys" in doing documentation. That does not diminish its importance, however. There are at least five reasons why we need to do documentation. These are given in Figure 17.2

- Reference for future changes in deliverables
- Historical record for estimating item and cost on future projects, activities, and tasks
- Training resource for new project managers
- Input for further training and development of the project team
- Input for performance evaluation by the functional managers of the project team members

Figure 17.2 Purpose of documentation.

1. Project Overview Statement
2. Project Proposal and backup data
3. Original and revised project schedules
4. Minutes of all project meetings
5. Copies of all status reports
6. Design documents
7. Copies of all change notices
8. Copies of all written communications
9. Outstanding issues reports
10. Final report
11. Sample deliverables (if appropriate)
12. Client acceptance documents
13. Postimplementation audit report

Figure 17.3 Contents of documentation.

Contents of Documentation

The list given in Figure 17.3 is the "whole enchilada." For a given project, the project manager will have to determine what documentation is appropriate. We always refer back to value added considerations. If the document has value, and many will have good value for future projects, then include it in the documentation. Note also that the list contains very little that does not arise naturally in the conduct of the project. All that is really needed is to appoint someone to care and feed the project notebook. This involves collecting the documents at the time of their creation, ensuring that they are in a retrievable form (electronic is a must).

Postimplementation Audit

The postimplementation audit is an evaluation of the project's goals and activity achievement as measured against the project plan, budget, time deadlines, quality of deliverables, specifications, and client satis-

1. **Was the project goal achieved?**
   a. **Does it do what the project team said it would do?**
   b. **Does it do what the client said it would do?**
2. **Was the project work done on time, within budget, and according to specification?**
3. **Was the client satisfied with the project results?**
4. **Was business value realized? (Check success criteria.)**
5. **What were the lessons learned about project management methodology?**

Figure 17.4 Why conduct a postimplementation audit?

faction. The log of the project activities serves as baseline data for this audit. There are four important questions to be answered, as shown in Figure 17.4.

The postimplementation audit is seldom done, which is unfortunate because it does have great value for all stakeholders. Some of the reasons for skipping the audit are listed in Figure 17.5.

The Final Report

The Final Project Report serves as the memory or history of the project. It is the file that others can check to study the progress and impediments of the project. There are many formats that can be used for a final report. The items listed in Figure 17.6 are usually included in a final report.

- **Managers don't want to know.**
- **Managers don't want to pay the cost.**
- **Not a high priority.**
- **Too much other billable work to do.**

Figure 17.5 Why postimplementation audits are not done.

- **Overall success of the project**
- **Organization of the project**
- **Techniques used to get results**
- **Project strengths and weaknesses**
- **Project team recommendations**

Figure 17.6 Contents of the final report.

Celebrating Success

There must be some recognition of the project team at the end of the project. This may be as simple as a commemorative mug, t-shirt, pizza party, tickets to the ball game, or something more formal. We recall that when release 3 of Lotus 1-2-3 was delivered, each member of the project team was presented with a videotape showing the team at work during the last week of the project. That was certainly a good touch and one that will long be remembered by every member of the team.

PART 5

PREVIEW

We have presented a rather comprehensive treatment of the tools and techniques you will need in order to be an effective project manager. However, our job is not done. We have saved for Part 5 a discussion of the environment within which you will be practicing your newfound skills.

It will come as no surprise to you that the global village in which you work impacts every company. Not one single professional is untouched.

As we shall see, organizational structure has a lot to do with the likelihood of success or failure of projects. The traditional project, functional, matrix, and task force forms are discussed in relation to effective project management. Each has advantages and disadvantages. We also consider the present situation for project management in organizations that have become process oriented and those using self-managed teams. In both cases project management has taken on an important role.

There is a strong relationship between the project management life cycle and other processes. We discuss software development, new product development, and continuous quality improvement. In all three cases the tools and techniques of project management are important components in each of these life cycles.

In the pages that follow we attempt to put project management in the context of the information age enterprise. We discuss how organizational structure can be a hindrance or help for the project manager. We also show how project management relates to a number of other contemporary methodologies.

OVERVIEW

PART 5

Enterprise Considerations

LEARNING OBJECTIVES

As a result of participating in the learning experiences in this part you will be able to:

1. Explain the relationship between organization structure and project management.
2. Understand the issues concerned with managing projects that cross organizational boundaries.
3. Use project management tools and techniques in the systems development life cycle.
4. Use project management tools and techniques in new product development.
5. Know how project management contributes to continuous quality improvement programs.

Organizational Designs and Their Impact on Project Management

The environment in which the project team must function can be a great help or hindrance to successful project management. In Part 5 we examine this and other issues. Given that you must operate within a given structure you will at least understand the advantages and disadvantages relative to project management. To the extent that you can influence organization structure, this section will help you form your recommendations.

Project Structure

It goes without saying that the project structure (Figure 1) is most supportive of effective project management. In this organizational structure the project team works full-time on the project until the project is complete. The project manager has line responsibility for the team members. For the project manager this means having the responsibility for team skills development and deployment. Having the authority to assign and reassign team members to project activities as the needs of the project schedule dictate and not having to negotiate resource reassignment with another manager is a big plus.

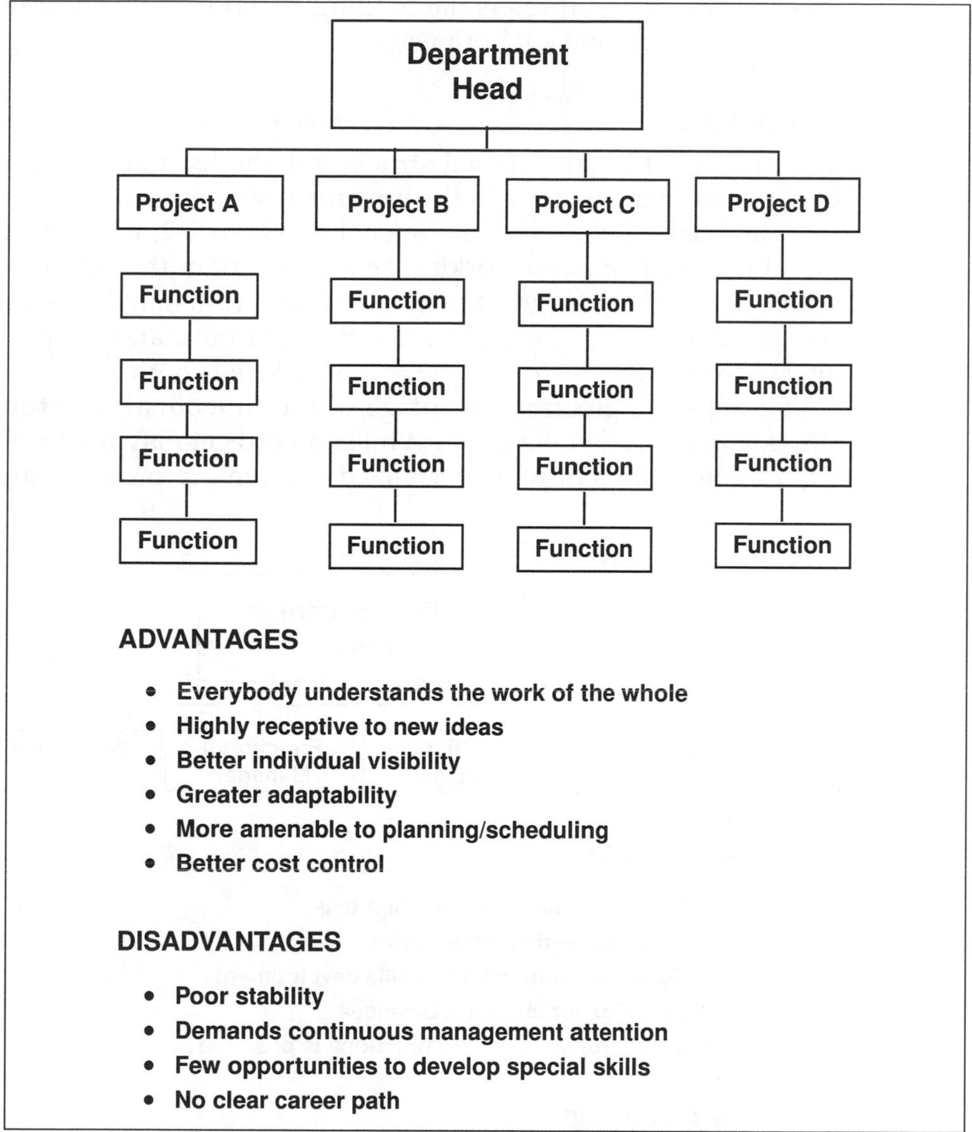

Figure 1 The project structure.

On the other hand, the major disadvantage of the project structure is the inefficient use of resources. We have already discussed the trade-off between time to market and resource utilization. If time to market is the dominant constraint, then resource efficiency suffers. However, if the efficient use of resources is the binding constraint, then time to market suffers. You can't have it both ways!

Functional Structures

The functional organizational structure is the least supportive of effective project management. In the functional structure, projects frequently have no identity of their own. Referring to Figure 2, when the first functional manager finishes working on an activity in the project, the deliverable is *thrown over the transom* to the next functional manager, so the process continues. The project has no champion and no project manager, so to speak. Obviously the risk of failure is high.

Perhaps the greatest advantage of the functional structure falls on the side of skills development. While one project may not be able to justify the development of a specialized skill, many projects can. As long

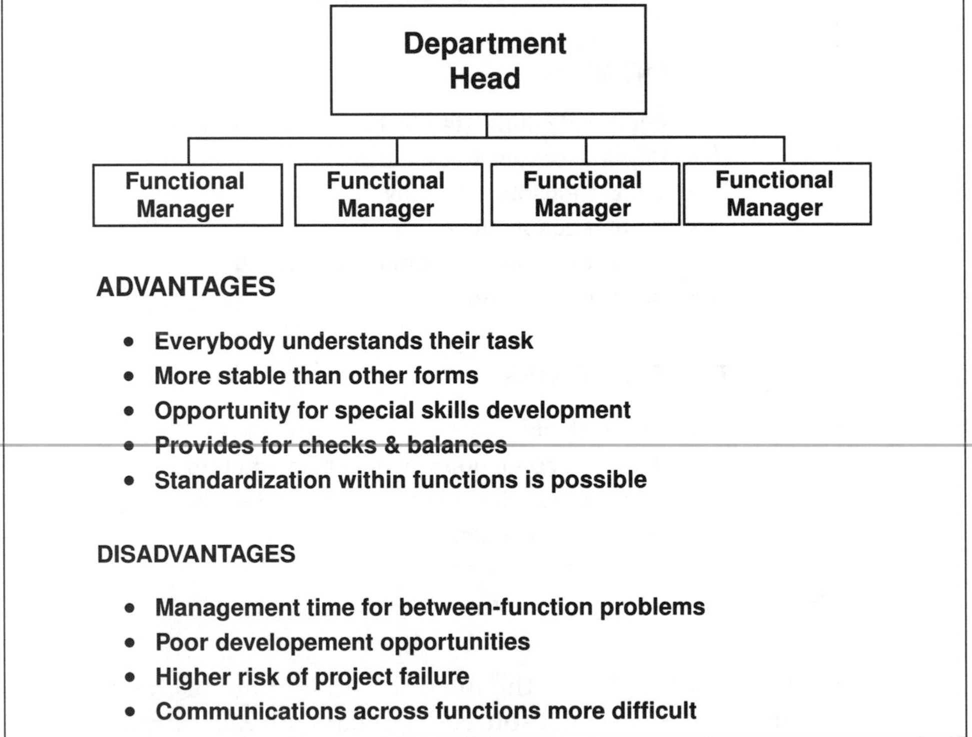

Figure 2 The functional structure.

as there is some way to marshall the forces to collaborate on the use of the special skills, they can be developed. The functional structure does just that.

Matrix Structures

The matrix structure is probably the most common form found in today's organizations, although there is strong evidence that that is changing and businesses are moving toward a hybrid form of project structure. More on that later. The movement toward downsizing or rightsizing (or, in some cases, capsizing) has brought with it the need to use resources more efficiently. At the same time it is important that projects retain their identity and visibility. The structure that accomplishes this best is the matrix structure Figure 3).

To a large degree the matrix structure has all of the advantages of the functional and project structures with few of their disadvantages. Unfortunately it is not that simple or every organization would follow a matrix form. Along with the matrix structure comes a good dose of political baggage. The functional manager is responsible for staff development and deployment. The project manager is responsible for getting projects done on time, within budget, and according to specification. These two sets of responsibilities are often at odds with one another. The project manager will always want to negotiate for the A Team, while the functional manager will want to use project work for on-the-job training. The situation is further complicated when the functional manager is also a project manager. To whose projects is the A Team assigned?

There are several variations of the matrix structure that you should be aware of. The matrix structure given in Figure 3 is one in which functional units are strong relative to projects. This form is called a *functional matrix structure*. If we rotate the structure so that projects are strong relative to functional units, then the functional units provide a support role to projects. These structures are called *project matrix structures*. Obviously, functional managers would prefer the functional matrix, while project managers would prefer the project matrix. Between these two forms there is a third called the *balanced matrix*. In this form the project managers report through a project office, which reports to the general manager responsible for functional units. Balance is achieved in that both the project managers and the functional managers ultimately report to the same line manager.

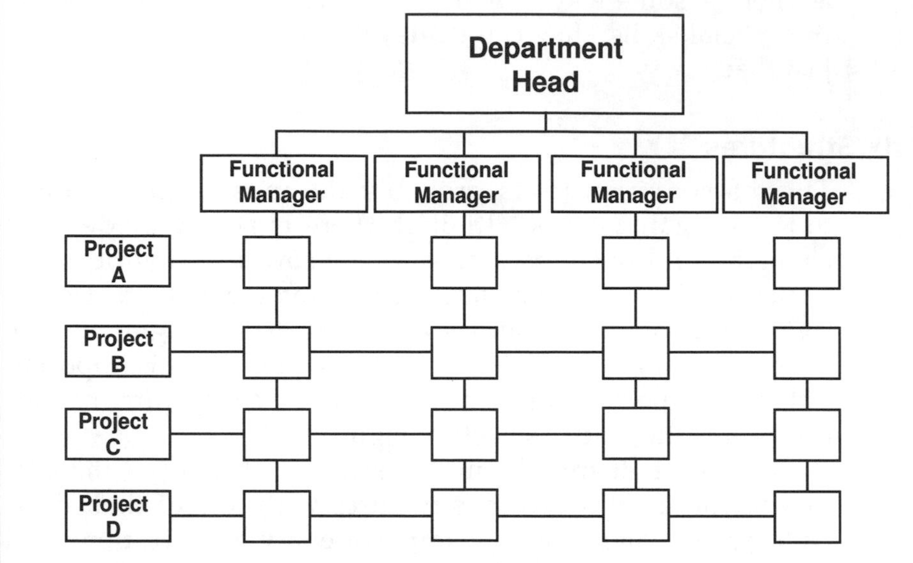

POTENTIAL ADVANTAGES

- Better assessment of skill and development needs
- Better utilization of specialized skills
- Flexible and adaptive to changing environments
- Few communication problems (dual reporting)
- Everybody understands the work of the whole
- Project objectives are clear and visible
- Morale is high
- Develops future project managers
- Project shutdown is not too traumatic

POTENTIAL DISADVANTAGES

- Success depends on manager interactions
- Project management difficult (no line authority)
- Greater potential for politics
- Each project team member has two bosses
- Conflicting goals (project vs. function)
- Potential balance of power conflicts
- Higher management costs
- More complex than other forms

Figure 3 The matrix structure.

Task Forces

Along with all of the changes we are witnessing in organizations, hybrid forms of organizational structures are beginning to emerge. Many of these are the direct result of downsizing efforts and empowerment of the worker. We collect these new forms under the name *task force* but recognize that there are several variations. The first distinction is that task forces may be permanent or temporal structures. We generally think of task forces as taking on some responsibility or charge. Once the charge has been met, the task force is dissolved. These situations are not unlike a project structure except that the team members are generally assigned to the task force on a part-time basis.

The more interesting variation is the permanent task force; Figure 4 depicts the situation. Here the task force has a specific responsibility, acts independently of the department, and draws upon the functional areas for advice and training. The functional areas perform a support role only. The most common example of this structure is the self-managed or self-directed team. In this situation the team has all of the skills it needs to carry out its assigned mission. If any skills are missing, the team is responsible for training its members in the needed skills or acquiring additional team members with the requisite skills. Teams will often have profit/loss responsibility, and hiring and firing authority. In a sense, they are a business within a business. Obviously, this structure is very supportive of effective project management. In fact, effective project management is a prerequisite of good performance of these task forces. Since the team is a permanent structure it shares the same advantages of the project structure.

Project Management in Contemporary Organizational Environments

There is a trend in organizations to structure themselves such that cross-functional teams are commonly used. This adds several areas of concern for the project manager. While cross-functional teams are common in those enterprises that focus on business process rather than business function and those that are more customer-centered than in prior years, they do bring some new issues to the table for the project manager, as discussed in the following. Project managers and team members who manage projects within larger organizations must communicate, sell ideas, negotiate, problem solve, and resolve conflicts

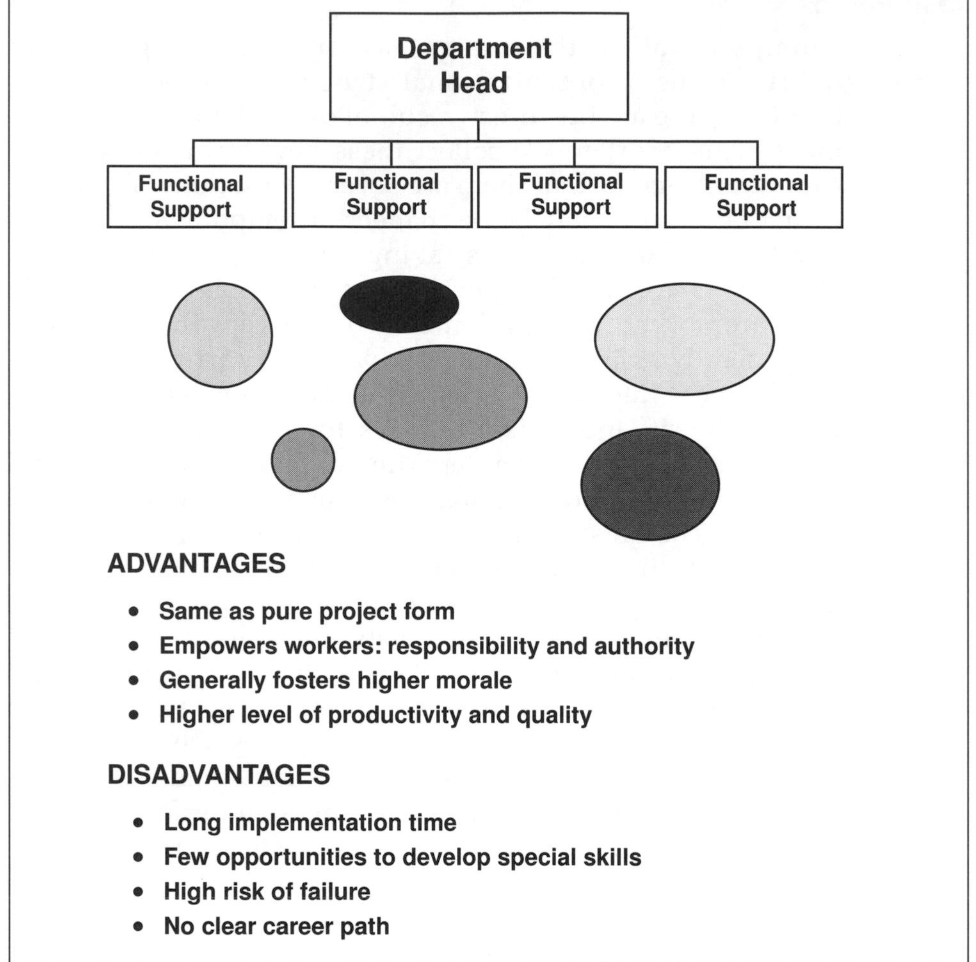

Figure 4 The task force structure.

across functional and sometimes geographic boundaries. Since the project manager and team are almost always *between* authority and control structures in the larger organization, their people skills must be adept. Having more than one boss is a given in projects.

Ownership

Companies that have evolved to a process focus will often have identified a process owner—a manager who has the responsibility and authority over the process from end to end. Project teams can function very successfully in these environments. Companies that are new to the process structure may not have made such delegations. The project manager may face difficulties in managing the project because there is no clear line of authority. The task force or self-managed team approach may mitigate some of these problems.

Commitment

As would be the case with contracted team members, commitment to the project can be a problem for the project manager unless steps are taken to build that commitment. Those who do not have a vested interest in the project may simply see themselves as hired help on the project. The project manager should take steps to see that these professionals understand their role in the success of the project. For example, they should know the importance of their work on the project, for example, that their activity is on the critical path, or how the output of their efforts contributes to the project objectives. They need to know the consequences of their efforts, both good and bad. If possible involve them in the planning process. Give them an opportunity to contribute their expertise to what is to be done, how it is to be done, and what resource requirements they have for successfully completing their project work.

Authority

Perhaps the major issue in cross-functional teams is line of authority. It should not happen by default. The stakeholders, especially the contracted team members and resource managers, must have formal statements from the project champion or customer as to who has the authority and responsibility for the project . A formal kickoff presentation, led by the project champion or customer, will include an announcement (verbal and in writing) as to the lines of authority for the project. Having done this at the beginning of the project, there is little chance of confusion or problems downstream in the project.

Process Oriented

With the need to focus the organization's efforts more on customer satisfaction, organizations have turned themselves on their side to reconfigure from functional to process structures. In the process structure there are process owners and process teams. These teams could be product-based, that is, they have total responsibility from R&D through customer support and for everything in between. In these situations the project team is a permanent entity and can develop a solid base for project work. The team has the opportunity to establish its own work habits, skill set, meeting format, reporting structure, problem resolution method, and other tools, techniques, and procedures to make project management truly effective. Other organizational structures do not avail the team of these opportunities. Therefore, project management in a process-oriented organization has every reason to be successful.

Self-Managed Teams

Closely related to the process-oriented format are self-managed teams. Generally they will have responsibility for a function or subfunction but otherwise share the same strengths as the process structure. They are self-contained in that all of the skills they need are present in the team. They are devoid of the usual command and control features and will generally function just as independently as in the process structures.

Interenterprise

Electronic commerce, the information highway, and electronic data interchange have given rise to new forms of doing business. They are evidenced by the emergence of trading partnerships between suppliers and customers and other neighboring pairs in the food chain. Within these alliances has come the need for new application systems that span organizational boundaries. For example, the vendor has access to its customer's inventory system and can trigger a reorder whenever inventory levels have reached previously established reorder points. Invoicing and payment of invoices is moving toward electronic transactions under the control of both parties' computer systems.

In these situations project management is treading new waters. Some of the issues to consider are:

- Which organization provides the project manager, or are there two project managers?
- Who owns the system?
- How are the differences between technology infrastructures to be reconciled?
- What about public network security? Do we use a private network?

Interenterprise systems development is in its infancy. The project management tools to support it are only now beginning to be developed. We can only guess at the problems to be encountered and hope that their solution will be easily forthcoming.

Relationship between Project Management and Other Methodologies

Software Development Life Cycle

Those of our readers who are systems development professionals will have recognized many similarities between the project management life cycle and the systems development life cycle. The two do in fact have many things in common. Many organizations that claim to be practicing project management have basically adapted their systems development methodology to a pseudoproject-management methodology. While this may work, in our experience several problems arise because of the lack of specificity in some parts of the systems development methodology. We also find that most systems development methodologies do not give enough how-to details to support good project management practices. Figure 5 shows the commonality that exists between the project management life cycle and a typical systems development life cycle.

New Product Development Life Cycle

New product development can benefit from a well-defined project management methodology. Just as there is similarity between systems development and project management there also is similarity between the product development life cycle and project management. To see this, consider Figure 6, which shows the parallelism between the two.

Time to Market

Time to market is a critical success factor in new product development. We have given examples of several project management tools and techniques that can reduce time-to-market techniques. For the project manager this means that the time side of the triangle is fixed and resource efficiency is not a binding constraint. Much of what we have taught you about project management works very comfortably in the product development arena.

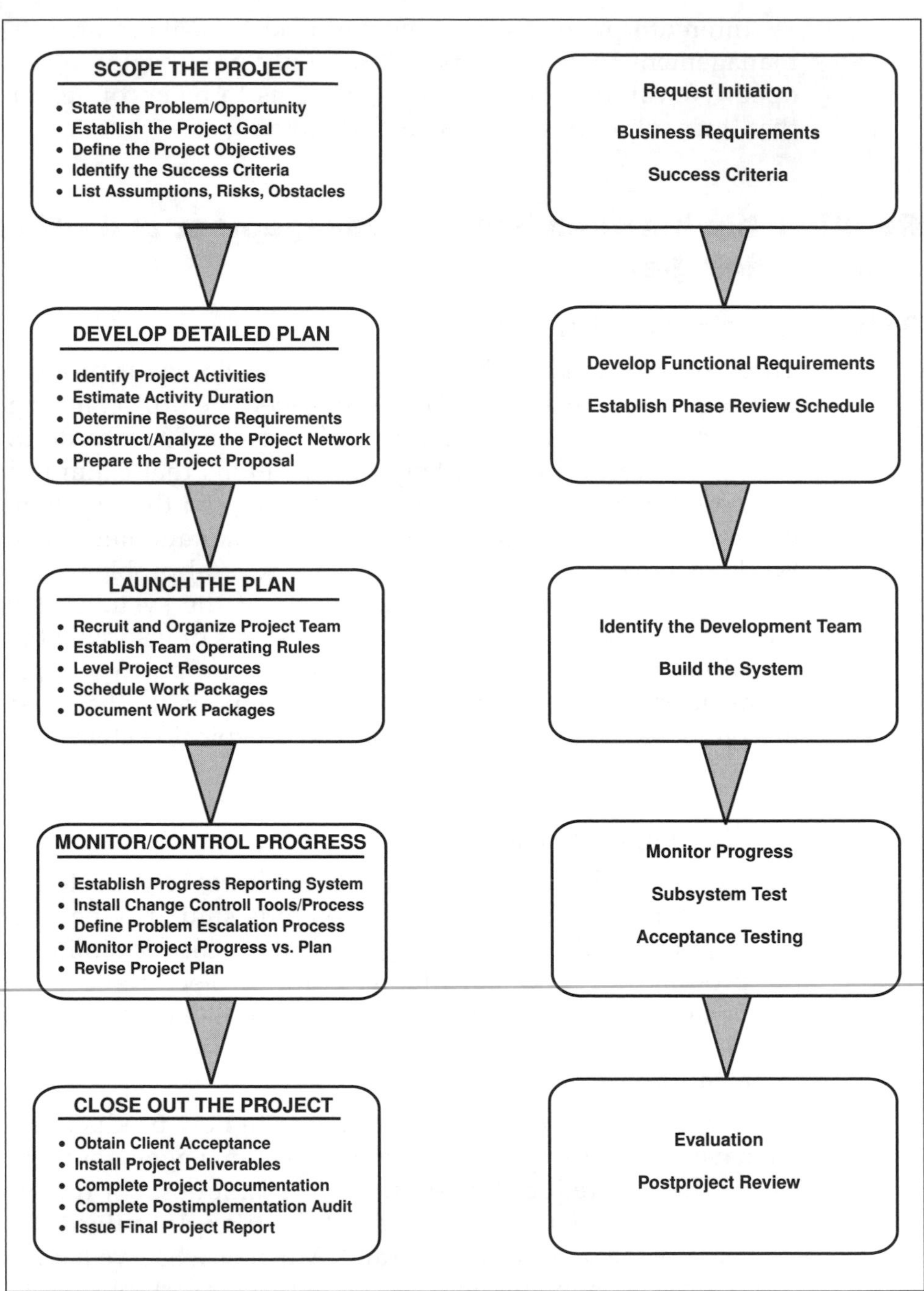
SCOPE THE PROJECT
• State the Problem/Opportunity
• Establish the Project Goal
• Define the Project Objectives
• Identify the Success Criteria
• List Assumptions, Risks, Obstacles
DEVELOP DETAILED PLAN
• Identify Project Activities
• Estimate Activity Duration
• Determine Resource Requirements
• Construct/Analyze the Project Network
• Prepare the Project Proposal
LAUNCH THE PLAN
• Recruit and Organize Project Team
• Establish Team Operating Rules
• Level Project Resources
• Schedule Work Packages
• Document Work Packages
MONITOR/CONTROL PROGRESS
• Establish Progress Reporting System
• Install Change Controll Tools/Process
• Define Problem Escalation Process
• Monitor Project Progress vs. Plan
• Revise Project Plan
CLOSE OUT THE PROJECT
• Obtain Client Acceptance
• Install Project Deliverables
• Complete Project Documentation
• Complete Postimplementation Audit
• Issue Final Project Report
Request Initiation
Business Requirements
Success Criteria
Develop Functional Requirements
Establish Phase Review Schedule
Identify the Development Team
Build the System
Monitor Progress
Subsystem Test
Acceptance Testing
Evaluation
Postproject Review

Figure 5 Project management and systems development.

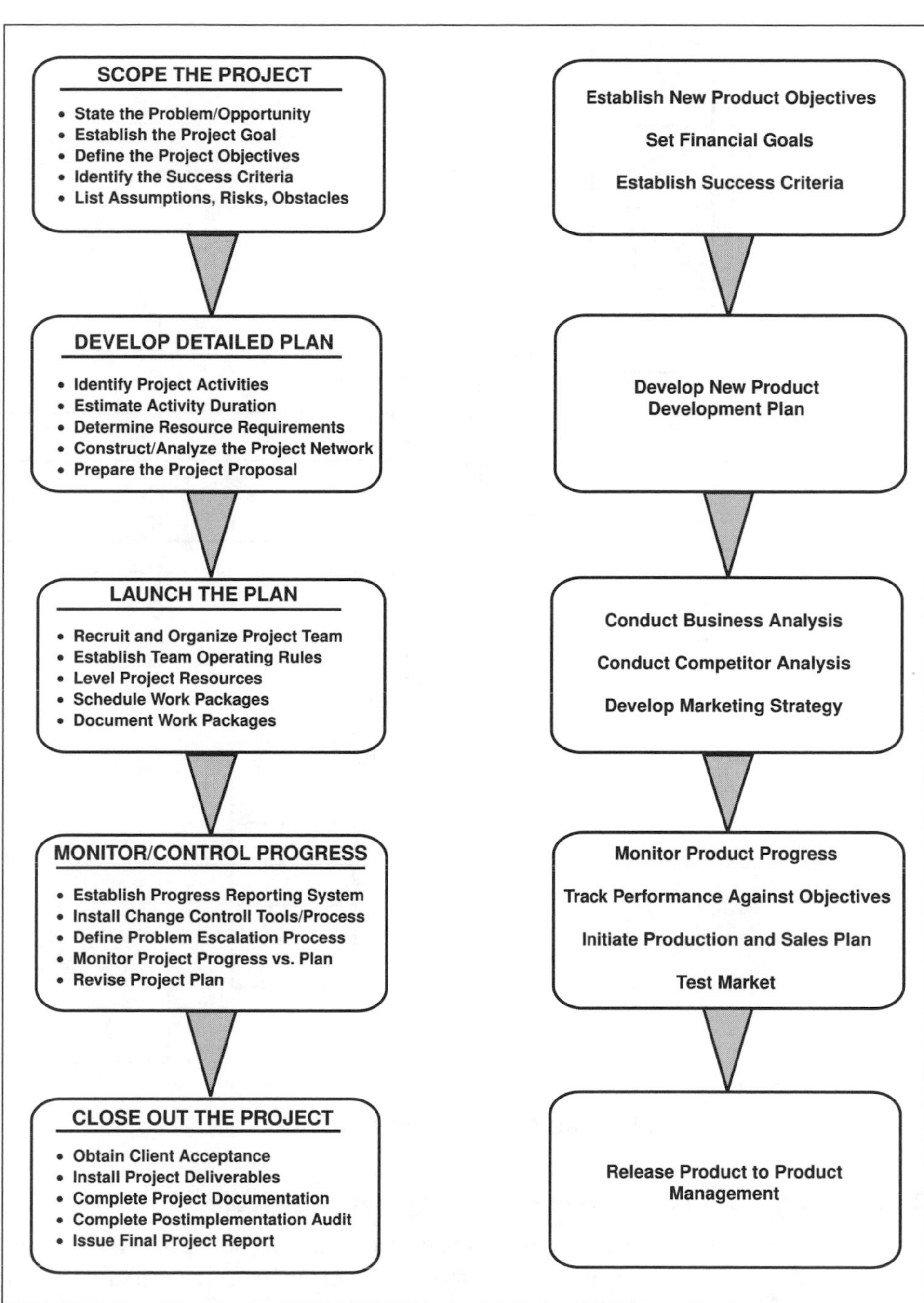
SCOPE THE PROJECT
• State the Problem/Opportunity
• Establish the Project Goal
• Define the Project Objectives
• Identify the Success Criteria
• List Assumptions, Risks, Obstacles
DEVELOP DETAILED PLAN
• Identify Project Activities
• Estimate Activity Duration
• Determine Resource Requirements
• Construct/Analyze the Project Network
• Prepare the Project Proposal
LAUNCH THE PLAN
• Recruit and Organize Project Team
• Establish Team Operating Rules
• Level Project Resources
• Schedule Work Packages
• Document Work Packages
MONITOR/CONTROL PROGRESS
• Establish Progress Reporting System
• Install Change Controll Tools/Process
• Define Problem Escalation Process
• Monitor Project Progress vs. Plan
• Revise Project Plan
CLOSE OUT THE PROJECT
• Obtain Client Acceptance
• Install Project Deliverables
• Complete Project Documentation
• Complete Postimplementation Audit
• Issue Final Project Report
Establish New Product Objectives
Set Financial Goals
Establish Success Criteria
Develop New Product Development Plan
Conduct Business Analysis
Conduct Competitor Analysis
Develop Marketing Strategy
Monitor Product Progress
Track Performance Against Objectives
Initiate Production and Sales Plan
Test Market
Release Product to Product Management

Figure 6 Product development life cycles and project management.

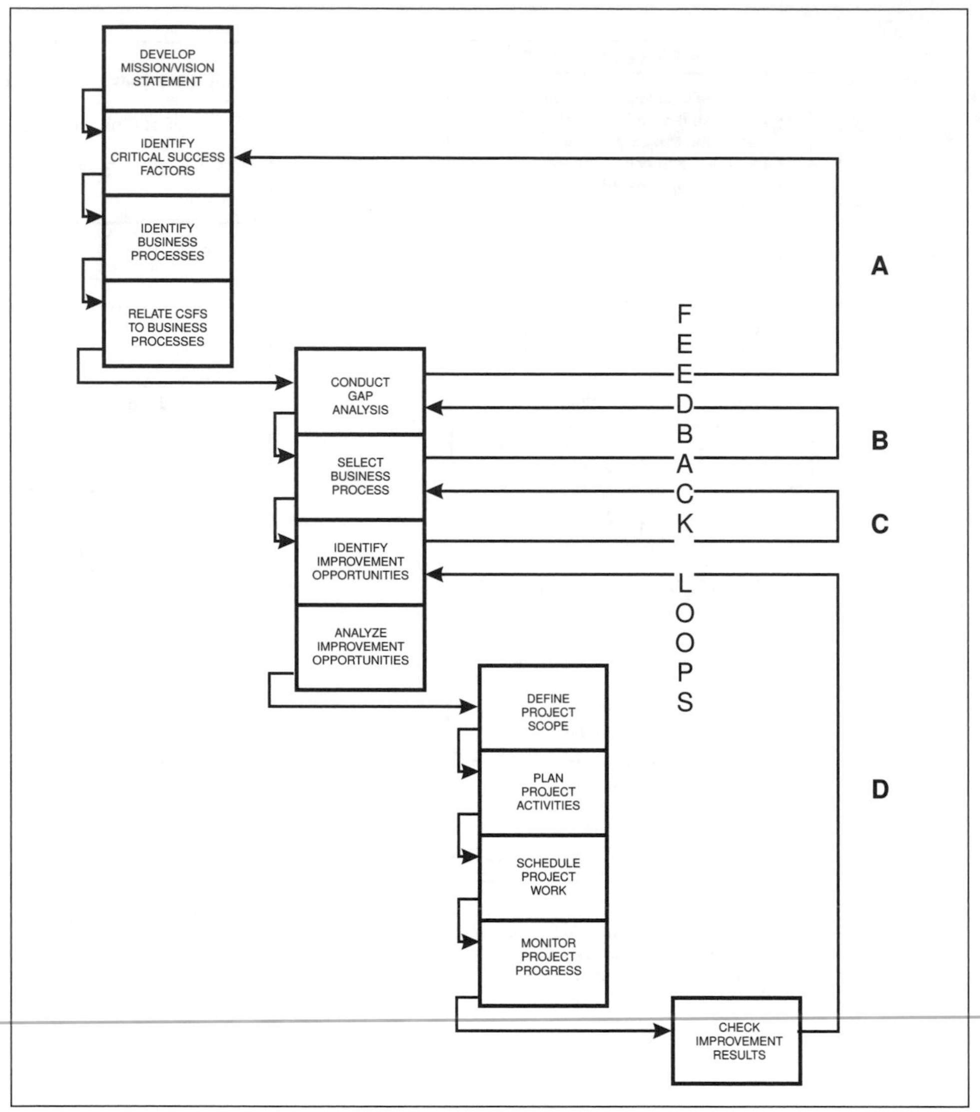

Figure 7 Continuous quality management model.

Continuous Quality Improvement Program Life Cycle

Continuous quality management is a way of life in those enterprises that want to attain and sustain a competitive position in the fast-paced information technology industry. This is most evident in those organizations that are customer driven. Levi Strauss, Motorola, and Xerox are but a few. The list of companies that have applied for or won the coveted Baldrige Award are also on the list. In this section we examine a model for continuous quality improvement (Figure 7), with emphasis on the role of project management in that model.

Figure 7 is a schematic of the Continuous Quality Management Model (CQMM) that we have used successfully in our project management engagements that involve quality improvement programs. The model is based on the assumption that the enterprise has documented its mission, vision, and critical success factors (CSFs). With these in place the processes that drive the business are identified and related to the CSFs. Next follows a Gap Analysis in which the management team

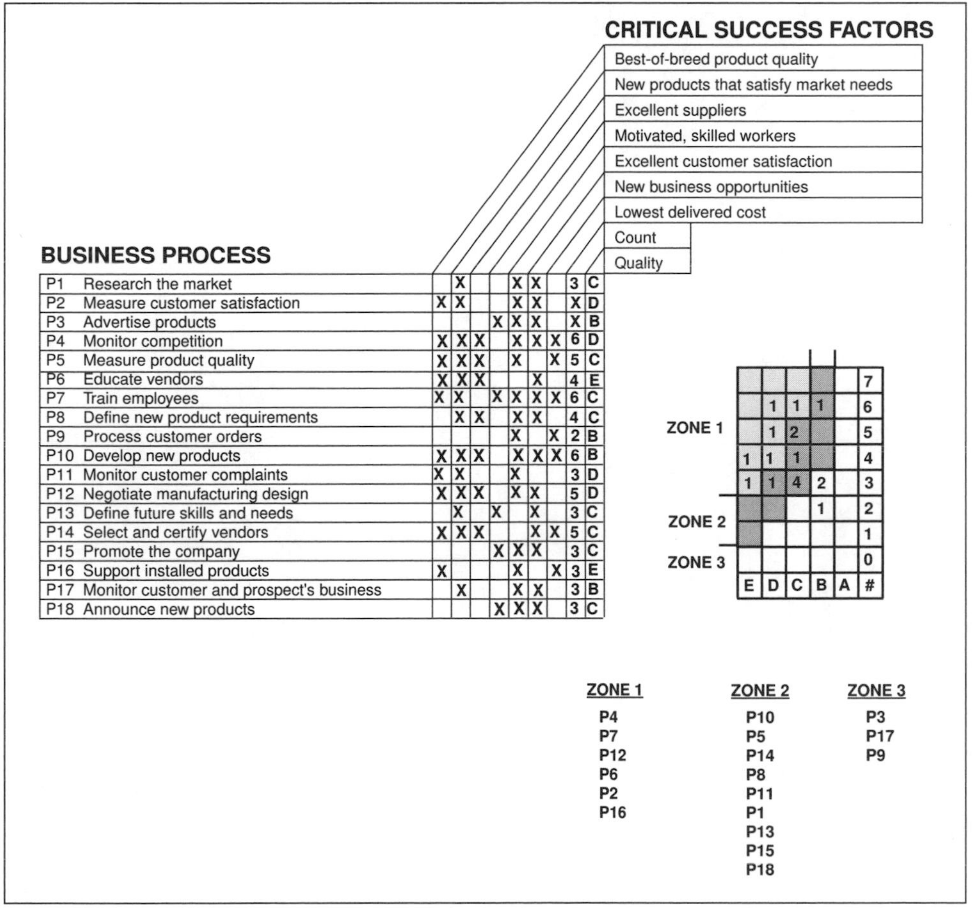

BUSINESS PROCESS	Best-of-breed product quality	New products that satisfy market needs	Excellent suppliers	Motivated, skilled workers	Excellent customer satisfaction	New business opportunities	Lowest delivered cost	Count	Quality
P1 Research the market		X			X	X		3	C
P2 Measure customer satisfaction	X	X			X	X		X	D
P3 Advertise products				X	X	X		X	B
P4 Monitor competition	X	X	X		X	X	X	6	D
P5 Measure product quality	X	X	X		X		X	5	C
P6 Educate vendors	X	X	X			X		4	E
P7 Train employees	X	X		X	X	X	X	6	C
P8 Define new product requirements		X	X		X	X		4	C
P9 Process customer orders					X		X	2	B
P10 Develop new products	X	X	X		X	X	X	6	B
P11 Monitor customer complaints	X	X			X			3	D
P12 Negotiate manufacturing design	X	X	X		X	X		5	D
P13 Define future skills and needs		X		X		X		3	C
P14 Select and certify vendors	X	X	X			X	X	5	C
P15 Promote the company				X	X	X		3	C
P16 Support installed products	X				X		X	3	E
P17 Monitor customer and prospect's business		X			X	X		3	B
P18 Announce new products				X	X	X		3	C

Figure 8 The process quality management matrix.

compares the enterprise's current performance with its desired performance in each business process. A grade of A (excellent) through E (embryonic) is assigned. By taking into account the process grade and the number of CSFs affected by the process, business processes can be ranked according to the priority needs for improvement programs (Figure 8). There then follows a problem analysis to identify and prioritize improvement opportunities for a given process. Out of this analysis a project idea emerges and the project management life cycle begins.

The model shown in Figure 7 is cyclical, as depicted by the feedback loops. Feedback Loop A occurs when there have been significant process changes and the relationship between CSFs and process may have changed. Feedback Loop B occurs when a business process may have changed and impacted the Gap Analysis. Feedback Loop C simply continues the priority scheme defined earlier and selects another business process for improvement. Feedback Loop D usually involves continued improvement efforts on the same business process. The results of the current project may not have been as expected, or new improvement ideas arose while conducting the current project. That is, the project management phase of the model is adaptive. Scope changes will often result from lessons learned during project execution.

In most management problems there are too many possibilities to expect experience, judgment, or intuition to provide good guesses even with perfect information.

Russell L. Ackoff

Out of intense complexities intense simplicities emerge.

Winston Churchill

Efficiency and economy imply employment of the right instrument and material as well as their right use in the right manner.

Louis Dembitz Brandeis
U.S. Supreme Court Justice

APPENDIX

EXTENSIONS TO MULTIPLE PROJECTS

Program Management vs. Multiproject Management

It must be clear at the outset that we are not dealing with program management. That is a separate topic altogether. In fact, program management is a special case of multiproject management in that it has a single goal or purpose (put a man on the moon), whereas multiproject management treats the case of independent multiple goals (develop a client-server based distribution system, install a new CIM package, and update the marketing information system).

Shared Resources: Combinations of People, Equipment, Space

Figure A.1 depicts the situation we will learn about in this module. The assumption is that there is some contention between projects that are vying for the same set of resources. Their only linkage is through those resources, which could be people, equipment, space, or any combination of the three. In any case they are limited resources that can be used only in one place at one point in time. That is, resource scheduling is the issue. A good example is the management of the systems and programming group in the MIS department. One way of envisioning the project management problem is as a matrix whose rows represent available resources and whose columns are the projects that require use of one or more of the resources. The manager's job is to make decisions on the use of those resources so that the project requirements for cost, time, and quality are met.

The extension to multiple projects adds a number of issues that are not present in single project management situations. For example, if the programming resource pool does not have enough hours available to meet all project requirements by the required deadlines, then one of four alternatives is available to management: Utilize slack time across projects to resolve the scheduling conflict, delay one or more projects, increase available hours in the programmer pool, or reduce the requirements of one or more projects. There may also be combinations of the three that are feasible. For example, some delay combined with additional hours in the resource pool may be less costly than any one of the strategies used by itself. In any case, all three strategies have far-reaching implications.

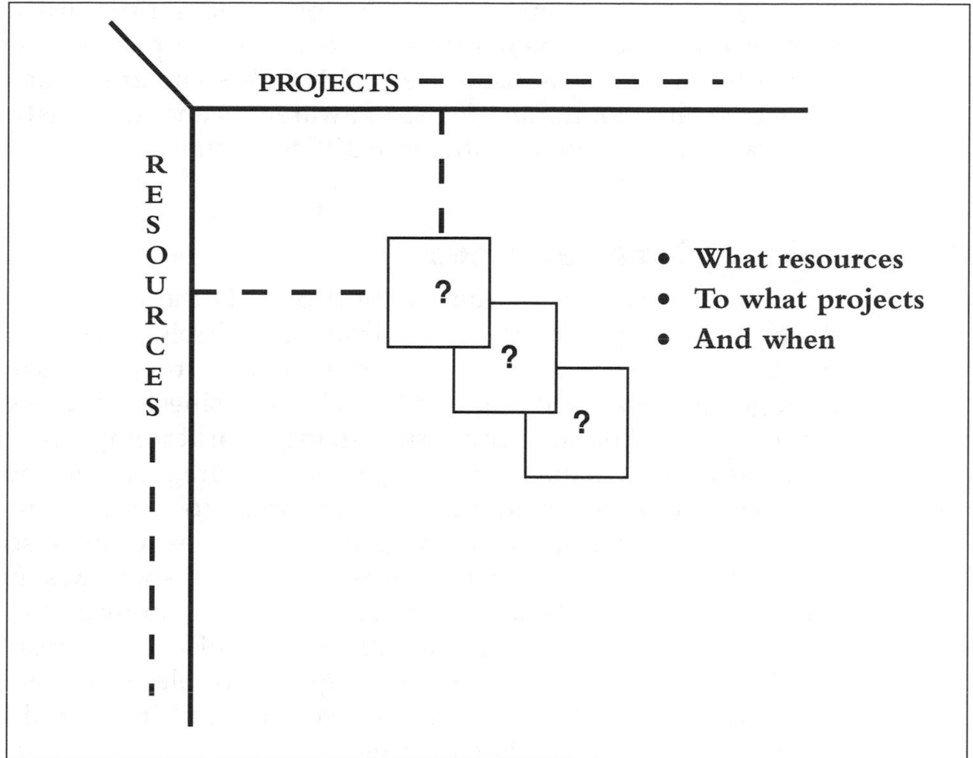

Figure A.1 A matrix visualization of the multiproject scenario.

There has been enough written on project management to fill the Bible and the Congressional Record several times over. Despite this wealth of information, there is precious little devoted to the problems of managing multiple projects. Few would disagree that the real world is not one-dimensional (one project). Rather we are faced with a number of projects competing for scarce resources, narrowing windows of opportunity, and the changing demands of internal and external customers. Projects are continually added, changed, and removed in response to business activity and changing market conditions. One thing is certain: The backlog of needed projects requires resources that exceed management's ability to provide. Of necessity, project priority changes are constant. Projects once scheduled now require schedule changes as any one of a number of parameters change. Out of this seeming chaos project managers and resource managers are expected to create order.

This appendix discusses a number of considerations arising in multiple project management situations. It is not the purpose here to present solutions to all issues raised (although some are recommended). Rather, we attempt to raise levels of awareness and appreciation among those who must contend with these difficult situations.

Organizational Considerations

The matrix structure, or some hybrid of it, is the preferred organizational form for planning and controlling multiple projects. The traditional functional structure does not provide the necessary project management oversight required by today's businesses and is somewhat contrary to the trend toward rightsizing, worker empowerment, and business process management. Organizations are trying to shorten time to market, and the functional structure tends to work counter to that. While the pure project structure greatly simplifies resource scheduling, it is easily seen as very inefficient resource utilization. Resources committed to one project may be underutilized and no formal mechanism exists to share excess capacity with other projects. The resulting cost inefficiencies are obvious. One could give examples of large projects in which the project structure has worked well, but in general these will be the exception rather than the rule.

The matrix structure has both advantages and disadvantages, which we have already discussed. We simply point out that, on balance, the matrix form is generally preferred in those organizations in which projects are an important component of departmental activity and where change and adaptability are expected.

There are two hybrids of the matrix structure to consider. The first occurs in those organizations in which the project managers and resource managers report to the same manager. This variation of the matrix structure is interesting because some of the political and decision-making situations that arise in the pure matrix structure do not exist here. The fact that one operational-level manager has span of control that encompasses the projects and the resources that are scheduled to work on the projects means that scheduling revisions and project priority decisions are vested in the same individual. Obviously much of the politics are avoided in this case.

The other hybrid arises when user managers function as project managers. As we move to client/server architectures and applications development at the user level, the project manager is more likely to come from the ranks of the user community. While this brings a lot of political baggage and fairly intense negotiation situations it does have a number of advantages. Probably the most significant advantage is a much lower risk of project failure than in the other hybrid we discussed. User managers will want the project to succeed. After all, one's reputation is on the line as is the success of the functional area. A related advantage is user buy-in. Commitment as project manager and buy-in as user go hand in hand. The major disadvantages occur in those organizations in which the user manager accepts the role of project manager in name only. This is usually signaled by the user manager deferring to the team members, and not really taking a leadership role. This often happens in cases in which senior management has not made a visible sign of endorsement and commitment to the project.

Of more recent vintage is the self-directed work team (SDWT). Peter Drucker, in a 1988 article in the *Harvard Business Review* ("The Coming of the New Organization," Jan/Feb 1988, pp. 45–53), writes of the emergence of a new organizational structure. It is based on information rather than the command and control structures that have dominated the business landscape since the turn of the century. Drucker argues for a leaner organization—one in which several layers of management are no longer needed because of the easy access to information for everyone on an as-needed basis. The article is required reading for any manager trying to redesign the organization to support the systems that are oriented to business processes rather than business functions. As the organization looks to improving customer service and empowering the work force, the notion of the SDWT coupled with Drucker's Task Force begins to make good sense.

A typical organizational structure that supports these ideas was discussed in Part 5. The functional areas are support to the self-directed project teams (SDPT). They provide very technical consulting and training, as requested. All SDPTs are self-contained in terms of the technology and business knowledge required to complete their work. It is important to note that SDPT members must be multidisciplined. In the ideal all team members can perform any task required of the team. This is a marked departure from the current notion of specialization characteristic of all other organizational structures. The migration toward SDPTs does not appear to be an option. As organizations consider a customer-services orientation and worker empowerment philosophy, they will come to realize that the SDPT, or some hybrid of it, is the only organizational design that makes sense.

Staffing Considerations

The notion of a *learning organization* as described by Peter Senge in his book *The Fifth Discipline* (New York: Doubleday/Currency, 1990), is quite compatible with good project management in the organization that uses a matrix or SDPT structure. Staff development has always been an issue; and with the migration away from centralized mainframe to client/server architectures, training and staff development are on the list of critical success factors. Of paramount importance is how to address the growing skills gap. The skills gap problem is further exacerbated by the focus on business processes rather than business functions. Information systems professionals soon realize that their skill set is lacking both in technology and business process knowledge.

In a matrix organization the managers of staff resources are responsible for developing the skill set in their staff that is required by the organization through the projects that it authorizes. The project is a good vehicle for staff development. Researchers have concluded that the job itself is the most influential motivator of information technology professionals. Challenge, opportunity for advancement, and recognition head the list of job design parameters that contribute to motivation. Those who manage staff resources might examine the skills required to complete each project task, examine the inventory of staff and their skills, and then assign the individual whose skill set almost matches requirements. The needed skills will be developed in conjunction with the project task—just-in-time training.

Of course, the project manager may not be all that willing to accept that model. Their priority is to get the project done on time, within budget, and according to specification. They are not particularly interested in the need for staff development unless it contributes directly to their ability to successfully complete projects.

Project-Related Considerations

There are two cases to consider. The first and most common situation is one where the resource pool is shared across multiple projects. In this case the projects are linked through one or more resources that they have in common. For example, they may both require the services of a telecommunications expert. When the scheduled use of the common resource on one project conflicts with the scheduled use of that same resource on one or more other projects, the dependency becomes quite obvious and the resource manager must solve the resource availability problem.

The second case involves a dependency between the schedule of two or more projects. The scheduled start date of an activity in one project may depend on the actual finish date of an activity in another project. There may in fact be multiple such dependencies. These dependencies are particularly significant when the completion date of the predecessor activity in one project affects the start date of a successor activity in another project, and that successor activity is on the critical path. In such cases, an early finish date on the sending activity is music to the ears of the receiving activity manager. Further issues deal with who owns the slack on the predecessor activity. For any successor activities that are on the critical path, the manager of the successor activity and the manager of the associated project will make a strong argument for claiming ownership of the slack.

It becomes obvious that, even for the simplest cases (say, two projects) the problem of resource scheduling may be intractable. The problem is further exacerbated in cases in which resources may be required on critical path activities of two projects whose schedules overlap. Let us step back from these multiple project scheduling problems and examine them in an orderly way.

Figure A.2 graphically displays the multiple project resource situation. The area of the triangle represents the collective specifications of currently scheduled projects. The sides of the triangle represent the

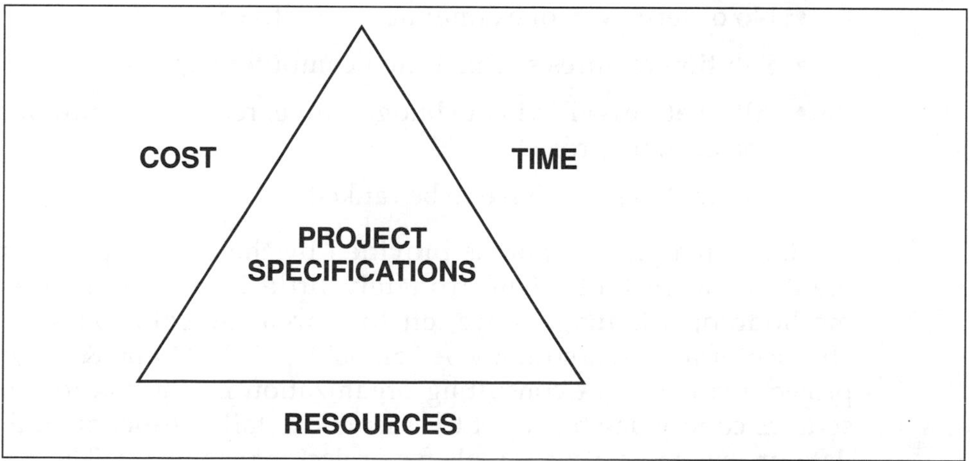

Figure A.2 Multiple project situation.

budget, time, and resources available in the IS department to complete the currently scheduled projects. If a new project is requested, or changes to an existing one made, the area enclosed by the three sides must be able to accommodate the request; or one of four things must happen:

- The request can be accommodated without affecting the completion date of the changed project or the completion dates of any other scheduled projects.
- The request can be accommodated but the scheduled completion of the changed project will be extended.
- The request can be accommodated but the scheduled completion of the changed project and at least one other project will be extended.
- The request cannot be accommodated with existing time, budget, and resources.

In all but the first case, negotiations will be required between the project manager, the requesting unit, resource managers, and other project managers. This is not strange turf for any of these managers. It happens in all multiple project environments. More basic to the situation is the determination of exactly which of these four situations characterizes the issue at hand. The analysis is obviously complex for a variety of reasons:

- Problem not well defined.
- No orderly way of examining alternatives.
- Solution requires sophisticated computer support.
- Alternatives will violate budget, time, resources, and/or specs on one or more projects.
- Alternatives will have to be ranked.

Some analytic support is provided by the typical project management software tools. Unfortunately little is offered in the way of methodology. Managers are left to search the solution space in the absence of a search strategy. As an aside, D. B. Crane & Associates, a project management consulting organization in Southboro, Massachusetts, is conducting a project to assemble detailed function and features data on existing software tools for project management. The results will soon be published in a database available on diskette.

Unfortunately there is no multiple project analog of CPM. Furthermore, it is unlikely that any manual process could be found to solve the scheduling or scheduling update problem. There is, however, an expert system solution. We are aware of one software tool from Erudite Corporation that purports to offer a solution. The package is called Sagacity and is described in a recent book by Richard E. Westney (*Computerized Management of Multiple Small Projects*, New York, NY: Marcel Dekker, 1992). Sagacity uses an expert systems approach called Assignment Modeling. Sagacity interacts with the decision maker to propose resource scheduling alternatives for multiple project scheduling problems. The system requires the decision maker to specify a series of prioritization rules based on a user-supplied criteria. The rules are generally duration driven or effort driven. Duration-driven rules calculate the total work-hours of effort using inputs on the duration and resources required. Effort-driven rules calculate activity duration from inputs on the total work effort required and then calculate the resources required and activity duration. Sagacity uses the user-determined prioritization rules to sequentially schedule projects based on their relative priority. The system can be used to establish initial project schedules as well as to update existing project schedules.

Slack Management

We will spend some time later in the module examining the tactical issues discussion. For now it is sufficient to know that the first strategy for the project manager or the manager of project managers is to examine the available slack. In the case of a single project the available slack was embedded within the project, but in the case of multiple projects the slack is distributed across several projects. The project manager will have to look for opportunities to reschedule start and end dates for activities to make the slack available to other projects. Alternatively, the project manager might use slack time to train others in the skills needed to resolve the conflict. As in the case of single projects, the project manager will want to exhaust all possibilities before going to upper management with a request for additional resources, extended deadlines, or reduced project requirements.

Project Delay

Imposing project delays may affect customer relations, cause severe financial penalties for missed deadlines, affect other projects that are dependent upon timely completion of the subject projects, and increase the risk of meeting customer requirements. In deciding whether this strategy makes sense, management will have to weigh the penalties for a delay in one project or some combination of projects. Before reaching a decision of this scope, the project managers will have to have exhausted other possibilities for using slack time for noncritical path activities to resolve conflicts.

Strategic and Tactical Issues

The strategic issues listed in Figure A.3 cannot be resolved by the project managers. They are issues that must be dealt with at a higher level. In some cases the manager of the project managers may be able to suggest alternative strategies. In the final analysis the client will take part in the decision. This will occur for certain if the projects are for internal clients. When the projects are for external clients, their involvement may not be perfunctory. That is, the performance contract will often include penalty clauses for late completion or out-of-specification deliverables. The strategic decision will follow from a weighing of tangible (e.g., financial) and intangible (e.g., customer relations) factors.

- **What data and information is needed by senior management for strategic decision making?**
- **How do I communicate clearly to stakeholders?**
- **How do I decide which projects to delay given insufficient resources to meet cost, time, and specification constraints?**
- **How do I determine the training and hiring mix for developing and inventorying staff skills?**
- **What are the strategic planning issues over the project management life cycle?**

Figure A.3 Multiproject management strategic issues.

- **How do I identify interproject dependencies and their impact on project completion?**
- **How do I schedule my resources across projects?**
- **How do I add new projects to an existing schedule of projects?**
- **How do I determine the percentage of resources to allocate to projects and the percentage to contingengies?**
- **When do I use automated tools for planning and/or control?**

Figure A.4 Multiproject management tactical issues.

Multiproject Management Tactical Issues

The tactical issues shown in Figure A.4 will generally be settled at the midmanager level (manager of project managers, resource managers, project managers).

We have only introduced the topic of multiple project management. Unfortunately there is little in the theory and application of project management to help the project manager with multiple project situations. Some of the project management software packages offer some help in resource scheduling but only as a *what-if* functionality.

Control over computing belongs with users.

Brandt Allen
University of Virginia

A computer won't clean up the errors in your manual of procedures.

Sheila M. Eby
Business writer
Inc. Magazine's
***Guide to Small Business Success*, 1987**

APPENDIX B

PROJECT MANAGEMENT SOFTWARE PACKAGES

Project Management Software Packages

We have spent considerable time assembling information on the microcomputer software packages available commercially. In our research we discovered more than 125 such packages. At some point in time you will have to face the decision as to which package is best for you or your organization. This is no easy matter, for there are several approaches to project management that these packages might be based on. There are also the algorithms used to calculate project variables. Again each package designer made certain assumptions in developing their package.

Realizing the significance of the decision, we decided to build a database containing as much information as we could reasonably collect from the vendors. The resulting database contains information on over 280 variables for over 60 products. To collect such data we developed a list of questions and asked the vendors to respond. The data is therefore vendor-supplied and we bear no responsibility for its accuracy or completeness.

In this appendix we report only a small portion of the data. Those who would like to obtain a complete copy of the database should contact the authors at:

D. B. Crane & Associates
78 Oak Hill Road
Southboro, MA 01745

	Product / Company	Address	Contact
1	Micro Planner X-Pert V.2.0.5 (MAC) Micro Planning International	958 Edwards Ave. Santa Rosa, CA 95401	Brad Pirrung 800-200-7648 707-545-7648
2	TimePhaser Global Work Sched. V.5 (OS2) Timephaser Corporation	4141 Jutland Dr., Suite 201 San Diego, CA 92117	Robert D. Krintzman 619-554-1023 619-554-1028

TimePhaser (TM) Global Work Scheduler (TM) consists of four tightly coupled application solutions and tools which are designed to provide managers with easy-to-use, real-time status and schedule and cost control capabilities.

Enterprise To-Do-Lists (TM) is an enterprise-wide work scheduler. It is designed to schedule all of the work in a company, not just the large jobs. It allows users to update their own individual prioritized To-Do-List at any time, eliminating the current requirement common to all other CPM scheduling systems that all progress for a job be reported and updated as of a single cut-off date. And it can schedule activities that involve multiple decisions and/or approvals and which could previously only be planned with flow charts.

Management DataView (TM) is an enterprise-wide, management information system which provides a rich assortment of summary and detailed reports for all work at all levels of detail to all authorized management.

Application Integrator (TM) is a seamless integration tool that provides an intelligent pathway for the integration of data between TimePhaser Global Work Scheduler and other software applications throughout an organization.

Platform Navigator (TM) is a connectivity tool that enables TimePhaser Global Work Scheduler to operate with the same "look and feel" across all major computing platforms, such as IMB mainframe, AS/400, PC/LAN (DOS, OS/2, Windows and Windows NT), RS/6000, UNIX, DEC/VAX, DG/MB BULL, Wang/VS, S/36 and Macintosh.

	Product / Company	Address	Contact
3	Micro Planner X-Pert V.2.0.5 (UNIX) Micro Planning International	958 Edwards Ave. Santa Rosa, CA 95401	Brad Pirrung 800-200-7648 707-545-7648
4	Micro Planner Manager V.1.0 (UNIX) Micro Planning International	958 Edwards Ave. Santa Rosa, CA 95401	Brad Pirrung 800-200-7648 707-545-7648

5	MISTER (UNIX) Shirley Software Systems	1930 La France Ave. South Pasedena, CA 91030	Walter Shirely 818-441-5121
6	TimePhaser Global Work Sched. V.5 (DOS) Timephaser Corporation	4141 Jutland Dr., Suite 201 San Diego, CA 92117	Robert D. Krintzman 619-554-1023 619-554-1028

TimePhaser (TM) Global Work Scheduler (TM) consists of a suite of four tightly coupled application solutions and tools which are designed to provide managers with an easy-to-use, real-time status and schedule and cost control capabilities.

Enterprise To-Do Lists (TM) is an enterprise-wide work scheduler. It is designed to schedule all of the work in a company, not just the large jobs. It allows users to update their own individual prioritized To-Do List at any time, eliminating the current requirement common to all other CPM scheduling systems that all progress for a job be reported as of a single cut-off date. And it can schedule activities that invilove multiple decisions and/or approvals and which could previously only be planned with flow charts.

Management Data View (TM) is an enterprise-wide, mangement information system which provides a rich assortment of summary and detailed reports for all levels of detail to all authorized management.

Application Integrator (TM) is a seamless integration tool that provides an intelligent pathway for the integration of data between TimePhaser Global Work Scheduler and other software applications throught an organization.

Platform Navigator (TM) is a connectivity tool that enables TimePhaser Global Work Scheduler to operate with the same "look and feel" across all major computing platforms, such as IBM mainframe, AS/400, PC/LAN (DOS, OS/2, Windows and Windows NT), RS/6000, UNIX, DEC/VAX, DG/MB BULL, Wang/VS, S/36 and Macintosh.

7	MISTER (DOS) Shirley Software Systems	1930 La France Ave. South Pasedena, CA 91030	Walter Shirley 818-441-5121
8	Microsoft Project for Windows V. 4.0 Microsoft Corporation	1 Microsoft Way Redmond, CA 98052	206-882-8080 206-883-8010

Project planning is rarely easy, but Microsoft Project version 4.0 offers breakthrough features that make it dramatically easier to plan, manage, and communicate any kind of project.

8 Microsoft Project for Windows V. 4.0 (continued)

Regardless of your project planning experience, Microsoft Project helps you get started quickly. Those familiar with Microsoft Office programs will find that they and Micrsoft Project will work alike, so once you're familiar with Microsoft Office, you're well on your way to knowing Microsoft Project. If you're a new user, Cue Cards give you step-by-step instructions that stay on-screen while you're creating your plans. To make your plans look great without a lot of effort, choose your favorite format and let the GanttChartWizard do the work for you. PlanningWizards monitor your actions and offer planning and scheduling suggestions and alternatives, which can be automatically incorporated into your plan.

Microsoft Project does a lot of the work for you. Just like the best-selling programs in the Microsoft Office family, it features InteliSense (TM) technology-built-in intelligence that senses what you want to do and produces the results you have in mind. So routine tasks, like scheduling monthly status reports, are automatic. And complex jobs, like assessing resource needs across multiple projects, are easier.

If you're an experienced project manager, you'll find powerfull scheduling features to help manage every stage of any kind of project - from planning a special event to developing and marketing a new product. Plans inevitably change, and Microsoft Project makes it easier to see the implications and keep your projects on track. You can communicate information using a monthly calendar, a Gantt or PERT chart, or create a customized report that gives your projects the attention they deserve.

Microsoft Project makes it easy to collaborate on projects within your workgroup. You can delegate tasks, send and receive status updates, even assign "to do" lists via your e-mail system. Microsoft Project automatically customizes your message to each team member so that it includes all relevant task assignments.

One look at Microsoft Project and you'll quickly see why it's the best-selling project management program in the world.

9 TimePhaser Global Work Sched. V.5 (WIN)
Timephaser Corporation
4141 Jutland Dr., Suite 201
San Diego, CA 92117
Robert D. Krintzman
619-554-1023
619-554-1028

TimePhaser (TM) Global Work Scheduler (TM) consists of a suite of four tightly coupled application solutions and tools which are designed to provide managers with easy-to-use, real-time status and schedule and cost control capabilities.

Enterprise To-Do lists (TM) is an enterprise-wide work scheduler. It is designed to schedule all of the work in a company, not just the large jobs. It allows users to update their own individual prioritized to-Do List at any time, eliminating the current requirement common to all other CPM scheduling systems that all progress for a job be reported and updated as of a single cut-off date. And it can schedule activities that involve multiple decisions and/or approvals and which could preiouvsly only be planned with flow charts.

Management DataView (TM) is an enterprise-wide, management information system which provides a rich assortment of summary and detailed reports for all work at all levels of detail to all authorized management.

9 TimePhaser Global Work Sched. V.5 (WIN) (continued)

Application Integrator (TM) is a enterprise-wide, management information system which provides a rich assortment of summary and detailed reports for all work at all levels of detail to authorized management.

Application Integrator (TM) is a seamless integration tool that provides an intelligent pathway for the integration of data between TimePhaser Global Work Scheduler and other software application throughout an organization.

Platform Navigator (TIM) is a connectivity tool that enables TimePhaser Global Work Scheduler to operate with the same "look and feel" across all major computing platforms, such as IBM mainframe,AS/400, PC/LAN (DOS, OS/2, Windows and Windows NT), RS/6000, UNIX, DEC/VAX, DG/MB BULL, Wang VS, S/36 and Macintosh.

10	TimePhaser Global Work Sched. V.5 (UNIX) Timephaser Corporation	4141 Jutland Dr., Suite 201 San Diego, CA 92117	Robert D. Krintzman 619-554-1023 619-554-1028

TimePhases (TM) and Global Work Scheduler (TM) consists of a suite of four tightly coupled application solutions and tools which are designed to provide managers with easy-to-use, real-time status and schedule and cost control capabilities.

Enterprise to-Do Lists (TM) is an enterprise-wide work scheduler. It is designed to schedule all of the work in a company, not just the large jobs. It allows users to update their own individual priortized To-Do-List at any time eliminating the current requirement common to all other CPM scheduling systems that all progress for a job be reported and updated as of a single cut-off date. And it can schedule activities that involve multiple decisions and/or approvals and which could previously only be planned with flow charts.

Management DataView (TM) is an enterprise-wide, management information system which provides a rich assortment of summary and detailed reports for all work at all levels of detail to all authorized management.

Application Integrator(TM) is a seamless integration tool that provides an intelligent pathway for the integration of data between TimePhase Global Work Scheduler and other software applications throughout an organization.

Platform Navigator (TM) is a connectivity tool that enables TimePhaser Global Work Scheduler to operate with the same "look and feel" across all major computing platforms, such as IBM mainframe, AS/400, PC/LAN (DOS, OS/2, Windows and Windows NT), RS/6000, UNIX, DEC/VAX, DG/MB BULL, Wang/VS, S/36 and Macintosh.

11	Open Plan V.5.0 & OPERA (DOS) Welcom Software Technology Inc.	15995 N. Barkers Landing, Suite 275 Houston, TX 77079	Elizabeth Kuntz 713-558-0514 713-584-7828

12 Project/2 Series X (P/X) (WIN)
Project Software & Development, Inc.
20 University Road
Cambridge, MA 02138
Michael J. O'Neill
617-661-1444
617-661-1642

PROJECT/2 Series X (P/X) project management software is a powerful, client/server system designed specifically for enterprise-wide corporate and fedral use. Combining high-end functionality with low-end ease of use, P/X's flexibility suits large and small-scale projects alike. Key features include Graphical User Interface (GUI), integrated scheduling and cost functionality, extensive reports and graphics, and full data manipulation, system integration and customization capabilities. With P/X, files can be shared across platforms and stored in your ORACLE database. P/X is available across the most popular computing environments -- Personal Computers under Microsoft Windows, and DEC VAX/VMS and Sun UNIX, both under Motif. P/X also runs under leading LANS like Novell and PATHWORKS.

13 Texim Project for Windows V.2.0 (WIN)
Welcom Software Technology
15995 N. Barkers Landing, Suite 275
Houston, TX 77079
Elizabeth Kuntz
713-558-0514
713-584-7828

14 Project/2 Series X (P/X) (UNIX)
Project Software & Development, Inc.
20 University Road
Cambridge, MA 02138
Michael J. O'Neill
617-661-1444
617-661-1642

PROJECT/2 Series X (P/X) project management software is a powerful, client/server system designed specifically for enterprise-wide corporate and federal use. Combining high-end functionality with low-end ease of use, P/X's flexibility suits large and small-scale projects alike. Key features include Graphical User Interface (GUI), integrated scheduling and cost functionality, extensive reports and graphics, and full data manipulation, system integration, and customization capabilities. With P/X, files can be shared across platforms and stored in your ORACLE databse. P/X is available across the most popular computing environments -- Personal Computers under Microsoft Windows, and DEC VAX/VMS and Sun UNIX, both under Motif.

P/X also runs under leading LANSs like Novell and PATHWORKS.

15 Open Plan V.5.0 Extended (DOS)
Welcom Software Technology Inc.
15995 N. Barkers Landing, Suite 275
Houston, TX 77079
Elizabeth Kuntz
713-558-0514
713-584-7828

16 Open Plan V. 5.0 (DOS)
Welcom Software Technology Inc.
15995 N. Barkers Landing, Suite 275
Houston, TX 77079
Elizabeth Kuntz
713-558-0514
713-584-7828

17 Task Monitor 7.0 for MAC
Monitor Systems, Inc.
960 N. San Antonio Road
Suite 210
Los Altos, CA 94022
Al Ruiz
415-949-1688

18 The Intelligent Planner (WIN)
PlanView, Inc.
7320 N. Mopac, Suite 312
Austin, TX 78731
Phil Hagamire
512-346-8600

19 All-Tech Project Simulator (DOS)
Village Software
186 Lincoln Street
Boston, MA 02111
Debbie Pendleton
617-695-9332
617-695-1935

This template for use with Lotus 1-2-3 (TM), determines through simulation a probability distribution of the total time a project is likely to take, given the minimum, most likely and maximum times for each of up to 25 activities along the Critical Path of the project. It is NOT a scheduling program; instead, it uses the output of any scheduling program that provides Critical Path data. It produces valuable risk information that is unique and should be of great value to project leaders and sponsers dealing with projects involving uncertainties - projects that require experimentation or other activities whose duration is uncertain.

There are three working files on the disk: SIMULATN, TGANG, and TREPEAT. SIMULATN is the principal analysis. The input is the Minimum, Most Likely, and Maximum times for each of up to 25 activities on the Critical Path of the project. The time unit for each activity is unspecified, it can be an hour, a day or week.

The putput of SIMULATN is the Minimum, Average and Maximum times the entire project is likely to take, together with the Standard Deviation from the Average. A graph of the probability distribution is avalilable. TREPEAT provides a method for simulating failure/repeat probabilities for an activity.

TGANG presumes that completion of an experimental activity can be realized in less time and with greater certainty if duplicate efforts are undertaken simultaneously. TGANG provides for the parallel execution of up to four duplicate efforts simultaneously. The results show how much the Average and Maximum times of the project can be reduced.

20 Pro Trak Plus V.2.0 (DOS)
Village Software, Inc.
186 Lincoln Street
Boston, MA 01745
Debbie Pendleton
617-695-9332
617-695-1935

ProTrak 2.0 is a multiple-small project cost accounting system. For each project, it tracks budgets, actual committals and expenses, not

20 Pro Trak Plus V.2.0 (DOS) (continued)

hypothetical earned values, based on actual P.O.'s, work orders, invoices, timesheets, etc. using up to 20 user defineable codes. Final cost and cash flow forecasting are also provided. Schedule progress and physical percent complete can be tracked as macrovalues to assess budget and schedule compliance.

In combination with an included utility, ProTrak cab generate system-wide detailed and summary reporting with respect to costs and schedule.

21	CA-Super Project 3.0 for OS/2 Computer Associates International, Inc.	1 Computer Associates Plaza Islandia, NY 11788	516-342-6000 516-342-5392
22	CA-Super Project 3.0 for Windows Computer Associates International, Inc.	1 Computer Associates Plaza Islandia, NY 11788	516-342-6000 516-342-5329
23	CA-Super Project for DOS Computer Associates International, Inc.	1 Computer Associates Plaza Islandia, NY 11788	516-342-6000 516-342-5329
24	Primavera Project Planner 1.0 - Windows Primavera Systems, Inc.	Bala Plaza Bala Cynwd, PA 19004	Kristy Tan 215-660-5830 215-660-5857

Primavera Project Planner (P3) for Windows is project management software that integrates scheduling, resource allocation and leveling, cost control, and presentation graphics. P3 is true multi-user software that can be used in single-user mode or registered as part of a LAN work group.

P3 lets you summarize to any level, change focus from activities to resources to WBS in an instant. You can organize your projects with master and subprojects; 24 activity codes for selection, sequencing and filtering -- and as many as 16 custom data items to organize and track in further detail; fragnets; bar charts, pure logic diagrams, columns of activity data in any order you want; resource codes, WBS codes and color codes.

P3 starts with an extraordinary number of standard reports, lets you tailor each one with simple keystrokes and menu choices. True WYSIWYG capability shows it all on screen. You can customize with P3's set of drawing and editing tools.

P3 is fully integrated with Expedition contract control software, Parade performance measurement software and SureTrak Project Scheduler.

25	Primavera Project Planner Ver. 5.1 (DOS) Primavera Systems, Inc.	2 Bala Plaza Bala Cynwyd, PA 19004	Kristy Tan 215-660-5830 215-660-5857

25	Primavera Project Planner Ver. 5.1 (DOS) (continued)		
	Primavera Project Planner (P3) is the leading project management software for scheduling, resource management, cost control and presentation graphics. P3 is true multiuser software tht may be used in single-user mode or registered as part of a LAN workgroup. P3 allows you to access and maintain your project data 6 different ways, including its graphic user interface (GUI) and tabular mode of data entry. P3's custom report writer lets you modify the 100 predefined reports and create your own. You can preview and manipulate graphic output, including timescaled logic, Gantt, and resource and cost graphics.		
26	Project Workbench for Windows V.1.0 Applied Business Technology Corp.	361 Broadway New York, NY 10013	Sophia Zouras 212-219-8945 212-219-3567
27	MicroMan II (DOS) POC-IT Management Systems, Inc.	429 Santa Monica Blvd., Suite 460 Santa Monica, CA 90401	Sally Jacobs 310-393-4552 310-451-2888
	MicroMan II is an integrated project and staff management system designed specifically for information services organizations. It includes project management to schedule and track projects; staff management to monitor resource use and do staff planning; executive information for overall management of IS. MicroMan II handles an unlimited number of projects and resources and there are common project and resource databases. The scheduler considers resource availability, event dependencies, corporate and resource calendars, and other projects (mulit-project scheduling). The system includes an integrated time reporting function. Staff timesheets are produced or time can be enetered on-line for tracking project progress. There are over 65 standard reports and a custom report writer is included. Consolidated management reports show service to users, project status, backlog costs (can be used for chargeback), resource utilization and availability. The system runs standalone or multi-user on most networks, with full security features. MicroMan II is fully integrated with MicroMan Esti-Mate, a PC-based estimating and planning tool for information services projects used to calculate overall project effort and create project plans which include estimated hours to all events.		
28	Task Monitor 7.0 for PC Monitor Systems, Inc.	960 N. San Antonio Rd. Suite 210 Los Altos, CA 94022	Al Ruiz 415-949-1688

29 MicroMan for Windows (WIN)
POC-IT Management Services, Inc.
429 Santa Monica Blvd., Suite 460
Santa Monica, CA 90401
Sally Jacobs
310-393-4552
310-451-2888

MicroMan for Windows is an integrated project and staff management system designed specifically for information services organizations. It includes project management to schedule and track projects; staff management to monitor resource use and do staff planning; executive information for overall management of IS.

MicroMan for Windows handles an unlimited unmber of projects and resources and there are a common project and resource databases. The scheduler considers resource availibility, event dependencies, corporate and resource calendars, and other projects (mulit-project scheduling).

The system includes an intergrated time reporting function. Staff timesheets are produced or time can be entered on-line for tracking project progress. There are over 65 standard reports and a custom report writer is included. Consolidated management reports show service to users, project status, backlog, cost (can be used for chargebacks), resource utilization and availibility. The system runs standalone or multi-user on most networks, with full security features.

MicroMan for Windows is fully integrated with MicorMan Esti-Mate, a PC-based estimating and planning tool for information services projects used to calculate overall project effort and create project plans which include estimated hours for all project events.

30 Microsoft Project for Macintosh V 4.0
Microsoft Corporation
1 Microsoft Way
Redmond, CA 98052
206-882-8080
206-883-8010

Project planning is rarely easy, but Microsoft Project version 4.0 offers breakthrough features that make it dramatically easier to plan, manage, and communicate any kind of project.

Regardless of your project planning experience, Microsoft Project helps you get started quickly. Those familiar with Microsoft Office programs will find that they and Micrsoft Project will work alike, so once you're familiar with Microsoft Office, you're well on your way to knowing Microsoft Project. If you're a new user, Cue Cards give you step-by-step instructions that stay on-screen while you're creating your plans. To make your plans look great without a lot of effort, choose your favorite format and let the GanttChartWizard do the work for you. PlanningWizards monitor your actions and offer planning and scheduling suggestions and alternatives, which can be automatically incorporated into your plan.

Microsoft Project does a lot of the work for you. Just like the best-selling programs in the Microsoft Office family, it features InteliSense (TM) technology-built-in intelligence that senses what you want to do and produces the results you have in mind. So routine tasks, like scheduling monthly status reports, are automatic. And complex jobs, like assessing resource needs across multiple projects, are easier.

If you're an experienced project manager, you'll find powerfull scheduling features to help manage every stage of any kind of project - from

30 **Microsoft Project for Macintosh V 4.0** (continued)

planning a special event to developing and marketing a new product. Plans inevitably change, and Microsoft Project makes it easier to see the implications and keep your projects on track. You can communicate information using a monthly calendar, a Gantt or PERT chart, or create a customized report that gives your projects the attention they deserve.

Microsoft Project makes it easy to collaborate on projects within your workgroup. You can delegate tasks, send and receive status updates, even assign "to do" lists via your e-mail system. Microsoft Project automatically customizes your message to each team member so that it includes all relevant task assignments.

One look at Microsoft Project and you'll quickly see why it's the best-selling project management program in the world.

31 **MicroMan II (OS2)**
POC-IT Management Systems, Inc
429 Santa Monica Blvd., Suite 460
Santa Monica, CA 90401
Sally Jacobs
310-393-4552
310-451-2888

MicroMan II is an integrated project and staff management system designed specifically for information services organization. It includes project management to schedule and track projects; staff management to monitor resource use and do staff planning; executive information for overall management of IS.

MicrMan II handles an unlimited number of projects and resources and there are a common project and resource databases. The scheduler considers resource availability, event dependencies, corporate and resource calendars, and other projects (multi-project scheduling).

The system includes an integrated time reporting function. Staff timesheets are produced or time can be entered on-line for tracking project progress. There are over 65 standard reports and a custom report writer is included. Consolidated management reports show service to users, project status, backlog, costs (can be used for chargeback), resource utilization and avalibility. The system runs standalone or multi-user on most networks, with full security features.

MicrMan II is fully integrated with MicroMan Esti-Mate, a PC-based estimating and planning tool for information services projects used to calculate overall project effort and create project plans which include estimated hours for all projects.

32 **PROMIS LAN V.4 (DOS)**
Cambridge Management Systems, Inc.
50 Redfield Street, #206
Boston, MA 02122
Mark Almasian
617-288-2900
617-288-0606

33 **Project Scheduler 6 for Windows V.1.0**
Scitor Corporation
393 Vintage Park Drive, Suite 140
Foster City, CA 94404
Kim Momono
415-570-7700
415-570-7807

No.	Product / Company	Address	Contact
33	**Project Scheduler 6 for Windows V.1.0** (continued) Project Scheduler (TM) for Windows is an easy-to-use, yet powerful tool that will help you organize all of your project project management activities. From multi-project planning and tracking to analyzing and reporting, PS6 has the advanced feature set required for project managers. PS6 will streamline your planning with linked Gantt Charts, user configurable spreadsheets and one-touch icon views. With project grouping, you can view a master schedule of multiple projects and then seperate them for updates. Data can be arranged and summarized by Work Breakdown Structure (WBS), Organizational Breakdown Structure (OBS) or Resource Breakdown Structure (RBS). PS6 offers our unique Advanced Resource Tracking Spreadsheet (ARTS) (TM), which lets you evaluate resource costs and usage on a period by period basis. The Object-Oriented Report Writer has the power to create fully customized reports. PS6 offers detailed "what if" analysis, ODBC database connectivity, and network support for DOS-based workstations.		
34	HyperProject, V.1.4 MAC HyperProject, Inc.	12356 Jolette Ave. Granada Hills, CA 91344	Donald Kasper 818-831-0404 818-366-1769
35	Top Priority V.1.02 Spinnaker Software Corp.	201 Broadway Cambridge, MA 15241	Bob Miller 617-494-1200
36	Quick Schedule Plus Spinnaker Software Corp.	201 Broadway Cambridge, MA 02139	Bob Miller 617-494-1200
37	ALDERGRAF SCHEDULING SYSTEM V.5.2 AlderGraf Systems Inc.	10810 Old Katy Rd, #102 Houston, TX 77043	Leon C. Alderfer 713-467-8500 713-467-1062
38	FasTracs V.1.0 (WIN) Applied MicroSystems, Inc.	425 Crossville Rd., P.O. Box 832 Roswell, GA 30077	Russ Still 404-552-9000 404-552-0735
39	Time Line V. 5.0 (DOS) Symantic Corporation	7200 Redwood Boulevard Novato, CA 94945	Marion Barber Spector 415-898-1919 415-898-1297

40	Milestones, Etc. V.3.1a KIDSA Software, Inc. (WIN)	1114 Lost Creek Blvd., Suite 300 Austin, TX 78746	Sue Butler 800-765-0167 512-328-0247
41	SSP's PROMIS V.4.1 (DOS) Cambridge Management Systems, Inc.	50 Redfield Street, # 206 Boston, MA 02122	Mark Almasian 617-288-2900 617-288-0606
42	firstcase 3.2 AGS Management Systems, Inc.	1060 First Ave., Suite 400 King of Prussia, PA 19406	Mary Ellen Donatelli 215-565-2215

firstcase (R), a PC-based, client/server development management application, provides the following in an integrated framework.

fc methods (TM) - a family of methodologies that include:
- Client/Server Systems Development (CSSD), which provides the framework and guidance for developing client/server applications.
- Enterprise Architecture Planning (EAP), which gives guidlines for development of the strategic plan for Information Systems.
- Information Engineering, a methodology that focuses on the business needs and strategy of the enterprise.
- Structured Development, which stress a traditional approach to the development process that is concerned with the management of specific application development projects on an individual basis.

fc process (TM) - the process management element that provides an automated family of methodologies with the ability to customize the supplied methodologies, or to automate in-house standards or any other commercial methodology.

fc manager (TM) provides estimating (including Function Point Analysis) and project management. It equips the user with tools to plan, organize, monitor and direct an unlimited number of large or small projects of any complexity. Includes project templates and provides project simulation for "what if" scenarios, and resource-constrained scheduling across projects.

fc developer (TM) - a time and progress reporting module that provides a mechanism to initiate, guide and monitor the work activities of the project team. It automatically provides developers with a "to do" list and gives them instructions on the work that must be done to complete the activity, as well as guiding them in the use of the proper technique. It prompts the developers to report progress and provides real-time reporting.

Access to firstcase is through the workstation with a central library resident on the LAN file server. For small projects, firstcase can be used in stand-alone workstation environment.

43	PROJECT OUTLOOK V.4.0 (WIN) Cambridge Management Systems, Inc.	50 Redfield Street, #206 Boston, MA 02122	Mark Almasian 617-288-2900 617-288-0606
44	Dekker TRAKKER for Windows Dekker, Ltd.	Building 290, 636 East Brier San Bernadino, CA 92408	Susan Shroeder 909-384-9000
45	Dekker TRAKKER V.2.9 (DOS) Dekker, Ltd.	Building 260, 636 East Brier San Bernadino, CA 92408	Susan Shroeder 909-384-9000
46	Dekker TRAKKER V.2.8 (UNIX) Dekker, Ltd.	Building 260, 636 East Brier San Bernadino, CA 92408	Susan Shroeder 909-384-9000
47	PlanTRAC II-A.1 (DOS) Computerline, Inc.	21 Old Meetinghouse Rd. P.O. Box 639 Auborn, MA 01501	Paul Paine 508-832-9779 508-832-0955
48	Micro Planner Manager V.1.1 (MAC) Micro Planning International	958 Edwards Ave. Santa Rosa, CA 95401	Brad Pirrung 800-200-7648 707-545-7648
49	AutoPLAN II V.1.0 (UNIX) Digital Tools	18900 Stevens Creek Blvd. Cupertino, CA 95014	Jim O'Hare 408-366-6920 408-446-2140
50	Time Machine V.3.2 (WIN) Diversified Information Services, Inc.	4370 Tujunga Ave, Suite 130 Studio City, CA 91604	Jan Skone-Rees 818-506-7265 818-506-0949

51 SAS System for Info. Delivery (DOS)
SAS Institute, Inc.
SAS Campus Drive
Cary, NC 27513
Steve Becker
919-677-8000
919-677-8123

SAS/OR (R) software, a set of powerful management science tools, is an integral decision-support component of the SAS (R) System for Information Delivery. The software includes tools for mathematical programming, decision analysis, and project management. The project management tools give you the flexibility to plan, manage, and track projects through a single integrated system, The software is adept at handling complicated situations such as multiple project record-keeping, resource priorities, complex project calendars, substitutable rsources, multiple precedence relationships, activities deadlines, time and resource-constrained scheduling, and flexible reporting. Complementing the SAS/OR project management tools is the PROJMAN Menu System, a customizable and extendable point-and-click interface.

52 SAS System for Info. Delivery (WIN)
SAS Institute, Inc
SAS Campus Drive
Cary, NC 27513
Rene Samy
919-677-8000

SAS/OR (R) software, a set of powerful management science tools, is an integral decision-support component of the SAS (R) System for Information Delivery. The software includes tools for mathematical programming, decision analysis, and project management. The project management tools give you the flexibility to plan, manage, and track projects through a single integrated system. The software is adept at handling complicated situations such as multiple project record-keeping, resource priorities, complex project calendars, substitutable resources, multiple precedence relationships, activity deadlines, time and resource-constrained scheduling, and flexible reporting. Complementing the SAS/OR project management tools is the PROJMAN Menu System, a customizable and extendable point-and-click interface.

53 SAS System for Info. Delivery (OS2)
SAS Institute, Inc.
SAS Campus Drive
Cary, NC 27513
Steve Becker
919-677-8000
919-677-8123

SAS/OR (R) software, a set of powerful management science tools, is an integral decision-support component of the SAS (R) System for Information Delivery. The software includes tools for mathematical programming, decision analysis, and project management. The project management tools give you the flexibility to plan, manage, and track projects through a single integrated system. The software is adept at handling complicated situations such as multiple project record keeping, resource priorities, complex project calendars, substitutable resources, multiple precedence relationships, activity deadlines, time and resource-constrained scheduling, and flexible reporting. Complementing the SAS/OR project management tools is the PROJMAN Menu System, a customizable and extendable point-and-click interface.

54 Time Machine V.3.2 (DOS)
Diversified Information Services, Inc.
4370 Tujunga Ave.
Studio City, CA 91640
Jan Skone-Rees
818-506-7265
818-506-0949

	Product / Company	Address	Contact
55	SAS System for Info. Delivery (UNIX) SAS Institute, Inc.	SAS Campus Drive Cary, NC 27513	Steve Becker 919-677-8000

SAS/OR (R) software, a set of powerful management science tools, is an integral decision-support component of the SAS (R) System for Information Delivery. The software includes tools for mathematical programming, decision analysis, and project management. The project management tools give you the flexibility to plan, manage, and track projects through a single integrated system. The software is adept at handling complicated situations such as multiple project record keeping, resource priorities, complex project calendars, sustitutable resources, multiple precedence relationships, activity deadlines, time and resource-constrained scheduling, and flexible reporting. Complementing the SAS/OR project management tools is the PROJMAN Menu System, a customizable and extendable point-and-click interface.

	Product / Company	Address	Contact
56	ORO Project Management Sys. V.1.3 (DOS) Nichols & Company, Inc.	5855 Green Valley Circle, Suite 308 Culver City, CA 90230	Steve Jordan 310-670-6400 310-670-6409
57	MARK III MANAGEMENT SYSTEM V.4.1 (DOS) Program Control Corporation	749 Lakeland Road, Suite B Westlake Village, CA 91361	J.C. Jones 805-374-2722 805-374-2724

MARK III is a user friendly and extremely comprehensive project management system, designed to operate on a variety of computer systems, PC through the advanced mainframe. Project management data may be maintained in MARK III'S generic data base or in practically any spread sheet or data base system. The system is based on critical path precedence techniques and is designed to handle multiple projects. Interactions between tasks within or across projects is unlimited. The most visible MARK III outputs are high resolution graphics displaying Gantt type bar charts, network charts, resource cumulative curves and histograms. Output can be produced in a variety of formats for export to other packages. All project related computations (planned, expended, estimates at completion, etc.) are tabulated for display in a variety of user defined reports. Graphic output is compatible with HPGL plus a variety of other digitized electrostatic plotter systems. The strengths of MARK III are most apparent in construction management and life cycle management of programs such as large scale production, acquisition logistics management, manpower programs and integrated logistics support plans. MARK III data bases are interchangeable between host systems with no conversion requirements. The MARK III Management System is basic enough for use by the beginning project planner and comprehensive enough to handle the complexities required by the most experienced program manager. It meets all Cost/Schedule Control System Criteria (C/SCSC) required for Federal programs.

	Product / Company	Address	Contact
58	Everybody's Planner Ver. 2.3 (DOS) Abracadata, Ltd.	P.O. Box 2440 Eugene, OR 97402	John Blanchard 503-342-3030 503-683-1925

59	ORO Project Management Sys. V.1.3 (WIN) Nichols & Company, Inc.	5855 Green Valley Circle, Suite 308 Culver City, CA 90230	Steve Jordan 310-670-6400 310-670-6409
60	ARTEMIS Prestige for Windows Lucas Management Systems	12071 Fair Lakes Circle, Suite 350 Fairfax, VA 22033	Thomas G. Rogers 703-222-1111 703-222-8203
	Artemis prestige for Windows is an easy to use, client/server based, project management application running under Microsoft Windows. With Prestige's multi-user capabilities, many people can access or update data in the same project at the same time. Additionally, Artemis Presitge allows an unlimited number of multi-project combinations and has sophisticated resource leveling capabilities. Prestige operates on almost all the popular hardware platforms and uses industry databases.		
61	Great Gantt! V.1.4.6 (MAC) Varcon Systems, Inc.	10509 San Diego Mission Rd., Suite K San Diego, CA 92108	Janet Mika 619-563-6700 619-563-1986
62	Spectrum/Manager (DOS) Spectrum International, Inc.	2600 Boyce Plaza Road #100 Pittsburg, PA 15241	Gregory J. Zawacki 412-221-8580 412-221-8741
63	"PRIDE" Information Factory (OS/2) M. Bryce & Associates	777 Alderman Road Palm Habor, FL 34683	Tim Bryce 813-786-4567

Question	1 Micro Planner X-Pert V.2.0.5 (MAC)	2 TimePhaser Global Work Sched. V.5 (OS2)	3 Micro Planner X-Pert V.2.0.5 (UNIX)	4 Micro Planner Manager V.1.0 (UNIX)	5 MISTER (UNIX)	6 TimePhaser Global Work Sched. V.5 (DOS)	7 MISTER (DOS)
II.1 - What is the single user price of the program?	1995	750	1995	695	1000	750	1000
VIII.A.1 - Is a graphical user interface supported?	Yes	Yes	Yes	Yes	Yes	Yes	Yes
III.A.2 - Under which one of the following operating system does the program run, PC/MS DOS, DOS/Windows 3.x, OS2, MAC or UNIX?	Apple MacIntosh	OS/2	Unix	Unix	Unix	MS or PC DOS	MS or PC DOS
IV.1 - Does the program allocate processing between client and server processors? (Does it run in a client server environment?)	No	Yes	No	No	No	Yes	No
V.A.1 - Is the program data stored in a data base?	Yes	Yes	Yes	Yes	No	Yes	No
V.E.3 - What is the maximum number of resources supported by the program?	999999999	1000	999999999	999999999	100	1000	100
V.C.2 - What is the maximum number of activities supported by the program?	999999999	999999999	999999999	999999999	No Response to Question	999999999	No Response to Question
XIII.1 - Is scheduling in hours supported?	Yes	No	Yes	Yes	Yes	No	Yes
XV.1 - What is the maximum length of a project in years?	50	27	50	50	No Response to Question	27	No Response to Question
XVI.A.2 - Is the Precedence Diagraming Method supported?	Yes	Yes	Yes	Yes	Yes	Yes	Yes
XIX.B.1 - Is non-linear distribution of resources on a single activity supported?	Yes	No	Yes	Yes	No	No	No

Question	8 Microsoft Project for Windows V. 4.0	9 TimePhaser Global Work Sched. V.5 (WIN)	10 TimePhaser Global Work Sched. V.5 (UNIX)	11 Open Plan V.5.0 & OPERA (DOS)	12 Project/2 Series X (P/X) (WIN)	13 Texim Project for Windows V.2.0 (WIN)	14 Project/2 Series X (P/X) (UNIX)
II.1 - What is the single user price of the program?	695	750	750	6400	8000	995	8000
VIII.A.1 - Is a graphical user interface supported?	Yes	Yes	Yes	Yes	Yes	Yes	Yes
III.A.2 - Under which one of the following operating system does the program run, PC/MS DOS, DOS/Windows 3.x, OS2, MAC or UNIX?	DOS Windows 3.x	DOS Windows 3.x	Unix	MS or PC DOS	DOS Windows 3.x	DOS Windows 3.x	Unix
IV.1 - Does the program allocate processing between client and server processors? (Does it run in a client server environment?)	No	Yes	Yes	No	Yes	No	Yes
V.A.1 - Is the program data stored in a data base?	Yes	Yes	Yes	Yes	Yes	No	Yes
V.E.3 - What is the maximum number of resources supported by the program?	9999	1000	1000	999999999	32767	999999999	999999999
V.C.2 - What is the maximum number of activities supported by the program?	9999	999999999	999999999	999999999	32767	999999999	999999999
XIII.1 - Is scheduling in hours supported?	Yes	No	No	Yes	Yes	Yes	Yes
XV.1 - What is the maximum length of a project in years?	66	27	27	179	1020	250	1020
XVI.A.2 - Is the Precedence Diagraming Method supported?	Yes	Yes	Yes	Yes	Yes	Yes	Yes
XIX.B.1 - Is non-linear distribution of resources on a single activity supported?	Yes	No	No	Yes	Yes	No	Yes

	15 Open Plan V.5.0 Extended (DOS)	16 Open Plan V. 5.0 (DOS)	17 Task Monitor 7.0 for MAC	18 The Intelligent Planner (WIN)	19 All-Tech Project Simulator (DOS)	20 Pro Trak Plus V.2.0 (DOS)	21 CA-Super Project 3.0 for OS/2
II.1 - What is the single user price of the program?	6000	4200	895		45	99	650
VIII.A.1 - Is a graphical user interface supported?	Yes	Yes	No	Yes	NA	No	Yes
III.A.2 - Under which one of the following operating system does the program run, PC/MS DOS, DOS/Windows 3.x, OS2, MAC or UNIX?	MS or PC DOS	MS or PC DOS	Apple MacIntosh	DOS Windows 3.x	MS or PC DOS	MS or PC DOS	OS/2
IV.1 - Does the program allocate processing between client and server processors? (Does it run in a client server environment?)	No	No	No	Yes	No	No	No
V.A.1 - Is the program data stored in a data base?	Yes	Yes	No	Yes	No	No	No
V.E.3 - What is the maximum number of resources supported by the program?	999999999	999999999	999999999	999999999	NA	NA	999999999
V.C.2 - What is the maximum number of activities supported by the program?	999999999	999999999	999999999	999999999	No Response to Question	NA	64000
XIII.1 - Is scheduling in hours supported?	Yes	Yes	No	Yes	No Response to Question	NA	Yes
XV.1 - What is the maximum length of a project in years?	179	179	40	999999999	NA	NA	179
XVI.A.2 - Is the Precedence Diagraming Method supported?	Yes	Yes	Yes	Yes	No	NA	Yes
XIX.B.1 - Is non-linear distribution of resources on a single activity supported?	Yes	Yes	Yes	Yes	NA	NA	Yes

	22	23	24	25	26	27	28
	CA-Super Project 3.0 for Windows	CA-Super Project for DOS	Primavera Project Planner 1.0 - Windows	Primavera Project Planner Ver. 5.1 (DOS)	Project Workbench for Windows V.1.0	MicroMan II (DOS)	Task Monitor 7.0 for PC
II.1 - What is the single user price of the program?	650	650	4000	4000	1275	2895	895
VIII.A.1 - Is a graphical user interface supported?	Yes	Yes	Yes	Yes	Yes	Yes	No
III.A.2 - Under which one of the following operating system does the program run, PC/MS DOS, DOS/Windows 3.x, OS2, MAC or UNIX?	DOS Windows 3.x	MS or PC DOS	DOS Windows 3.x	MS or PC DOS	DOS Windows 3.x	MS or PC DOS	MS or PC DOS
IV.1 - Does the program allocate processing between client and server processors? (Does it run in a client server environment?)	No	No	Yes	Yes	No	No	No
V.A.1 - Is the program data stored in a data base?	No	No	Yes	Yes	Yes	Yes	No
V.E.3 - What is the maximum number of resources supported by the program?	999999999	999999999	999999999	999999999	900	999999999	999999999
V.C.2 - What is the maximum number of activities supported by the program?	16000	16000	999999999	999999999	10000	999999999	999999999
XIII.1 - Is scheduling in hours supported?	Yes	Yes	Yes	Yes	Yes	Yes	No
XV.1 - What is the maximum length of a project in years?	179	179	97	97	100	10	40
XVI.A.2 - Is the Precedence Diagraming Method supported?	Yes	Yes	Yes	Yes	Yes	NA	Yes
XIX.B.1 - Is non-linear distribution of resources on a single activity supported?	Yes	Yes	Yes	Yes	Yes	Yes	Yes

	29 MicroMan for Windows (WIN)	30 Microsoft Project for Macintosh V 4.0	31 MicroMan II (OS2)	32 PROMIS LAN V.4 (DOS)	33 Project Scheduler 6 for Windows V.1.0	34 HyperProject, V.1.4 MAC	35 Top Priority V.1.02
II.1 - What is the single user price of the program?	2895	695	2895	15000	695	345	80
VIII.A.1 - Is a graphical user interface supported?	Yes	Yes	Yes	Yes	Yes	Yes	No
III.A.2 - Under which one of the following operating system does the program run, PC/MS DOS, DOS/Windows 3.x, OS2, MAC or UNIX?	DOS Windows 3.x	Apple MacIntosh	OS/2	MS or PC DOS	DOS Windows 3.x	Apple MacIntosh	MS or PC DOS
IV.1 - Does the program allocate processing between client and server processors? (Does it run in a client server environment?)	No	No	No	Yes	No	No	No
V.A.1 - Is the program data stored in a data base?	Yes	Yes	Yes	Yes	No	No	No
V.E.3 - What is the maximum number of resources supported by the program?	999999999	9999	999999999	999999999	10000	0	NA
V.C.2 - What is the maximum number of activities supported by the program?	999999999	9999	999999999	999999999	999999999	999999999	999999999
XIII.1 - Is scheduling in hours supported?	Yes	Yes	Yes	No	Yes	No	Yes
XV.1 - What is the maximum length of a project in years?	10	66	10	100	100	999999999	99
XVI.A.2 - Is the Precedence Diagraming Method supported?	Yes	Yes	NA	Yes	Yes	Yes	No
XIX.B.1 - Is non-linear distribution of resources on a single activity supported?	Yes	Yes	Yes	Yes	Yes	No	No

	36 Quick Schedule Plus	37 ALDERGRAF SCHEDULING SYSTEM V.5.2	38 FasTracs V.1.0 (WIN)	39 Time Line V. 5.0 (DOS)	40 Milestones, Etc. V.3.1a	41 SSP's PROMIS V.4.1 (DOS)	42 firstcase 3.2
II.1 - What is the single user price of the program?	100	1475	250	699	189	3600	NA
VIII.A.1 - Is a graphical user interface supported?	No	No	Yes	No	Yes	Yes	Yes
III.A.2 - Under which one of the following operating system does the program run, PC/MS DOS, DOS/Windows 3.x, OS2, MAC or UNIX?	MS or PC DOS	MS or PC DOS	DOS Windows 3.x	MS or PC DOS	DOS Windows 3.x	MS or PC DOS	DOS Windows 3.x
IV.1 - Does the program allocate processing between client and server processors? (Does it run in a client server environment?)	No	No	No	No	No	NA	Yes
V.A.1 - Is the program data stored in a data base?	No	No	No	No	No	Yes	Yes
V.E.3 - What is the maximum number of resources supported by the program?	NA	999999999	No Response to Question	999999999	NA	999999999	999999999
V.C.2 - What is the maximum number of activities supported by the program?	999999999	32000+	10000	999999999	500	999999999	999999999
XIII.1 - Is scheduling in hours supported?	Yes	Yes	Yes	Yes	Yes	No	Yes
XV.1 - What is the maximum length of a project in years?	29	100	100	25	50	100	999999999
XVI.A.2 - Is the Precedence Diagraming Method supported?	No	Yes	No	Yes	Yes	Yes	Yes
XIX.B.1 - Is non-linear distribution of resources on a single activity supported?	No	No	NA	Yes	Yes	Yes	No

	43 PROJECT OUTLOOK V.4.0 (WIN)	44 Dekker TRAKKER for Windows	45 Dekker TRAKKER V.2.9 (DOS)	46 Dekker TRAKKER V.2.8 (UNIX)	47 PlanTRAC II-A.1 (DOS)	48 Micro Planner Manager V.1.1 (MAC)	49 AutoPLAN II V.1.0 (UNIX)
II.1 - What is the single user price of the program?	149	1500	2950	14,000 - 27,600	3000	695	1495
VIII.A.1 - Is a graphical user interface supported?	Yes	Yes	No	No	Yes	Yes	Yes
III.A.2 - Under which one of the following operating system does the program run, PC/MS DOS, DOS/Windows 3.x, OS2, MAC or UNIX?	DOS Windows 3.x	DOS Windows 3.x	MS or PC DOS	Unix	MS or PC DOS	Apple MacIntosh	Unix
IV.1 - Does the program allocate processing between client and server processors? (Does it run in a client server environment?)	NA	Yes	Yes	Yes	Yes	No	Yes
V.A.1 - Is the program data stored in a data base?	No	Yes	No	No	No	Yes	No
V.E.3 - What is the maximum number of resources supported by the program?	NA	999999999	999999999	999999999	999999999	99999999	999999999
V.C.2 - What is the maximum number of activities supported by the program?	RAM Dependent	999999999	999999999	999999999	999999999	999999999	999999999
XIII.1 - Is scheduling in hours supported?	No	Yes	No	No	Yes	Yes	Yes
XV.1 - What is the maximum length of a project in years?	100	999999999	999999999	999999999	999999999	50	50
XVI.A.2 - Is the Precedence Diagraming Method supported?	Yes	Yes	Yes	Yes	Yes	Yes	Yes
XIX.B.1 - Is non-linear distribution of resources on a single activity supported?	NA	Yes	Yes	Yes	Yes	Yes	Yes

	50 Time Machine V.3.2 (WIN)	51 SAS System for Info. Delivery (DOS)	52 SAS System for Info. Delivery (WIN)	53 SAS System for Info. Delivery (OS2)	54 Time Machine V.3.2 (DOS)	55 SAS System for Info. Delivery (UNIX)	56 ORO Project Management Sys. V.1.3 (DOS)
II.1 - What is the single user price of the program?	4500				4500		4800
VIII.A.1 - Is a graphical user interface supported?	Yes	Yes	Yes	Yes	Yes	Yes	Yes
III.A.2 - Under which one of the following operating system does the program run, PC/MS DOS, DOS/Windows 3.x, OS2, MAC or UNIX?	DOS Windows 3.x	MS or PC DOS	DOS Windows 3.x	OS/2	MS or PC DOS	Unix	MS or PC DOS
IV.1 - Does the program allocate processing between client and server processors? (Does it run in a client server environment?)	Yes	Yes	Yes	Yes	Yes	Yes	Yes
V.A.1 - Is the program data stored in a data base?	Yes	Yes	Yes	Yes	Yes	Yes	Yes
V.E.3 - What is the maximum number of resources supported by the program?	999999999	999999999	999999999	999999999	999999999	999999999	999999999
V.C.2 - What is the maximum number of activities supported by the program?	999999999	999999999	999999999	999999999	999999999	999999999	999999999
XIII.1 - Is scheduling in hours supported?	Yes	Yes	Yes	Yes	Yes	Yes	Yes
XV.1 - What is the maximum length of a project in years?	999999999	999999999	999999999	999999999	999999999	999999999	78
XVI.A.2 - Is the Precedence Diagraming Method supported?	Yes	Yes	Yes	Yes	Yes	Yes	Yes
XIX.B.1 - Is non-linear distribution of resources on a single activity supported?	Yes	No	No	No	Yes	No	Yes

	57 MARK III MANAGEMENT SYSTEM V.4.1 (DOS)	58 Everybody's Planner Ver. 2.3 (DOS)	59 ORO Project Management Sys. V.1.3 (WIN)	60 ARTEMIS Prestige for Windows	61 Great Gantt! V.1.4.6 (MAC)	62 Spectrum/Manager (DOS)	63 "PRIDE" Information Factory (OS/2)
II.1 - What is the single user price of the program?	1595	99	4800	7775	195	5000	25000
VIII.A.1 - Is a graphical user interface supported?	Yes	Yes	Yes	Yes	Yes	No	Yes
III.A.2 - Under which one of the following operating system does the program run, PC/MS DOS, DOS/Windows 3.x, OS2, MAC or UNIX?	MS or PC DOS	MS or PC DOS	DOS Windows 3.x	DOS Windows 3.x	Apple MacIntosh	MS or PC DOS	OS/2
IV.1 - Does the program allocate processing between client and server processors? (Does it run in a client server environment?)	Yes	No	Yes	Yes	No	NA	Yes
V.A.1 - Is the program data stored in a data base?	Yes	No	Yes	Yes	No	Yes	Yes
V.E.3 - What is the maximum number of resources supported by the program?	999999999	1000	999999999	999999999	NA	999999999	999999999
V.C.2 - What is the maximum number of activities supported by the program?	999999999	1870	999999999	999999999	999999999	999999999	999999999
XIII.1 - Is scheduling in hours supported?	No	No	Yes	Yes	Yes	Yes	Yes
XV.1 - What is the maximum length of a project in years?	30	9	78	100	30	999999999	999999999
XVI.A.2 - Is the Precedence Diagraming Method supported?	No	No	Yes	Yes	No	No	Yes
XIX.B.1 - Is non-linear distribution of resources on a single activity supported?	No	No	Yes	Yes	NA	Yes	Yes

	1 Micro Planner X-Pert V.2.0.5 (MAC)	2 TimePhaser Global Work Sched. V.5 (OS2)	3 Micro Planner X-Pert V.2.0.5 (UNIX)	4 Micro Planner Manager V.1.0 (UNIX)	5 MISTER (UNIX)	6 TimePhaser Global Work Sched. V.5 (DOS)	7 MISTER (DOS)
XIX.D.1 - Is resource leveling supported?	Yes	Yes	Yes	Yes	Yes	Yes	Yes
XVI.I.1 - Can risk analysis be performed using Monte Carlo or other similar sampling techniques?	No	No	No	No	No	No	No
XXIV.A.6 - Are detail level planned schedules summarized to summary activities?	Yes	Yes	Yes	Yes	No Response to Question	Yes	No Response to Question
XXIV.B.1 - Is a sub-project capability supported?	Yes	Yes	Yes	Yes	No Response to Question	Yes	No Response to Question
XXV.1 - Are schedule dependencies between multiple projects, not in the same data file (set) supported?	Yes	Yes	Yes	Yes	No	Yes	No
XXVI.1 - Is resource leveling across multiple projects supported?	Yes	Yes	Yes	Yes	Yes	Yes	Yes
XXIII.A.4 - How many total reports both tabular and graphic are provided?	Customizable	100	Customizable	Customizable	No Response to Question	100	No Response to Question
XXIII.A.2 - Is column and header formatting supported?	Yes	Yes	Yes	Yes	No	Yes	No
XXVII.1 - Is the same reporting capability that exists for single projects, available across multiple projects?	Yes	Yes	Yes	Yes	Yes	Yes	Yes

Question	8 Microsoft Project for Windows V. 4.0	9 TimePhaser Global Work Sched. V.5 (WIN)	10 TimePhaser Global Work Sched. V.5 (UNIX)	11 Open Plan V.5.0 & OPERA (DOS)	12 Project/2 Series X (P/X) (WIN)	13 Texim Project for Windows V.2.0 (WIN)	14 Project/2 Series X (P/X) (UNIX)
XIX.D.1 - Is resource leveling supported?	Yes	Yes	Yes	Yes	Yes	Yes	Yes
XVI.I.1 - Can risk analysis be performed using Monte Carlo or other similar sampling techniques?	No	No	No	Yes	No	Yes	No
XXIV.A.6 - Are detail level planned schedules summarized to summary activities?	Yes	Yes	Yes	Yes	Yes	Yes	Yes
XXIV.B.1 - Is a sub-project capability supported?	Yes	Yes	Yes	Yes	Yes	Yes	Yes
XXV.1 - Are schedule dependencies between multiple projects, not in the same data file (set) supported?	Yes	Yes	Yes	Yes	Yes	No	Yes
XXVI.1 - Is resource leveling across multiple projects supported?	Yes	Yes	Yes	Yes	Yes	Yes	NA
XXIII.A.4 - How many total reports both tabular and graphic are provided?	13	100	100	90	42	80	42
XXIII.A.2 - Is column and header formatting supported?	Yes	Yes	Yes	Yes	Yes	Yes	Yes
XXVII.1 - Is the same reporting capability that exists for single projects, available across multiple projects?	Yes	Yes	Yes	Yes	Yes	Yes	Yes

	15 Open Plan V.5.0 Extended (DOS)	16 Open Plan V. 5.0 (DOS)	17 Task Monitor 7.0 for MAC	18 The Intelligent Planner (WIN)	19 All-Tech Project Simulator (DOS)	20 Pro Trak Plus V.2.0 (DOS)	21 CA-Super Project 3.0 for OS/2
XIX.D.1 - Is resource leveling supported?	Yes	Yes	No Response to Question	Yes	NA	NA	Yes
XVI.I.1 - Can risk analysis be performed using Monte Carlo or other similar sampling techniques?	No	No	Yes	No	Yes	NA	No
XXIV.A.6 - Are detail level planned schedules summarized to summary activities?	Yes	Yes	Yes	Yes	NA	NA	Yes
XXIV.B.1 - Is a sub-project capability supported?	Yes	Yes	Yes	Yes	NA	NA	Yes
XXV.1 - Are schedule dependencies between multiple projects, not in the same data file (set) supported?	Yes	Yes	Yes	NA	NA	NA	Yes
XXVI.1 - Is resource leveling across multiple projects supported?	Yes	Yes	No Response to Question	Yes	NA	NA	Yes
XXIII.A.4 - How many total reports both tabular and graphic are provided?	90	90	No Response to Question	80	NA	6	125
XXIII.A.2 - Is column and header formatting supported?	Yes	Yes	Yes	Yes	No	No Response to Question	Yes
XXVII.1 - Is the same reporting capability that exists for single projects, available across multiple projects?	Yes	Yes	No	Yes	NA	Yes	Yes

	22 CA-Super Project 3.0 for Windows	23 CA-Super Project for DOS	24 Primavera Project Planner 1.0 - Windows	25 Primavera Project Planner Ver. 5.1 (DOS)	26 Project Workbench for Windows V.1.0	27 MicroMan II (DOS)	28 Task Monitor 7.0 for PC
XIX.D.1 - Is resource leveling supported?	Yes	Yes	Yes	Yes	Yes	Yes	No Response to Question
XVI.I.1 - Can risk analysis be performed using Monte Carlo or other similar sampling techniques?	No	No	No	No	No	No	Yes
XXIV.A.6 - Are detail level planned schedules summarized to summary activities?	Yes	Yes	Yes	Yes	Yes	Yes	Yes
XXIV.B.1 - Is a sub-project capability supported?	Yes	Yes	Yes	Yes	Yes	No	Yes
XXV.1 - Are schedule dependencies between multiple projects, not in the same data file (set) supported?	Yes	Yes	No	No	No	Yes	Yes
XXVI.1 - Is resource leveling across multiple projects supported?	Yes	Yes	Yes	Yes	Yes	Yes	No Response to Question
XXIII.A.4 - How many total reports both tabular and graphic are provided?	125	125	100 +	100 +	76	65	No Response to Question
XXIII.A.2 - Is column and header formatting supported?	Yes	Yes	Yes	Yes	Yes	Yes	Yes
XXVII.1 - Is the same reporting capability that exists for single projects, available across multiple projects?	Yes	Yes	Yes	Yes	Yes	Yes	No

	29 MicroMan for Windows (WIN)	30 Microsoft Project for Macintosh V 4.0	31 MicroMan II (OS2)	32 PROMIS LAN V.4 (DOS)	33 Project Scheduler 6 for Windows V.1.0	34 HyperProject, V.1.4 MAC	35 Top Priority V.1.02
XIX.D.1 - Is resource leveling supported?	Yes	Yes	Yes	Yes	Yes	No	Yes
XVI.I.1 - Can risk analysis be performed using Monte Carlo or other similar sampling techniques?	No	No	No	No	No	No	No
XXIV.A.6 - Are detail level planned schedules summarized to summary activities?	Yes	Yes	Yes	Yes	Yes	No	No
XXIV.B.1 - Is a sub-project capability supported?	No	Yes	No	Yes	Yes	No	Yes
XXV.1 - Are schedule dependencies between multiple projects, not in the same data file (set) supported?	Yes	Yes	Yes	No	Yes	No	Yes
XXVI.1 - Is resource leveling across multiple projects supported?	Yes	Yes	Yes	Yes	Yes	No	No
XXIII.A.4 - How many total reports both tabular and graphic are provided?	65	13	65	70 +	30	8	5
XXIII.A.2 - Is column and header formatting supported?	Yes	Yes	Yes	Yes	Yes	Yes	No
XXVII.1 - Is the same reporting capability that exists for single projects, available across multiple projects?	Yes	Yes	Yes	Yes	Yes	No	Yes

Question	36 Quick Schedule Plus	37 ALDERGRAF SCHEDULING SYSTEM V.5.2	38 FasTracs V.1.0 (WIN)	39 Time Line V. 5.0 (DOS)	40 Milestones, Etc. V.3.1a	41 SSP's PROMIS V.4.1 (DOS)	42 firstcase 3.2
XIX.D.1 - Is resource leveling supported?	No	No	No	Yes	No	Yes	Yes
XVI.I.1 - Can risk analysis be performed using Monte Carlo or other similar sampling techniques?	No	No	No	No	No	No	No
XXIV.A.6 - Are detail level planned schedules summarized to summary activities?	No	NA	No	Yes	No	Yes	Yes
XXIV.B.1 - Is a sub-project capability supported?	No	No	Yes	No	No	Yes	Yes
XXV.1 - Are schedule dependencies between multiple projects, not in the same data file (set) supported?	Yes	No	No	No	No	No	Yes
XXVI.1 - Is resource leveling across multiple projects supported?	No	No	No	Yes	No	Yes	Yes
XXIII.A.4 - How many total reports both tabular and graphic are provided?	2	15	14	16	1	70	25
XXIII.A.2 - Is column and header formatting supported?	Yes	Yes	Yes	Yes	Yes	NA	Yes
XXVII.1 - Is the same reporting capability that exists for single projects, available across multiple projects?	No	No	Yes	Yes	No	Yes	Yes

	43 PROJECT OUTLOOK V.4.0 (WIN)	44 Dekker TRAKKER for Windows	45 Dekker TRAKKER V.2.9 (DOS)	46 Dekker TRAKKER V.2.8 (UNIX)	47 PlanTRAC II-A.1 (DOS)	48 Micro Planner Manager V.1.1 (MAC)	49 AutoPLAN II V.1.0 (UNIX)
XIX.D.1 - Is resource leveling supported?	NA	Yes	Yes	Yes	Yes	Yes	Yes
XVI.I.1 - Can risk analysis be performed using Monte Carlo or other similar sampling techniques?	No	Yes	No	No	Yes	No	No
XXIV.A.6 - Are detail level planned schedules summarized to summary activities?	Yes	Yes	Yes	Yes	Yes	Yes	Yes
XXIV.B.1 - Is a sub-project capability supported?	Yes	Yes	Yes	Yes	Yes	Yes	Yes
XXV.1 - Are schedule dependencies between multiple projects, not in the same data file (set) supported?	No	Yes	Yes	Yes	Yes	Yes	Yes
XXVI.1 - Is resource leveling across multiple projects supported?	NA	Yes	Yes	Yes	Yes	Yes	Yes
XXIII.A.4 - How many total reports both tabular and graphic are provided?	3	100	32	32	20+	Customizable	16
XXIII.A.2 - Is column and header formatting supported?	No	Yes	Yes	Yes	Yes	Yes	Yes
XXVII.1 - Is the same reporting capability that exists for single projects, available across multiple projects?	NA	Yes	Yes	Yes	Yes	Yes	Yes

	50 Time Machine V.3.2 (WIN)	51 SAS System for Info. Delivery (DOS)	52 SAS System for Info. Delivery (WIN)	53 SAS System for Info. Delivery (OS2)	54 Time Machine V.3.2 (DOS)	55 SAS System for Info. Delivery (UNIX)	56 ORO Project Management Sys. V.1.3 (DOS)
XIX.D.1 - Is resource leveling supported?	Yes	Yes	Yes	Yes	Yes	Yes	Yes
XVI.I.1 - Can risk analysis be performed using Monte Carlo or other similar sampling techniques?	No	Yes	Yes	Yes	No	Yes	No
XXIV.A.6 - Are detail level planned schedules summarized to summary activities?	Yes	NA	No	NA	Yes	No	Yes
XXIV.B.1 - Is a sub-project capability supported?	Yes	Yes	Yes	Yes	Yes	Yes	Yes
XXV.1 - Are schedule dependencies between multiple projects, not in the same data file (set) supported?	Yes	Yes	Yes	Yes	Yes	Yes	Yes
XXVI.1 - Is resource leveling across multiple projects supported?	Yes	Yes	Yes	Yes	Yes	Yes	Yes
XXIII.A.4 - How many total reports both tabular and graphic are provided?	Yes	80	80	80	Yes	80	3+ Million
XXIII.A.2 - Is column and header formatting supported?	Yes	Yes	Yes	Yes	Yes	Yes	Yes
XXVII.1 - Is the same reporting capability that exists for single projects, available across multiple projects?	Yes	Yes	Yes	Yes	Yes	Yes	Yes

Question	57 MARK III MANAGEMENT SYSTEM V.4.1 (DOS)	58 Everybody's Planner Ver. 2.3 (DOS)	59 ORO Project Management Sys. V.1.3 (WIN)	60 ARTEMIS Prestige for Windows	61 Great Gantt! V.1.4.6 (MAC)	62 Spectrum/Manager (DOS)	63 "PRIDE" Information Factory (OS/2)
XIX.D.1 - Is resource leveling supported?	Yes	No	Yes	Yes	NA	Yes	No
XVI.I.1 - Can risk analysis be performed using Monte Carlo or other similar sampling techniques?	No	No	No	No	No	No	No
XXIV.A.6 - Are detail level planned schedules summarized to summary activities?	Yes	Yes	Yes	Yes	Yes	Yes	Yes
XXIV.B.1 - Is a sub-project capability supported?	Yes	No	Yes	Yes	Yes	Yes	Yes
XXV.1 - Are schedule dependencies between multiple projects, not in the same data file (set) supported?	Yes	No	Yes	Yes	No	No	No
XXVI.1 - Is resource leveling across multiple projects supported?	Yes	No	Yes	Yes	No	Yes	Yes
XXIII.A.4 - How many total reports both tabular and graphic are provided?	Multipule	7	3+ Million	70	1	200	14
XXIII.A.2 - Is column and header formatting supported?	Yes	No	Yes	Yes	Yes	No	Yes
XXVII.1 - Is the same reporting capability that exists for single projects, available across multiple projects?	Yes	NA	Yes	Yes	Yes	Yes	Yes

Ignorance never settles a question.

Benjamin Disraeli

Those who have read of everything are thought to understand everything, too; but it is not always so—reading furnishes the mind only with materials of knowledge; it is thinking that makes what is read ours. We are of the ruminating kind, and it is not enough to cram ourselves with a great load of collections; unless we chew them over again, they will not give us strength and nourishment.

John Locke

APPENDIX

PROJECT MANAGEMENT BIBLIOGRAPHY

Project Management Bibliography

The following listed books are simply a collection from our project management libraries. They will be of particular interest to information systems professionals who have project management responsibility, are members of project teams, or simply have a need to learn about the basics of sound project management. The focus of many of the books is systems and software development because that is our primary interest, although several also treat the basic concepts and principles of project management.

Awani, Alfred. 1983. *Project Management Techniques*. New York, NY: Petroteil Books.

Bennatan, E. M. 1992. *On Time, Within Budget: Software Project Management Practices and Techniques*. Wellesley, MA: QED Publishing Group. (ISBN 0-89435-408-6)

Block, R. 1983. *The Politics of Projects*. New York, NY: Yourdon Press.

Burman, J. 1972. *Precedence Networks for Project Planning and Control*. New York, NY: McGraw-Hill.

Charette, Robert N. 1989. *Software Engineering Risk Analysis and Management*, New York, NY: McGraw-Hill. (ISBN 0-07-010719-X)

Cleland, D. I., and W. R. King, eds. 1983. *Project Management Handbook*. New York, NY: Van Nostrand Reinhold.

Clifton, D. S. 1975. *Project Feasibility Analysis*. New York, NY: John Wiley & Sons.

Dekom, Anton K. 1994. *Practical Project Management*. New York, NY: Random House Business Division. (ISBN 0-394-55077-3)

De Marco, T. 1982. *Controlling Software Projects*. New York, NY: Yourdon Press.

De Marco, Tom, and Timothy Lister. 1987. *Peopleware: Productive Projects and Teams*. New York, NY: Dorsett House Publishing. (ISBN 0-932633-05-6)

Fleming, Quentin W., John W. Bronn, and Gary C. Humphreys. 1987. *Project & Production Scheduling*. Chicago, IL: Probus Publishing. (ISBN 0-917253-63-9)

Frame, J. Davidson. 1987. *Managing Projects in Organizations.* San Francisco, CA: Jossey-Bass.

Gilbreath, Robert D. 1986. *Winning at Project Management: What Works, What Fails, and Why.* New York, NY: John Wiley & Sons. (ISBN 0-471-83910-8)

Grady, Robert B. 1992. *Practical Software Metrics for Project Management and Process Improvement.* Englewood Cliffs, NJ: Prentice Hall. (ISBN 0-13-720384-5)

Harrison, F. L. 1984. *Advanced Project Management.* New York, NY: John Wiley & Sons.

Haynes, Marion E. 1989. *Project Management: From Idea to Implementation.* Los Altos, CA: Crisp Publications. (ISBN 0-931961-75-0)

Hoare, H. R. 1973. *Project Management Using Network Analysis.* New York: McGraw-Hill.

House, Ruth Sizemore. 1988. *The Human Side of Project Management.* Reading, MA: Addison-Wesley.

Kerzner, Harold. 1982. *Project Management for Executives.* New York, NY: Van Nostrand Reinhold.

Kerzner, Harold. 1984. *Project Management: A Systems Approach to Planning, Scheduling and Controlling.* New York, NY: Van Nostrand Reinhold.

King, David. 1992. *Project Management Made Simple.* Englewood Cliffs, NJ: Yourdon Press Computing Series. (ISBN 0-13-717729-1)

Lewis, James P. 1993. *The Project Manager's Desk Reference.* Chicago, IL: Probus Publishing. (ISBN 1-55738-461-4)

Lientz, Bennet P., and Kathryn P. Rea. 1995. *Project Management for the 21st Century.* New York, NY: Academic Press. (ISBN 0-12-449965-1)

Lowery, Gwen. 1994. *Managing Projects with Microsoft Project 4.0.* New York, NY: Van Nostrand Reinhold. (ISBN 0-442-01768-5)

Meredith, Jack R., and Samuel J. Mantel, Jr. 1989. *Project Management: A Managerial Approach.* New York, NY: John Wiley & Sons.

Microsoft Press. 1994. *Microsoft Project 4 for Windows: Step by Step.* Redmond, WA. (ISBN 1-55615-595-6)

Miller, Dennis. 1994. *Visual Project Planning & Scheduling*. Boca Raton, FL: The 15th Street Press. (ISBN 0-9640630-1-8)

Moder, J. J. 1983. *Project Management with CPM, Pert, and Precedence Diagramming*. New York, NY: Van Nostrand Reinhold.

Norris, Mark, Peter Rigby, and Malcolm Payne. 1993. *The Healthy Software Project: A Guide to Successful Development and Management*. Chichester, England: John Wiley & Sons, Ltd. (ISBN 0-471-94042-9)

Page-Jones, Meilir. 1985. *Practical Project Management: Restoring Quality to DP Projects and Systems*. New York, NY: Dorsett House Publishing. (ISBN 0-932633-00-5)

Putnam, Lawrence H., and Ware Myers. 1992. *Measures for Excellence: Reliable Software On Time, Within Budget*. Englewood Cliffs, NJ: Yourdon Press Computing Series. (ISBN 0-13-56794-0)

Pyron, Tim. 1994. *Using Microsoft Project 4 for Windows*. Wellesley, MA: QED Publishing Group. (ISBN 1-56529-594-3)

Raferty, John. 1994. *Risk Analysis in Project Management*. London, England: E & FN SPON. (ISBN 0-419-18420-1)

Randolph, W. Allen, and Barry Z. Posner. 1988. *Effective Project Planning & Management: Getting the Job Done*. Englewood Cliffs, NJ: Prentice Hall. (ISBN 0-13-244815-7)

Roetzheim, William H. 1988. *Structured Computer Project Management*. Englewood Cliffs, NJ: Prentice Hall. (ISBN 0-13-853532-9)

Russell, Archibald. 1976. *Managing High Technology Programs and Projects*. New York, NY: John Wiley & Sons.

Smith, Preston G., and Donald G. Reinertsen. 1991. *Developing Products in Half the Time*. New York, NY: Van Nostrand Reinhold. (ISBN 0-442-00243-2)

Spinner, M. 1981. *Elements of Project Management*. Englewood Cliffs, NJ: Prentice Hall.

Stuckebruck, C., ed. 1981. *The Implementation of Project Management: The Professional's Handbook*. Reading, MA: Addison-Wesley.

Thomsett, R. 1980. *People & Project Management*. New York, NY: Yourdon Press.

Thomsett, R. 1993. *Third Wave Project Management*. Englewood Cliffs, NJ: Yourdon Press Computing Series. (ISBN 0-13-915299-7)

Turner, W. S III. 1980. *Project Auditing Methodology*. Amsterdam: North Holland.

Weiss, Joseph W., and Robert K. Wysocki. 1992. *5-Phase Project Management: A Practical Planning and Implementation Guide*. Reading, MA: Addison Wesley. (ISBN 0-201-56316-9)

Weist, J. D., and F. Levey. 1977. *A Management Guide to PERT/CPM*, 2d ed. Englewood Cliffs, NJ: Prentice Hall.

Westney, Richard E. 1992. *Computerized Management of Multiple Small Projects*. New York, NY: Marcel Dekker. (ISBN 0-8247-8645-9)

Whitten, Neal. 1990. *Managing Software Development Projects*. New York, NY: John Wiley & Sons. (ISBN 0-471-51255-9)

Zeldman, M. 1978. *Keeping Technical Projects on Target*. New York, NY: AMACOM Books.

Zells, Lois. 1990. *Managing Software Projects: Selecting and Using PC-Based Project Management Systems*. Wellesley, MA: QED Information Sciences. (ISBN 0-89435-275-X)

A computer will not make a good manager out of a bad manager. It makes a good manager better faster and a bad manager worse faster.

Edward M. Esber
CEO, Ashton-Tate
***Fortune*, March 2, 1987**

Control over computing belongs with users.

Brandt Allen
University of Virginia
***Harvard Business Review*,**
January/February 1987

APPENDIX

Project Management Simulator

Project Management Simulator

Project Management Simulator (PMSIM) is contained on the CD-ROM you received with this book. In order to run PMSIM you simply need to have a system that is running MS Project Version 4 for Windows. Everything else you will need is contained in the enclosed disk. To run PMSIM simply:

1. Insert the disk into your CD-ROM drive.
2. In Windows, choose Run from the File menu.
3. In Windows, type, **d:setup** (where "d" is the letter of your CD-ROM drive), then press **Enter**.
4. Follow the on-screen prompts.

We have tried to create a number of realistic situations that will test your understanding of the tools and techniques of good project management. Once you have read and understood the material in Chapters 1 through 16, you are ready to try your new found skills. There are 13 lessons of increasing complexity to test your skills. Each lesson describes a situation through a project file which you will analyze using MS Project. You do not need any prior understanding of MS Project. PMSIM is self-contained. Once your analysis is complete, there will be a number of questions to test your understanding of the situation and offer additional helpful information should you need it. Since the lessons are of increasing complexity, you should begin with the first lesson and work your way through all 13.

User Assistance and Information

John Wiley & Sons, Inc., is pleased to provide assistance to users of this CD-ROM. Should you have questions regarding the installation or use of this package, please call our technical support number at 212-850-6194 weekdays between 9 A.M. and 4 P.M. Eastern Time.

To place orders for additional copies of this book, including the software, or to request information about other Wiley products, please call 800-879-4539.

Good luck!

Index

C

N

O

P

Q

R

S

T

U

V